Nikon® D60 Digital Field Guide

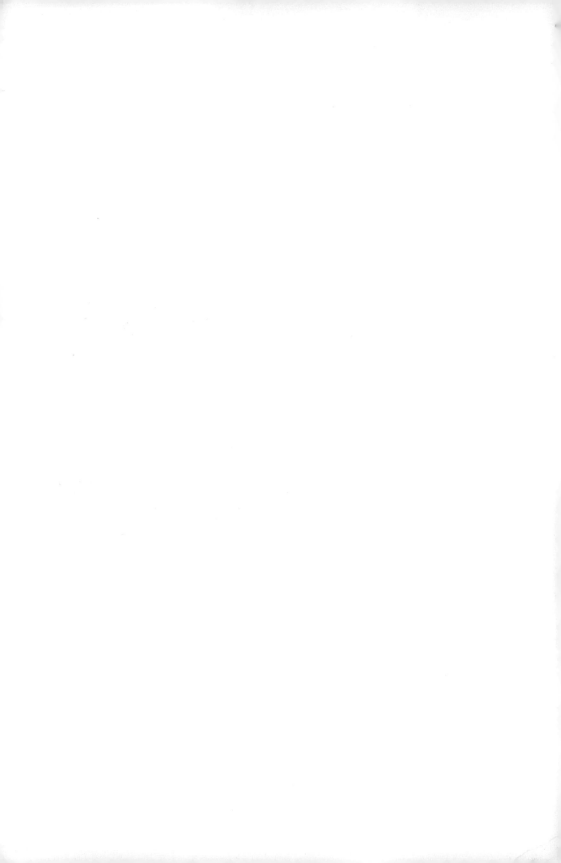

Nikon® D60 Digital Field Guide

J. Dennis Thomas

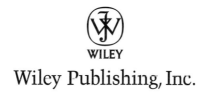

WILEY

Wiley Publishing, Inc.

Nikon® D60 Digital Field Guide

Published by
Wiley Publishing, Inc.
10475 Crosspoint Blvd.
Indianapolis, IN 46256
www.wiley.com

Copyright © 2008 by Wiley Publishing, Inc., Indianapolis, Indiana

Published simultaneously in Canada

ISBN: 978-0-470-38312-4

Manufactured in the United States of America

10 9 8 7 6 5 4 3 2 1

For general information on our other products and services or to obtain technical support, please contact our Customer Care Department within the U.S. at (800) 762-2974, outside the U.S. at (317) 572-3993 or fax (317) 572-4002.

Wiley also publishes its books in a variety of electronic formats. Some content that appears in print may not be available in electronic books.

Library of Congress Control Number: 2008929127

WILEY

About the Author

J. Dennis Thomas, has been interested in photography since his early teens when he found some of his father's old photography equipment and photographs of the Vietnam War. Fortunately, he was able to take photography classes with an amazing teacher who started him on a path of learning that has never stopped.

His first paying photography gig was in 1990 when he was asked to do promotional shots for a band being promoted by Warner Bros. Records. Although he has pursued many different career paths through the years, including a few years of being a musician, his love of photography and the printed image has never waned.

With the advent of digital photography, although he was resistant to give up film, Dennis realized there was yet more to learn in the realm of photography. It was just like starting all over. Photography was fresh and exciting again. Realizing that the world of digital photography was complex and new, he decided to pursue a degree in photography in order to learn the complex techniques of digital imaging with the utmost proficiency.

Eventually Dennis decided to turn his life-long passion into a full time job. He currently owns his own company, Dead Sailor Productions, a photography and graphic design business. He does freelance work for companies including RedBull Energy Drink, Obsolete Industries, Secret Hideout Studios, and Digital Race Photography. He continues to photograph bands, including LA Guns, the US Bombs, Skid Row, Quiet Riot, Echo & the Bunnymen, Dick Dale, Link Wray, Willie Nelson, Bo Diddley, and the Rolling Stones. He has been published in several regional publications and continues to show his work in various galleries throughout the country.

He is also the author of the *Nikon Creative Lighting System Digital Field Guide,* the *Nikon COOLPIX Digital Field Guide*, the *Canon Speedlite System Digital Field Guide*, and the *Nikon D300 Digital Field Guide*, all from Wiley.

Credits

Acquisitions Editor
Courtney Allen

Senior Project Editor
Cricket Krengel

Technical Editor
Ben Holland

Copy Editor
Kim Heusel

Editorial Manager
Robyn B. Siesky

Vice President & Group Executive Publisher
Richard Swadley

Vice President & Publisher
Barry Pruett

Business Manager
Amy Knies

Senior Marketing Manager
Sandy Smith

Project Coordinator
Lynsey Stanford

Graphics and Production Specialists
Alissa D. Ellet

Quality Control Technician
Jessica Kramer

Proofreading
Melissa D. Buddendeck

Indexing
Christine Spina Karpeles

Special Help
Jama Carter
Chris Wolfgang

To all my friends...

Acknowledgments

Thanks to everyone who has helped me out while working on these books. An extra special thanks to Courtney, Cricket, and Laura, at Wiley for keeping me busy.

Contents at a Glance

Contents

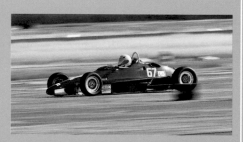

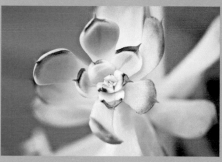

Chapter 3: Setting up the Nikon D60   49

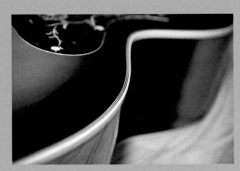

Part II: Capturing Great Images with the Nikon D60   69

Chapter 4: Essential Photography Concepts   71

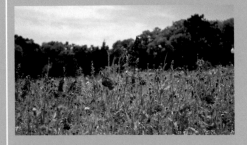

Chapter 5: Selecting and Using Lenses   85

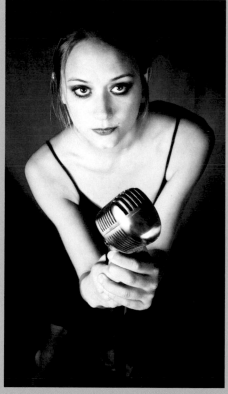

Chapter 6: Working with Light   105

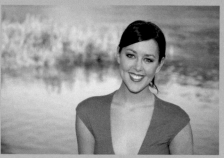

Chapter 7: Real World Applications   135

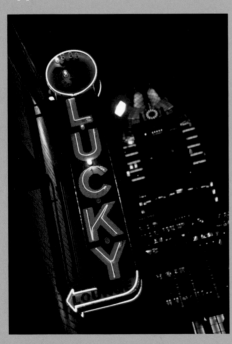

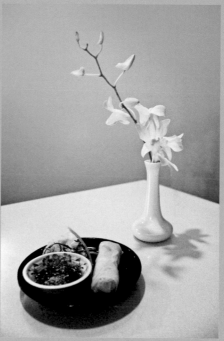

Part III: Appendixes 219

Appendix A: Accessories 221

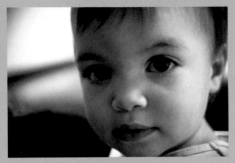

Appendix B: Online Resources 227

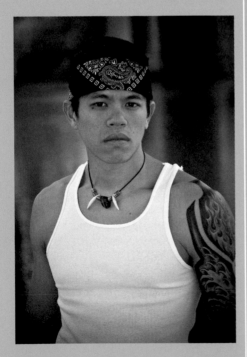

Glossary 231

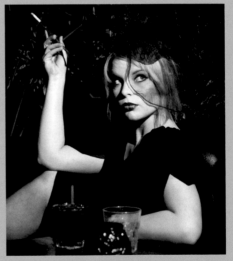

Index 239

Introduction

This book is intended to get you familiarized with all of the features and functions of the Nikon D60 dSLR camera. Although it covers a lot of the same material as the User's Manual, this book presents it in a format that is easier to comprehend and is much more interesting to read. In addition to covering the technical details I include some practical real world advice, tips and tricks, and explanations of how to set up your equipment to achieve interesting and compelling images.

The intention of this book is to offer something for a wide range of readers, from amateur photographers who are buying the D60 as their first dSLR to more advanced photographers who have upgraded from another camera and are looking to expand the scope of their photography.

About the D60

The D60 is Nikon's newest consumer level dSLR camera. So far it is Nikon's smallest dSLR camera. But, don't let the small size fool you, great things come in small packages and the D60 is no exception.

The D60 is packed with features including a big, bright 2.5 inch LCD monitor, a 10.2 megapixel CCD image sensor, Active D-lighting to expand tonal range, and two — count 'em, two — methods of dust reduction, a first in any camera of any level!

The D60 has a multitude of shooting modes for almost any situation from the Digital Vari-Program modes that make it simple to shoot in almost any situation to the more hands on Manual and Semi-Automatic modes that are available on all professional cameras.

The Nikon D60 kit comes bundled with one or two of Nikon's amazing Vibration Reduction (VR) lenses. You can get the 18-55mm lens or a kit with both an 18-55mm and a 55-200mm lens these lenses cover almost all of the ranges you will need. This is the first time that Nikon has offered VR lenses with a camera at this price. Nikon lenses are world renowned for their quality and durability. Although the D60 is limited to using Nikon's Silent Wave motor lenses, also known as AF-S lenses, for full functionality, you can also attach almost any lens Nikon has made for the past 70 years and get some functionality out of it, which I discuss later in the book. Nikon's line of AF-S lenses has dozens of options for you to choose from.

With the D60, you can take advantage of Nikon's current line-up of Speedlights, the SB-400, SB-600, and the SB-800 as well as the R1C1 macro lighting kit. You can also take advantage of the Nikon Creative Lighting System that allows you to control a number of flashes off-camera for the ultimate control of your light. The D60 can even be used with some of the older Nikon Speedlights (with limited functionality, of course).

All in all, the D60 is a sturdy, but lightweight and compact, dSLR camera that will allow you to capture great images for many years to come.

Quick Tour

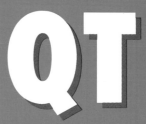

The Quick Tour is designed to cover the basic functions you need to know to get you started using your D60 right away. It is by no means meant to be an in-depth look at the menus and modes, so if you're ready for that information, you can just give this section a quick once-over and move on to the later chapters, where everything is discussed in more detail.

If you already use a Nikon dSLR (digital single lens reflex), a lot of this may be familiar to you. In fact, if you use a D40/D40X, the setup for the D60 is very similar. If you are upgrading from a compact digital camera, you probably should read the entire Quick Tour to familiarize yourself with the camera.

This Quick Tour assumes that you have already unpacked the camera, read the manual, charged the batteries, mounted a lens, and inserted the memory card. If you haven't done these things, do them now.

I'm sure you're ready to get out there and shoot some photos with your new D60, so get going!

Selecting a Shooting Mode

The great thing about the D60 is that you can start taking great photos nearly right out of the box. The D60 has some automatic shooting modes that choose the proper settings for you. All you really have to do is point the camera at something and shoot!

The first thing you need to do is turn the camera on. The on/off switch is located right on top off the camera with the shutter release button.

On/off switch

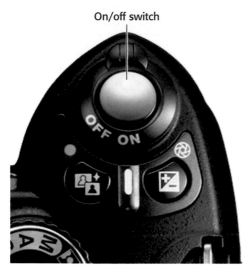

Image courtesy of Nikon, Inc.
QT.1 The on/off switch in the on position

Changing the shooting mode is simple: Rotate the Mode dial located on the top of the camera. The shooting mode will also appear on the top-left corner of the LCD when the shooting info is displayed. The D60 has quite a few shooting modes ranging from fully automatic to completely manual.

The D60 offers two fully automatic modes:

 Auto. This is a "point and shoot" mode in which the camera controls all of the settings, including shutter speed, aperture, and ISO. If the camera deems it necessary, the built-in flash automatically activates as well.

 Auto (flash off). This mode is similar to the Auto mode; the camera controls all settings. However, in this mode, the flash is disabled. This is a mode to use when natural lighting is preferred or the use of flash is not allowed (such as in a museum).

The D60 employs what Nikon terms Digital Vari-Program (DVP) modes (also called *scene modes*). These modes apply settings that are optimized to the type of scene you're shooting, and include modes for shooting portraits, sports, children, and a few others. The DVP modes are as follows:

 Portrait. This mode uses a wider aperture, allowing the background to be soft while giving you sharp focus on your subject.

 Landscape. This mode chooses a smaller aperture to ensure that focus is achieved throughout the image. The camera also enhances blues and greens to accentuate the sky and foliage in the scene.

 Child. This mode optimizes skin tones and boosts the saturation a bit for more vivid colors.

 Sports. With this mode, the camera chooses a higher shutter speed to freeze the action.

 Close-up. This mode provides sharp details on the subject while allowing the background to soften to draw attention to the subject.

 Night Portrait. This mode uses flash to capture your subject while maintaining a longer shutter speed to capture the ambient light of the background; this results in an evenly balanced, more natural-looking exposure.

The DVP modes take care of all of the settings for you, including activating the flash. These modes are handy when you're starting out but you're limited when it comes to fine-tuning the settings. Once you get more familiar with camera settings such as aperture and shutter speed, you may find yourself eschewing these DVP modes in favor of choosing the more flexible P, S, A, or M modes.

- ✦ **P.** Programmed Auto is a fully automatic shooting mode in which the camera decides both the aperture setting and shutter speed. You can use the Command dial to adjust the aperture and shutter to better suit your needs. This is known as flexible program, and it allows you to control the settings while maintaining the same exposure. Use this mode when taking snapshots or when controlling the shutter speed and the aperture is not as important as simply getting the photo.

- ✦ **S.** *Shutter Priority* is a semiautomatic mode in which you decide the shutter speed to use and the camera chooses the appropriate aperture. Use this mode when you need fast shutter speeds to freeze action or slow shutter speeds to show motion blur.

- ✦ **A.** *Aperture Priority* is another semiautomatic mode where you adjust the aperture to control how much of the image is in focus (the depth of field). Use this mode when you want to isolate a subject by focusing on it and letting the background go soft, or if you want to be sure that everything in the picture is in sharp focus.

- ✦ **M.** With *Manual mode*, you decide the shutter speed and aperture. You can use this mode when you want to completely control the exposure to achieve a certain tonality in your image by purposefully over- or underexposing the image. When using this mode, it's helpful to check the D60 light meter in the viewfinder.

Programmed modes

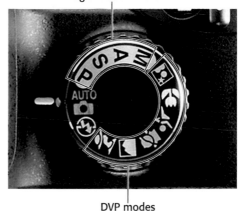

DVP modes

Image courtesy of Nikon, Inc.

QT.2 Rotate the Mode dial to select a shooting mode.

Focusing

Your Nikon D60 camera can automatically focus on the subject when using the lens that comes with the D60 kit. If you bought the camera body only, you need a Nikon AF-S lens to achieve autofocus (AF). Nikon's AF-S lenses have a built-in AF motor that allows the lens to focus without the use of an in-camera motor drive. Older Nikon AF lenses that are designated AF or AF-D require the use of a focus motor drive located in the camera body. In order to make the D60 the smallest and lightest camera that Nikon offers, the D60 does not have a focus motor built in to the camera. Therefore, you have to manually focus any older AF lenses that don't carry the AF-S designation.

The lens that comes with the D60 kit is the AF-S DX Nikkor 18-55mm f/3.5-5.6G VR. You can focus this lens either automatically or manually. To use the AF feature, you must first be sure that the switch on the lens is set to A.

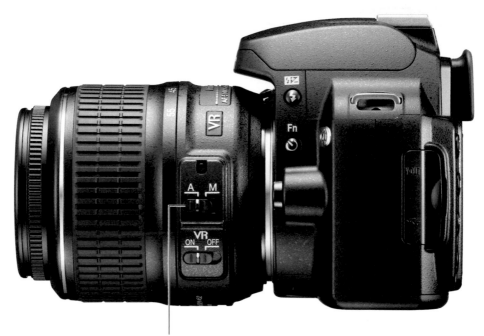

Autofocus/manual focus switch

Image courtesy of Nikon, Inc.
QT.3 The A/M switch on the kit lens

To autofocus the camera, you simply press the Shutter Release button halfway. The focus areas that are used to determine focus appear in the viewfinder as a series of three brackets. One or more of these brackets momentarily lights up in red when the camera achieves focus.

By default, the camera automatically focuses on the closest subject in all modes except for the Close-Up DVP mode, in which the camera uses the center focus point, and the Sports DVP mode, in which the camera uses all three focus points.

Once the camera has locked focus, a small green light in the bottom-left corner of the viewfinder lights up and a beep sounds. Now you can just press down fully on the Shutter Release button to take your picture.

If you want to lock focus and exposure settings so you can recompose your photo while maintaining the focus and exposure readings, you can press the Auto exposure/Autofocus lock (AE-L/AF-L) button that is found to the right of the viewfinder.

Playback

After you shoot some images with your D60, you can look at them on the big, bright 2.5-inch LCD screen. To view your images, press the Play button on the back of the camera; it's the top button to the left of the viewfinder. The most recent photo taken is the first image displayed.

To scroll through the images that are stored on the memory card, press the multiselector button left or right. Pressing the button to the right allows you to view the images in the sequence that they were taken. Pressing the button to the left displays the images in reverse order. Pressing the button up and down enables you to check the exposure settings and histogram.

 Cross-Reference *For more information on exposure settings and histograms see Chapter 4.*

There are a few other options available to you when the camera is in Playback mode:

✦ **Press the Thumbnail/Zoom out button to view thumbnails.** You can choose to view either four or nine images at a time. When in Thumbnail mode, use the multiselector to navigate among the thumbnails to highlight one. You can then press the OK button to bring the selected image to a full-size preview.

✦ **Press the Zoom in button to magnify the image.** This button allows you to check for sharpness or look for details. Pressing this button also takes you out of the thumbnail preview.

✦ **Press the Protect button to save images from being deleted.** The Protect button (denoted by a key) locks the image to prevent you from accidentally erasing it when editing your images in the camera.

 Caution *When the card is formatted, all images including the protected ones are erased.*

✦ **Use the multiselector to view image data.** To see what settings were used when a photograph was taken, press the multiselector up or down. This also allows you to check the histogram, which is a visual representation of the tonality of the image.

 Cross-Reference *For more detailed information on histograms, see Chapter 2.*

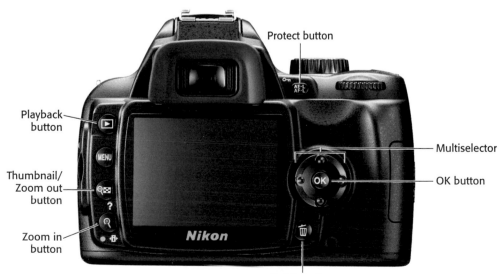

Protect button

Playback button

Multiselector

Thumbnail/ Zoom out button

OK button

Zoom in button

Nikon

Delete button

Image courtesy of Nikon, Inc.

QT.4 You can use these buttons in the Playback mode for a variety of functions.

✦ **Press the OK button to do in-camera photo editing.** Pressing the OK button brings you to a menu that allows you to do some rudimentary in-camera editing such as applying D-lighting, fixing red-eye, and cropping.

Cross-Reference *For more detailed information on in-camera editing, see Chapter 8.*

✦ **Press the Delete button to erase images.** The Delete button has an icon shaped like a trashcan on it. Press this button to permanently erase the image from your memory card. When the Delete button is pressed, the camera asks for confirmation. Press the Delete button again to complete the deletion.

Cross-Reference *For more detailed information on settings, see Chapter 2 for modes and Chapter 3 for menu settings.*

Downloading

When you fill up a card or you're ready to do some post-processing of your images, you want to download them off your memory card and onto your computer for storage. You can either download the images straight from the camera to your computer or you can remove the memory card from the camera and use a card reader to transfer the images.

To download images from the camera using the USB cable, follow these steps:

1. **Turn off the camera.** Be sure that the camera is off when connecting it to the computer to ensure that the camera's or computer's electronics are not damaged.

2. **Open the rubber cover that conceals the D60's output connections.** On the left side of the camera (with the back facing you) is a cover that hides the camera's USB video out ports.

3. **Connect the camera to the USB cable.** Inside the box that your D60 came in, there is a USB cable. Plug the small end of the cable into the camera and plug the other end into a USB slot on your computer.

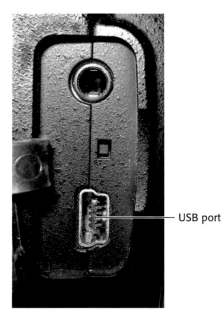

USB port

QT.5 The camera's USB port

4. Turn the camera on. Once turned on, your computer should recognize the camera as a mass storage device. You can then drag and drop your files or you can use a software program, such as Nikon View or Adobe Bridge, to transfer your files.

To download images using a SD card reader, follow these steps:

1. Turn off the camera. Be sure that the camera is off to avoid damaging the SD card upon removal.

2. Remove the memory card. Open the memory card door cover and press the SD card in and release to eject.

3. Insert the SD card into the card reader. Be sure that the reader is connected to your computer. Your computer should recognize the card as a mass storage device, and you can drag and drop the files or you can use a software program, such as Nikon View or Adobe Bridge, to transfer your files.

Note *Depending on your software and how your computer is set up, your computer may offer to automatically transfer the files to a predetermined destination.*

Cross-Reference *For more detailed information on downloading and transferring images see Chapter 8.*

Using the Nikon D60

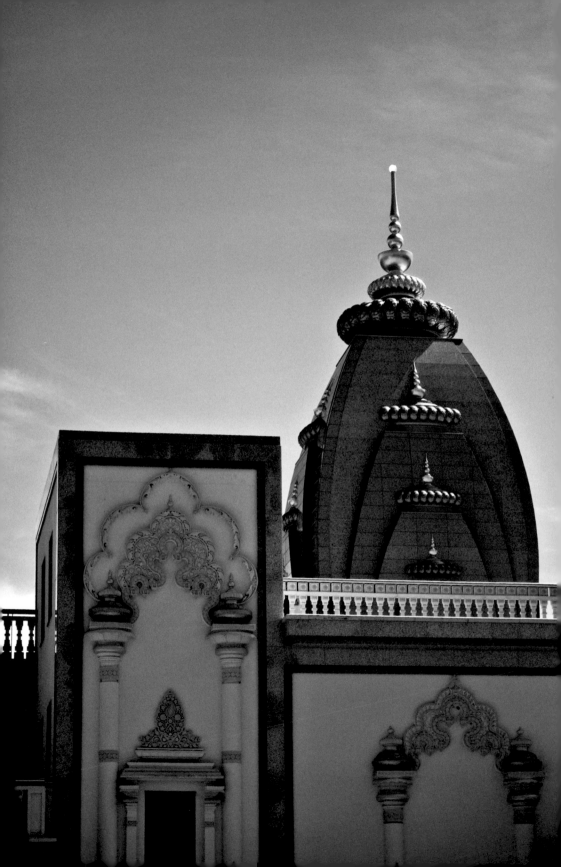

Exploring the Nikon D60

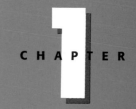
This chapter covers the key components of the Nikon D60. These are the features that are most readily accessible because they are situated on the outside of the camera: the buttons, knobs, switches, and dials.

If you are upgrading or switching from another dSLR, some of this may be a review, but there are some new features that you may or may not be aware of, so a quick read-through is a good idea even if you are an experienced Nikon dSLR user.

For those who may be just beginning in the world of dSLRs, this chapter is a great way to get acquainted with some of the terms that are used in conjunction with your new camera.

So fasten your seatbelts, and get ready to explore the D60!

Key Components of the D60

If you've read the Quick Tour, you should be pretty familiar with the basic buttons and switches that you need to do the essential settings. In this section, you look at the camera from all sides and break down the layout so that you know what everything on the surface of the camera does.

This section doesn't cover the menus, only the exterior controls. Although there are many features you can access with just the push of a button, oftentimes you can change the same setting inside of a menu option. Although the D60 doesn't have the same amount of buttons as some of its bigger siblings in the Nikon line, it does have quite a few of them. Knowing exactly what these buttons do can save you loads of time and help you get the shot.

Top of the camera

The top of the D60 is where you find some of the most important buttons and dials. This is where you can change the shooting mode and press the Shutter Release button to take your photo. Also included in this section is a brief description of some of the things you find on the top of the lens. Although your lens may vary, most of the features are quite similar from lens to lens.

✦ **Shutter Release button.** In my opinion, this is the most important button on the camera. Halfway pressing this button activates the camera's autofocusing and light meter. When you fully depress this button the shutter is released and a photograph is taken. When the camera has been idle and has "gone to sleep," lightly pressing the Shutter Release button wakes up the camera. When the image review is on, lightly pressing the Shutter Release button turns off the LCD and prepares the camera for another shot.

✦ **On/Off switch.** This switch, located around the Shutter Release button, is used to turn the camera on and off. Push the switch all the way to the left to turn off the camera. Pull the switch to the right to turn your camera on.

✦ **Mode dial.** This is an important dial. Rotating this dial allows you to quickly change your shooting mode. You can choose one of the Digital Vari-Program modes, one of the semiautomatic modes, or you can choose to set the exposure manually.

> **Cross-Reference** *For a detailed description of all of the exposure modes, see Chapter 2.*

✦ **Exposure compensation/ Aperture button.** Pressing this button in conjunction with spinning the Command dial (the Command dial is the wheel on the rear of the camera) allows you to modify the exposure that is set by the D60's light meter or the exposure you set in Manual exposure mode. Turning the Command dial to the right decreases exposure, while turning the dial to the left increases the exposure. This button also doubles as the Aperture button when the camera is set to Manual exposure mode. Pressing the button while rotating the Command dial allows you to adjust your lens aperture. Additionally, when pressing this button in conjunction with the flash mode you can adjust your flash exposure compensation by rotating the Command dial.

✦ **Active D-Lighting.** Pressing this button and rotating the command dial allows you to quickly turn on and off the Active D-Lighting function. Active D-Lighting helps to keep your highlights and shadow areas from being too dark or too light in high contrast situations.

✦ **Focal plane mark.** The focal plane mark shows you where the plane of the image sensor is inside the camera. When doing certain types of photography, particularly macro photography using a bellows lens, you need to measure the length of the bellows from the front element of the lens to the focal plane. This is where the focal plane mark comes in handy.

✦ **Hot shoe.** This is where an accessory flash is attached to the camera body. The hot shoe has an electronic contact that tells the flash to fire when the shutter is released. There are also a number of other electronic contacts that allow the camera to communicate with the flash to enable the automated features of a dedicated flash unit such as the SB-600.

✦ **Focus ring.** Rotating the focus ring enables you to manually focus the camera. With some lenses, such as the high-end Nikkor AF-S lenses, you can manually adjust the focus at any time. With the kit lens you must set the lens to Manual focus using the Focus mode switch on the side of the lens. Rotating the focus ring while the lens is set to autofocus can damage your lens.

✦ **Zoom ring.** Rotating the zoom ring allows you to change the focal length of the lens. Prime lenses do not have a zoom ring.

✦ **Focal length indicators.** These numbers indicate which focal length in millimeters your lens is zoomed to.

 Cross-Reference *For more information on lenses, see Chapter 4.*

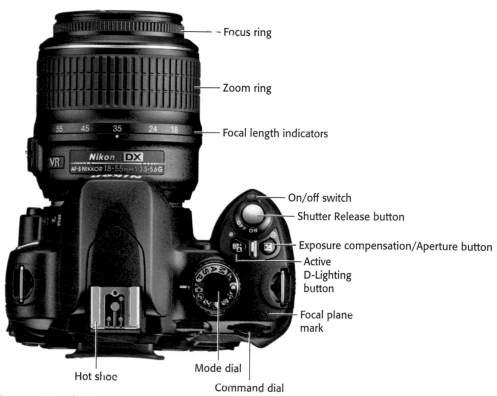

Focus ring

Zoom ring

Focal length indicators

On/off switch

Shutter Release button

Exposure compensation/Aperture button

Active D-Lighting button

Focal plane mark

Hot shoe

Mode dial

Command dial

Image courtesy of Nikon, Inc.

1.1 Top-of-the-camera controls

Back of the camera

The back of the camera is where you find the buttons that mainly control playback and menu options, although there are a few buttons that control some of the shooting functions. Most of the buttons have more than one function – a lot of them are used in conjunction with the Command dial or the multiselector. On the back of the camera you also find several key features, including the all-important viewfinder and LCD.

✦ **LCD.** This is the most obvious feature on the back of the camera. This 2.5-inch, 230,000-dot liquid crystal display (LCD) screen is a very bright, high-resolution screen. The LCD is where you view all of your current camera settings as well as review your images after shooting.

✦ **Eye sensor.** This sensor detects when you put the camera's viewfinder up to your eye. This is used to automatically turn off the shooting information displayed on the LCD and turn on the Viewfinder shooting information.

✦ **Viewfinder.** This is what you look through to compose your photographs. Light coming through the lens is reflected from a single front-silvered mirror and a pentaprism enabling you to see exactly what you're shooting. Around the viewfinder is a rubber eyepiece that gives you a softer place to rest your eye and to block any extra light from entering the viewfinder as you compose and shoot your images.

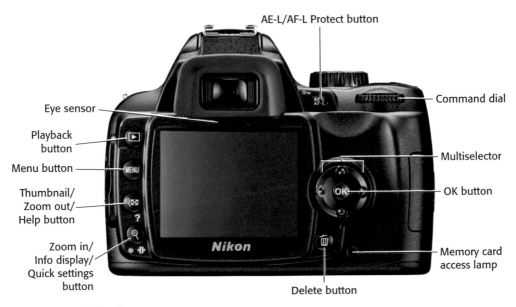

AE-L/AF-L Protect button

Eye sensor

Command dial

Playback button

Menu button

Multiselector

Thumbnail/ Zoom out/ Help button

OK button

Zoom in/ Info display/ Quick settings button

Memory card access lamp

Delete button

Image courtesy of Nikon, Inc.

1.2 Back-of-the-camera controls

✦ **Diopter adjustment control.** Just to the right of the viewfinder, hidden behind the eyecup, is the Diopter adjustment control. Use this control to adjust the viewfinder lens to suit your individual vision differences (not everyone's eyesight is the same). To adjust this, look through the viewfinder, and press the Shutter Release button halfway to focus on something. If what you see in the viewfinder isn't quite sharp, slide the Diopter adjustment up or down until everything appears in focus. The manual warns you not to put your finger or fingernail in your eye. I agree that this might not be a good idea.

✦ **AE-L/AF-L/Protect.** The Auto-Exposure/Auto-Focus lock button is used to lock the auto exposure (AE) and autofocus (AF). You can also customize the button to lock only the AE or only the AF, or you can set the button to initiate AF (this setting is in the Custom Settings Menu, CSM-12). When in playback mode this button can be pressed to lock an image to protect it from being deleted. A small key icon will be displayed in the upper left-hand corner of images that are protected.

Cross-Reference *For more information on the Custom Settings menu see Chapter 3.*

✦ **Command dial.** This dial is used to change a variety of settings depending on which button you are using in conjunction with it. By default, it is used to change the shutter speed when in Shutter Priority and Manual mode or the aperture when in Aperture Priority mode. It is also used to adjust Exposure compensation and change the Flash mode.

✦ **Multiselector.** The multiselector is another button that serves a few different purposes. In Playback mode, the multiselector is used to scroll through the photographs you've taken, and it can also be used to view image information such as histograms and shooting settings. When in certain Shooting modes, the multiselector can be used to change the active focus point when in Single point or Dynamic area AF mode. This is the button used to navigate through the menu systems.

✦ **OK button.** When in the Menu mode, press this button to select the menu item that is highlighted.

✦ **Delete button.** When reviewing your pictures, if you find some that you don't want to keep you can delete them by pressing this button marked with a trashcan icon. To prevent accidental deletion of images the camera displays a dialog box asking you to confirm that you want to erase the picture. Press the Delete button a second time to permanently erase the image.

✦ **Playback button.** Pressing this button displays the most recently taken photograph. You can also view other pictures by pressing the multiselector left and right.

✦ **Menu button.** Press this button to access the D60 menu options. There are a number of different menus including Playback, Shooting, Custom Settings, and Retouch. Use the multiselector to choose the menu you want to view.

✦ **Thumbnail/Zoom out/Help button.** In Playback mode, pressing this button allows you to go from full-frame playback (or viewing the whole image) to viewing thumbnails. The thumbnails can display either four images or nine images on a page. When viewing the menu options, pressing this button displays a help screen that explains the functions of that particular menu option. When in Shooting mode, pressing this button explains the functions of that particular mode.

✦ **Zoom in/Info display/Quick settings button.** When reviewing your images you can press the Zoom in button to get a closer look at the details of your image. This is a handy feature for checking the sharpness and focus of your shot. When zoomed in, use the multiselector to navigate around within the image. To view your other images at the same zoom ratio you can rotate the Command dial. To return to full-frame playback, press the Zoom out button. You may have to press the Zoom out button multiple times depending on how much you have zoomed in. When the camera is "asleep" pressing this button displays the Shooting info. When the Shooting info is displayed, pressing the button again gives you access to the Quick Settings menu. When in the Quick Settings menu, use the multiselector to highlight the desired setting to change then press the OK button to access the options.

Note The Zoom in / Info display / Quick settings button is one of two buttons that has a green dot beside it. The other button is the Active D-Lighting button. Pressing and holding these two buttons at the same time for 2 seconds resets all camera menus and settings to camera default.

Cross-Reference For more detailed information on the Quick Settings menu, see Chapter 3.

✦ **Memory card access lamp.** Located just to the right of the Delete button is the memory card access lamp. This light will flash green when the camera is saving to the memory card. Under no circumstances should you try to remove the memory card when this lamp is lit. You can damage your card and/or camera and lose your images.

Front of the camera

The front of the D60 (lens facing you) is where you find the buttons to quickly adjust the flash settings as well as some camera-focusing options, and with certain lenses you will find some buttons that control focusing and Vibration Reduction (VR).

✦ **Flash pop-up/Flash mode/Flash Exposure compensation button.** Press this button to open and activate the built-in Speedlight. Pressing this button and rotating the Command dial on the rear of the camera allows you to choose a flash mode. You can choose from among Front-curtain sync, Red-eye reduction, Red-eye reduction with slow sync, Slow sync, and Rear curtain sync. After the flash pops up, pressing this button in conjunction with the Exposure compensation button and rotating the Command dial allows you to adjust the Flash Exposure Compensation (FEC). FEC allows you to adjust the flash output to make the flash brighter or dimmer, depending on your needs.

Cross-Reference *For more information on flash modes see Chapter 6.*

✦ **Self-timer/Function (Fn) button.** By default, pressing this button activates the camera's self-timer. When the self-timer is on, the camera delays the shutter release to allow you to get into the picture or to reduce vibration caused by shaking the camera when pressing the Shutter Release button while

the camera is attached to a tripod. This button can also be set to provide other functions. You can set the button to quickly change from single to continuous shot, image quality, ISO sensitivity, or white balance via the Quick settings menu. Pressing the Fn button and rotating the Command dial changes the settings for the specific function assigned. The Fn button can be assigned to a specific function in CSM 11.

Cross-Reference *For more information on the Custom Settings menu (CSM), see Chapter 3.*

✦ **Lens release button.** This button disengages the locking mechanism of the lens, allowing the lens to be rotated and removed from the lens mount.

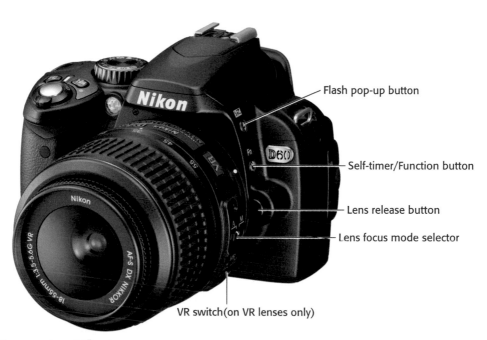

Flash pop-up button

Self-timer/Function button

Lens release button

Lens focus mode selector

VR switch(on VR lenses only)

Image courtesy of Nikon, Inc.
1.3 Front right camera controls

✦ **Lens Focus mode selector.** This switch is used to choose between using the lens in Auto or Manual focus.

✦ **VR switch.** If your lens features Vibration Reduction (VR) technology, this switch allows you to turn the VR on or off. When shooting in bright light it's best to turn the VR off to reduce battery consumption.

✦ **Built-in flash.** This option is a handy feature that allows you to take sharp pictures in low-light situations. Although not as versatile as one of the external Nikon Speedlights such as the SB-800 or SB-600, the built-in flash can be used very effectively and is great for snapshots.

✦ **AF-assist illuminator.** This is an LED that shines on the subject to help the camera focus in dim lighting. The AF-assist illuminator only lights when in Single focus mode (AF-S) or Automatic focus mode (AF-A).

✦ **Infrared receiver.** This allows you to wirelessly control the camera's shutter release using the optional ML-L3 infrared transmitter.

Sides and bottom of camera

The sides and bottom of the camera have places for connecting and inserting things such as cables, batteries, and memory cards.

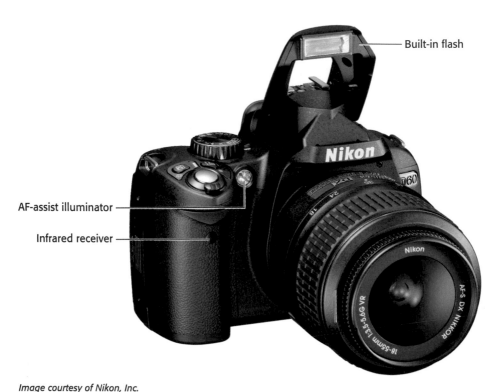

Built-in flash

AF-assist illuminator

Infrared receiver

Image courtesy of Nikon, Inc.
1.4 **Left front camera controls**

Right side

On the right side of the camera (with the lens facing you), are the D60's output terminals. These are used to connect your camera to a computer or to an external source for viewing your images directly from the camera. These terminals are hidden under a plastic cover that helps keep out dust and moisture.

✦ **Video out.** This connection, officially called Standard video output, is used to connect the camera to a standard TV or VCR for viewing your images on-screen. The D60 is connected with the EG-D100 video cable that is supplied with the camera.

✦ **USB port.** This is where the USB cable plugs in to attach the camera to your computer to transfer images straight from the camera. The USB cable is also used to connect the camera to the computer when using Nikon's optional Camera Control Pro 2 software.

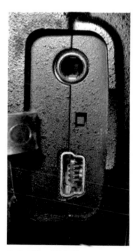

1.5 The D60's output terminals

Left side

On the left side of the camera (lens facing you) is the memory card slot cover. Sliding this door toward the back of the camera opens it so you can insert or remove your memory card.

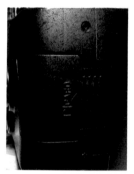

1.6 Memory card slot cover

Bottom

The bottom of the camera has a couple of features that are quite important.

✦ **Battery chamber cover.** This covers the chamber that holds the EN-EL9 battery that is supplied with your D60.

✦ **Tripod socket.** This is where you attach a tripod or monopod to help steady your camera.

Viewfinder Display

When looking through the viewfinder not only do you see the image you are composing, but there is also a lot of useful information about the photo you are setting up. Here is a complete list of all the information you can get from the viewfinder display.

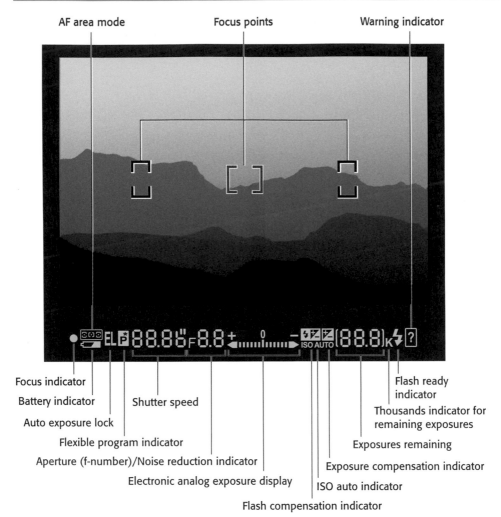

AF area mode   Focus points   Warning indicator

Focus indicator
Battery indicator
Auto exposure lock
Flexible program indicator
Aperture (f-number)/Noise reduction indicator
Electronic analog exposure display
Flash compensation indicator
ISO auto indicator
Exposure compensation indicator
Exposures remaining
Thousands indicator for remaining exposures
Flash ready indicator
Shutter speed

1.7 Viewfinder display showing all icons

✦ **Focus indicator.** This is a green dot that lets you know if the camera detects that the scene is in focus. When focus is achieved, the green dot lights up; when the scene is not in focus, the green dot blinks.

✦ **Focus point display.** When in Dynamic-area or Single Point AF modes this shows you which AF point is chosen by showing it with a bracket around it. When set to Closest Subject mode no AF point is chosen

✦ **EL lock.** When this is lit you know that the auto exposure has been locked.

✦ **Flexible program indicator.** When this is lit it lets you know that the exposure has been modified from the original settings defined when using the Programmed Auto exposure mode. To return to the default settings rotate the Command dial until this indicator disappears.

✦ **Shutter speed display/noise reduction indicator.** This shows how long your shutter is set to stay open. When the camera is performing noise reduction "job nr" is displayed here.

✦ **Aperture/f-stop display.** This shows what your current lens opening setting is.

✦ **Electronic analog exposure display/Exposure compensation/ Rangefinder.** Although Nikon gives this feature a long and confusing name, in simpler terms this is your light meter. When the bars are in the center you are at the proper settings to get a good exposure; when the bars are to the right you are underexposed; and when the bars are to the left you are overexposing your image. This feature is especially handy when using Manual exposure. When the Exposure Compensation button is pressed this indicates how much over- or underexposure is being set. When the Rangefinder option is turned on (CSM 19) this shows you a bar graph that indicates distance. When the subject is in focus there is one bar on either side of a 0. When the bars are displayed to the left this indicates that you are focused in front of the subject; bars to the right indicate that the focus is falling behind the subject. Use the focus ring to adjust the focus. The Rangefinder display is not available when shooting in Manual exposure mode. The range finder function is only available in Manual focus mode and is automatically activated when you attach a non-CPU manual focus lens.

✦ **FEC indicator.** When this is displayed your Flash exposure compensation is on.

✦ **Exposure compensation indicator.** When this appears in the viewfinder, Exposure compensation is activated, and you may not get a correct exposure.

✦ **Remaining exposures.** This set of numbers lets you know how many more exposures can fit on the memory card. The actual number of exposures may vary according to file information and compression. When the Shutter Release button is half-pressed, the display changes to show how many exposures can fit in the camera's *buffer* before the buffer is full and the frame rate slows down. The buffer is in-camera memory that stores your image data while the data is being written to the memory card. This area also indicates that the white balance is ready to be set by flashing PRE it displays the amount of exposure compensation and FEC when the exposure compensation button is pressed. It tells you whether the Active D-Lighting is on or off when the Active D-Lighting button is pressed, and also indicates when your camera is attached to a computer.

✦ **Flash ready indicator.** When this is displayed the flash, whether it is the built-in flash or an external Speedlight attached to the hot shoe, is fully charged and ready to fire at full power.

✦ **Warning indicator.** When this question mark icon is flashing the camera is warning you that there may be a problem with your settings. Press the Help button to view the warning.

✦ **Battery indicator.** This appears when the battery is low. When the battery is completely exhausted this icon blinks and the shutter release is disabled.

✦ **Auto ISO indicator.** This is displayed when the automatic ISO setting is activated to let you know that the camera is controlling the ISO settings.

✦ **K.** This lets you know that there are more than 1,000 exposures remaining on your memory card.

Shooting Info Display

When the camera is turned on the Shooting info is automatically displayed on the LCD monitor screen. The Shooting info display shows some of the same shooting information that appears in the viewfinder, but there are also some settings that are only displayed here. When this is displayed on the LCD you can view and change the settings without looking through the viewfinder. The Shooting info remains on display until no buttons have been pushed for about 8 seconds, your eye is put up to the viewfinder, or the Shutter Release button is pressed.

This display shows you everything you need to know about your camera settings. Additionally, the camera has a built-in sensor that knows when the camera is being held vertically and the Shooting info is displayed upright no matter which way you hold your camera.

The camera also allows you a number of options on how the information is displayed. You can choose between Classic, Graphic, and Wallpaper. You can also change the color of the Shooting info display. You can choose black, blue, or orange. You can also choose a different display for the DVP and P, S, A, and M modes. These setting can be accessed in the Setup menu under the Info display format menu.

 Cross-Reference *For more info on the Set-up menu, see Chapter 3.*

✦ **Shooting mode.** This displays the shooting mode that your camera is currently set to. This can be one of the DVP modes, in which case the display will be the appropriate icon or one of the semiauto modes such as P, S, A, or M, in which case the display shows the corresponding letter. This display changes when the Mode dial is rotated.

✦ **Shutter speed.** This shows in seconds or fractions of seconds how long your shutter will stay open when the Shutter Release button is pressed.

✦ **Aperture (f- number).** This tells you how wide your aperture or lens opening is. The terms *aperture* and *f-stop* are interchangeable. Higher f-numbers denote smaller openings while lower f-numbers mean that the opening is wider, letting in more light.

✦ **Shutter speed display.** When set to the Graphic mode this gives you a visual idea about the length of your shutter speed.

✦ **Aperture display.** When set to Graphic mode this shows you approximately what your lens opening looks like.

✦ **Electronic analog exposure display/Exposure compensation.** This is your light meter. When the bars are in the center, you are at the proper settings to get a good exposure; when the bars are to the right, you are underexposed; when the bars are to the left, you are overexposing your image. This feature comes in especially handy when using Manual exposure.

✦ **Flash exposure compensation.** This shows you the amount, if any, of flash exposure compensation. Flash exposure compensation (FEC) is used to make the flash more or less bright. FEC is set by simultaneously pressing the Flash mode button, the Exposure compensation button, and rotating the Command dial.

✦ **Flash sync mode.** This shows which mode your flash is set to. You can change the flash mode by pressing the Flash button and rotating the Command dial.

✦ **Exposure compensation value.** This shows the amount of exposure compensation, if any, that has been set. Exposure compensation is used to increase or decrease the amount of exposure to fine-tune your image.

✦ **Help indicator.** When this icon is flashing there may be a problem with one of your settings. Pressing the Help/Zoom out button displays information on rectifying the problem.

✦ **Active D-Lighting indicator.** This shows whether you have Active D-Lighting on or off. Active D-Lighting can be set by pressing the Active D-Lighting button and rotating the Command dial.

✦ **Number of remaining exposures/Preset white balance recording indicator/Capture mode indicator.** This shows you approximately how many exposures can be saved to your memory card. When the Preset White Balance is ready to be set this blinks PRE.

✦ **K.** This icon appears when you have more than 1,000 exposures remaining on your memory card.

✦ **Metering mode.** This displays which metering mode your camera is set to: Matrix, Center-weighted, or Spot.

✦ **AF-area mode.** This tells you which AF-area mode is selected: Closest subject, Dynamic area, or Single point.

✦ **Focus mode.** This tells you which focus mode your camera is set to: AF-A (Automatic), AF-C (Continuous), or AF-S (Single).

✦ **Release mode.** This lets you know what release mode your camera is set to: Single frame, Continuous, Self-timer, Delayed remote, or Quick response remote.

✦ **ISO sensitivity.** This tells you what your current ISO setting is.

✦ **White balance mode.** This displays which white balance setting you are currently using.

✦ **Image size.** This tells you the size of the image you are recording.

✦ **Image quality.** This display shows the quality or compression of the JPEG or shows that you are recording a RAW image.

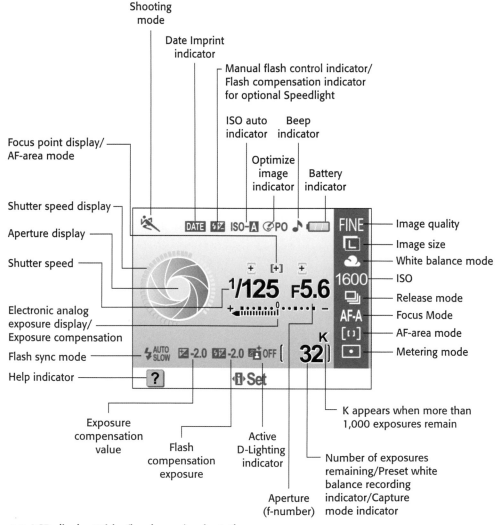

1.8 LCD display Wide (landscape) orientation

✦ **Focus point display/AF-area mode.** This indicates which focus point is currently active. This also shows the AF-area mode currently in use.

✦ **Battery indicator.** This shows you the remaining charge on your battery.

✦ **Beep indicator.** This icon tells you whether you have the camera set to beep when focus is achieved.

✦ **Optimize image indicator.** This option lets you know which Optimize image setting your camera is currently set to. The options are Normal (N), Softer (SO), Vivid (VI), More vivid (VI*), Portrait (PO), Black-and-white (BW), or Custom.

✦ **ISO auto indicator.** When this icon is shown the camera is set to Auto ISO.

✦ **Manual flash control indicator/Flash compensation for optional Speedlight indicator.** When this is displayed the camera's built-in flash is being set manually. This icon also appears when an optional Speedlight is attached and FEC has been set.

✦ **Date imprint indicator.** This icon is shown when the optional date imprint function is applied. This function prints the date at the bottom of the image as it's being recorded.

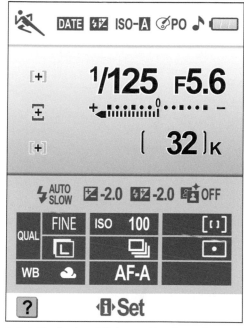

1.9 LCD display Tall (portrait) orientation

Nikon D60 Essentials

 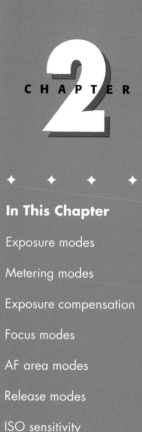

When you familiarize yourself with the basic layout of the D60 and all of the various dials, switches, and buttons, you should find it much easier to navigate to and adjust the settings that allow you to control and fine-tune the way the camera captures images. This chapter covers some of the most commonly changed settings of the camera, such as the exposure modes, metering, AF settings, white balance, and ISO. All of these settings combined are used to create your image, and you can tweak and adjust them to reflect your artistic vision or simply to be sure that your pictures come out right in tricky lighting situations.

Exposure settings covered in this chapter include the exposure modes and the metering modes. You also learn more about ISO, which also plays into exposure.

This chapter also explains the Autofocus modes, which determine which areas of the viewfinder are given preference when the camera is deciding what to focus on. Discussions of white balance, image quality, and file formats round out the chapter.

Exposure Modes

Exposure modes control how the camera chooses the aperture (f-stop), shutter speed, and ISO settings when determining the exposure. The camera gives aperture and shutter speed higher priority and adjusts the ISO accordingly depending on the lighting conditions. The D60 offers a wide variety of exposure modes ranging from fully manual, in which you completely determine the settings, to semiautomatic settings, in which you select the aperture or shutter speed, to fully automatic modes in which the camera determines all settings for you.

Digital Vari-Program

The Digital Vari-Program modes are more commonly called *scene modes*. These modes are for photographing specific scene types such as sports or portraits. The D60's scene modes allow you to capture the image with the settings that are best for what you are photographing. The camera has the parameters programmed into it so you can just rotate the Mode dial to the scene type. For example, when shooting sports you usually want to freeze the action, while when shooting a portrait you often want a wider aperture to blur out the background. With scene modes, you don't have to think about this and you can focus on capturing the moment rather than fretting over what the proper settings should be.

When using these scene modes, the camera controls all facets of the exposure process, including setting the shutter speed, aperture, and ISO. The camera also determines if there is enough light to make an exposure and activates the built-in flash if there is not enough light. Some of these scene modes, such as Auto (flash off) and Landscape, also make sure that the flash is not used even in low-light situations.

 Note *The Auto ISO setting can be overridden using the Quick settings display to change the ISO setting. If the Function button is set to ISO, the Auto ISO can be overridden as well. The override remains in effect unless the camera is changed to P, S, A, or M and returned to one of the DVP modes. When changing back to a DVP mode from P, S, A, or M the Auto ISO function is again activated.*

Auto

The Auto mode is basically a "point and shoot" mode. The camera takes complete control over the exposure. The camera's meter reads the light, the color, and the brightness of the scene and runs the information through a sophisticated algorithm. The camera uses this information to determine what type of scene you are photographing and chooses the settings that it deems appropriate for the scene. If there isn't enough light to make a proper exposure, the camera's built-in flash pops up when the Shutter Release button is half-pressed for focus. The flash fires when the shutter is released, resulting in a properly exposed image.

This mode is great for taking snapshots, when you simply want to concentrate on capturing the image and let the camera determine the proper settings.

Auto (flash off)

This mode functions in the same way as the Auto setting except it disables the flash even in low-light situations. In instances when the lighting is poor, the camera's AF-assist illuminator lights up to provide sufficient light to achieve focus. The camera uses the focus area of the closest subject to focus on.

This setting is preferable when you want to use natural or ambient light for your subject or in situations where you aren't allowed to use flash, such as museums or events such as weddings, where the flash may cause a distraction.

Portrait

This scene mode is for taking pictures of people. The camera automatically adjusts the colors to give natural-looking skin tones. The camera focuses on the closest subject. It also attempts to use a wide aperture, if possible, to reduce the depth of field. This draws attention to the subject of the portrait, leaving distracting background details out of focus.

The built-in flash and AF-assist illuminator automatically activate in low-light situations.

Landscape

This mode is used for taking photos of far-off vistas. The camera automatically adjusts the colors to apply brighter greens and blues to skies and foliage. The camera also automatically focuses on the closest subject and uses a smaller aperture to provide a greater depth of field to ensure focus throughout the entire image.

In this mode, the camera automatically disables the AF-assist illuminator and the flash.

Child

This mode is for taking great photos or candid shots of children. The camera automatically adjusts the colors to give more saturation while still giving a soft, natural skin tone. The camera automatically focuses on the closest subject and uses a fairly small aperture to capture background details. The built-in flash is automatically activated when the light is low.

Sports

This mode uses a high shutter speed to freeze the action of moving subjects. The camera focuses continuously as long as you have the Shutter Release button half-pressed. The camera also uses predictive focus tracking based on information from all of the focus areas in case the main subject moves from the center focus area.

The camera disables the built-in flash and AF-assist illuminator when this mode is selected.

Close-up

This scene mode is used for close-up or macro shots. It uses a fairly wide aperture to provide a soft background while giving the main subject a sharp focus. In this mode, the camera focuses on the subject in the center of the frame although you can use the multiselector to choose one of the other focus points to create an off-center composition. When light is low, the camera automatically activates the built-in flash. Be sure to remove your lens hood when using the flash on close-up subjects because the lens hood can cast a shadow on your subject by blocking the light from the flash.

Night Portrait

This mode is for taking portraits in low-light situations. The camera automatically activates the flash and uses a longer shutter speed to capture the ambient light from the background. This balances the ambient light and the light from the flash, giving you a more natural effect. I recommend using a tripod when you use this feature to prevent blur from camera shake that can occur during longer exposure times.

Programmed Auto

Programmed Auto, or P, mode is a fully automatic mode suitable for shooting snapshots and scenes where you're not very concerned about controlling the settings. This mode is similar to the Digital Vari-Program Auto mode, but doesn't automatically activate the flash in low light. It also allows you to adjust the ISO when your camera is set to the Auto-ISO off option. This mode also offers you the option of modifying the camera's settings to suit your specific needs.

When the camera is in P mode, the camera decides the settings for you based on a set of algorithms. The camera attempts to select a shutter speed that allows you to shoot handheld without suffering from camera shake while also adjusting your aperture so that you get good depth of field to ensure everything is in focus. When the camera body is coupled with an AF lens the camera automatically knows what focal length and aperture range the lens has. The camera then uses this lens information to decide what the optimal settings should be.

The P exposure mode chooses the widest aperture possible until it reaches the optimal shutter speed for the specific lens. Then the camera chooses a smaller f-stop, as well as increases the shutter speed as light levels increase. For example, when using a 17-55mm f/2.8 zoom lens, the camera keeps the aperture wide open until the shutter speed reaches about 1/40 second (the minimum shutter speed to avoid camera shake). Upon reaching 1/40 second, the camera adjusts the aperture to increase depth of field.

> **Cross-Reference** *For more information on aperture and shutter speed's effect on exposure see Chapter 4.*

The exposure settings selected by the camera appear on both the LCD monitor (when the Info button is pressed) and the viewfinder display. Although the camera chooses what it thinks are the optimal settings, the camera does not know what your specific needs are. You may decide that your hands are not steady enough to shoot at the shutter speed the camera has selected, or you may want a wider or smaller aperture for selective focus.

Fortunately, you aren't stuck with the camera's exposure choice. You can engage what is known as *flexible program*. Flexible

program allows you to deviate from the camera's aperture and shutter speed choice when you are in P mode. To automatically engage this feature, simply rotate the Command dial until the desired shutter speed or aperture is achieved. This allows you to choose a wider aperture/faster shutter speed when you rotate the dial to the right or a slower shutter speed/smaller aperture when you rotate the dial to the left. With flexible program, you can maintain the metered exposure while still having some control over the shutter speed and aperture settings.

A quick example of using flexible program would be if the camera has set the shutter speed at 1/60 second with an aperture of f/8 but you're shooting a portrait and want a wider aperture to throw the background out of focus. By rotating the Command dial to the right, you can open the aperture up to f/4, which causes the shutter speed to increase to 1/250 second. This is what is known as an *equivalent exposure*, meaning you get the same exact exposure but the settings are different.

When flexible program is on, an asterisk appears next to the P when the shooting info is displayed. Rotate the Command dial until the asterisk disappears to return to the default P settings.

 Caution *P, S, and A modes are not available when using a non-CPU lens. The camera must be set to M or Manual mode.*

 Note *If there is not enough light to make a proper exposure in P mode, the camera displays Lo instead of a shutter speed denomination.*

Aperture Priority

Aperture Priority, or A, mode is a semiautomatic mode. In this mode, you decide which aperture to use and the camera sets the shutter speed for the best exposure based on your chosen aperture. Situations where you may want to select the aperture include when you're shooting a portrait and want a wide aperture (small f-stop number) to blur the background, and when you're shooting a landscape and you want a small aperture (large f-stop number) to ensure the entire scene is in focus.

 If there is not enough light to make a proper exposure in A mode, the camera displays Lo in place of the shutter speed setting.

Shutter Priority

Shutter Priority, or S, mode is another semiautomatic mode. In this mode, you choose the shutter speed and the camera sets the aperture. This mode is good to use when shooting moving subjects or action scenes where you need to be sure to have a fast shutter speed to freeze the motion of your subject and prevent blur. You can also select a slower shutter speed to add motion blur as a creative photographic technique.

 If there is not enough light to make a proper exposure in S mode, the camera displays Lo in place of the aperture setting.

Manual

When in Manual, or M, mode, you set both the aperture and shutter speed settings. You can estimate the exposure, use a handheld light meter, or use the D60's electronic analog exposure display to determine the exposure needed.

 The D60's electronic analog exposure display only functions with lenses that have a CPU.

Probably the main question that people have about M mode is why use it when you have these other modes? There are a few reasons why you may want to set the exposure manually:

✦ **To gain complete control over exposure.** Most times, the camera decides the optimal exposure based on technical algorithms and an internal database of image information. Often what the camera decides to be optimal is not necessarily what is optimal in your mind. You may want to underexpose to make your image dark and foreboding, or you may want to overexpose a bit to make the colors pop (making colors bright and contrasty). If your camera is set to M, you can choose the settings and place your image in whatever tonal range you want without having to fool with Exposure compensation settings.

✦ **When using studio flash.** When using studio strobes or external nondedicated flash units, the camera's metering system isn't used. When using external strobes, a flash meter or manual calculation is necessary to determine the proper exposure. Using M mode, you can quickly set the aperture and shutter speed to the proper exposure; just be sure not to set the shutter speed above the rated sync speed of 1/200 second.

✦ **When using non-CPU lenses.** When you use older non-CPU lenses, you can only adjust the settings in M mode. You will also need to estimate the exposure settings or use an accessory light meter.

Metering Modes

The D60 has three metering modes that you can choose from to help you get the best exposure for your image: Matrix, Center-weighted, and Spot. Metering modes decide how the camera's light sensor collects and processes the information used to determine exposure. Each of these modes is useful for different types of lighting situations. You can change the modes by using the Quick Settings menu or changing the Custom Settings menu (CSM-5).

Matrix

The default metering system that Nikon cameras use is a proprietary system called 3D Color Matrix II, or Matrix metering for short. Matrix metering takes an evaluative reading of the light falling on the entire scene taking into account the color information. Then the camera runs the data through some sophisticated algorithms and determines the proper exposure for the scene. When using a current Nikkor D- or G-type lens, the camera also takes the focusing distance into consideration.

 Cross-Reference *For more info on lenses and lens specifications, see Chapter 5.*

The Matrix metering setting is highly intuitive, and Nikon has been refining it over a number of years, so it works very well for most subjects. I almost always have my camera set to Matrix.

Center-weighted

When the camera's metering mode is switched to Center-weighted, the meter takes a light reading of the whole scene, but bases the exposure settings mostly from the light falling on the center of the scene. The camera determines about 75 percent of the exposure from a circular pattern in the center of the frame and 25 percent from the edges.

Center-weighted metering is a very useful option. It works great when you're shooting photos where you know the main subject will be in the middle of the frame. It's useful when you're photographing a dark subject against a bright background, or a light subject against a dark background. And it works especially well for portraits where you want to preserve the background detail while exposing correctly for the subject.

Center-weighted metering can provide you consistent results without you having to worry about the fluctuations in exposure settings that can sometimes happen when using Matrix metering.

Spot

In Spot metering mode, the camera does just that: meters only a spot. This spot is only 3.5mm in diameter and only accounts for 2.5 percent of the entire frame. The spot is linked to the active focus point, which is good, so you can focus and meter your subject at the same time.

Spot metering is best when the subject is the only thing in the frame that you want the camera to expose for. For example, when you are photographing a subject on a completely white or black background, you need not be concerned with preserving detail in the background; therefore, exposing just for the subject works out perfectly. One example where this mode works well is in concert photography where the musician or singer is lit by a bright spotlight. You can capture every detail of the subject and just let the shadow areas go black.

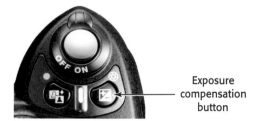

Exposure compensation button

2.1 The Exposure compensation button

Exposure Compensation

Your camera's meter is not always completely accurate. There are a lot of variables in most scenes, and large bright or dark areas can trick the meter into thinking a scene is brighter or darker than it really is, causing the image to be over- or underexposed. Exposure compensation is a feature of the D60 that allows you to fine-tune the amount of exposure to vary from what is set by the camera's exposure meter. If after taking the photograph you review it and it's too dark or too light, you can adjust the Exposure compensation and retake the picture to get a better exposure. You adjust Exposure compensation by pressing the Exposure compensation button, to the right of the Shutter Release button, and rotating the Command dial to the left for more exposure (+EV) or to the right for less exposure (-EV). The Exposure compensation is adjusted in 1/3 stops of light. You can adjust the Exposure compensation up to +5EV and down to -5EV, which is a large range of ten stops. To remind you that Exposure compensation has been set, the Exposure compensation indicator appears in the viewfinder display. It also appears on the rear LCD when the shooting info is being displayed.

Caution *Be sure to reset the Exposure compensation to 0 after you're done to avoid unwanted over- or underexposure.*

Histograms

The easiest way to determine if you need to adjust the Exposure compensation is to simply preview your image. If it looks too dark, add some Exposure compensation; if it's too bright, adjust the Exposure compensation down. This, however, is not the most accurate method of determining how much Exposure compensation to use. To accurately determine how much Exposure compensation to add or subtract, look at the *histogram*. A histogram is a visual representation of the tonal values in your image. Think of it as a graph that charts the lights, darks, and midtones in your picture.

The histogram charts a tonal range of about five stops, which is about the limit of what the D60's sensor can record. This range is broken down into 256 separate brightness levels from 0 (absolute black) to 255 (absolute white), with 128 coming in at middle, or 18 percent gray.

Ideally, with most average subjects that aren't bright white or extremely dark, you want to try to get your histogram to look

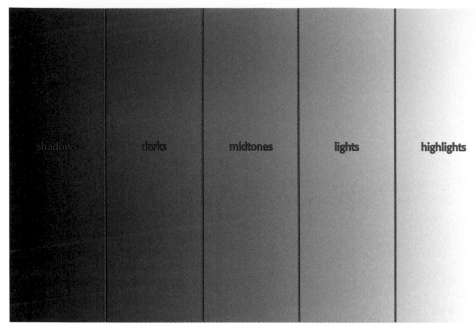

shadows   darks   midtones   lights   highlights

2.2 Representation of the tonal range of a histogram

sort of like a Bell curve, with most of the tones in the middle range tapering off as they get to the dark and light ends of the graph — so, you want to expose your subject so that it falls right about in the middle of the tonal range. But, this is only for most average types of images. As with almost everything in photography, there are exceptions to the rule. If you take a photo of a dark subject on a dark background (a *low-key* image), then naturally your histogram will have most of the tones bunched up on the left side of the graph. Conversely, if you take a photograph of a light subject on a light background (a *high-key* image), then the histogram will have most of the tones bunched up to the right.

The most important thing to remember is that there is no such thing as a perfect histogram. A histogram is just a factual representation of the tones in the image. The other important thing to remember is that although it's okay for the graph to be near one side or the other,

you usually don't want your histogram to have spikes bumping up against the edge of the graph; this indicates your image has *blown-out* highlights (completely white, with no detail) or *blocked-up* shadow areas (completely black, with no detail).

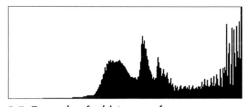

2.3 Example of a histogram from an over-exposed image (no highlight detail). Notice the spikes at the far right of the graph.

Now that you know a little bit about histograms, you can use them to adjust Exposure compensation. Here is a good order of operations to follow when using the histogram as a tool to evaluate your photos:

2.4 Example of a histogram from an under-exposed image (no shadow detail). Notice the spikes at the far left of the graph.

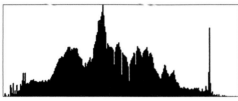

2.5 Example of a histogram from a properly exposed image. Notice that the graph does not spike against the edge on the left or the right, but tapers off.

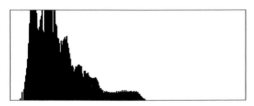

2.6 Example of a histogram from a low-key image. Notice that although the graph is mostly on the left, it does not spike against the edge, indicating that there is shadow detail in the image.

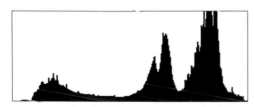

2.7 Example of a histogram from a high-key image. Notice that although the graph is mostly on the right, it does not spike against the edge, indicating that there is highlight detail in the image.

1. **After taking your picture, review its histogram on the LCD.** To view the histogram in the image preview, press the Playback button to view the image. Press the multi-selector up or down, until the histogram appears directly over the image preview.

2. **Look at the histogram.** An example of an ideal histogram is shown in figure 2.5.

3. **Adjust the Exposure compensation.** To move the tones to the right to capture more highlight detail, add a little Exposure compensation by pressing the Exposure compensation button and rotating the Command dial to the left. To move the tones to the left, press the Exposure compensation button and rotate the Command dial to the right.

4. **Retake the photograph if necessary.** After taking another picture, review the histogram again. If needed, adjust the Exposure compensation and try again until you achieve the desired exposure.

Bracketing

Another way to ensure that you get the proper exposure is to *bracket* your exposures. Bracketing is a photographic technique in which you vary the exposure of your subject over three or more frames. By doing this, you ensure you get the proper exposure in difficult lighting situationswhere your camera's meter can be fooled. Bracketing is usually done with at least one exposure under and one exposure over the metered exposure.

The following is a sequence of bracketed images. I shot five frames and used increments of 1EV to show the broad range of exposures you can get with bracketing.

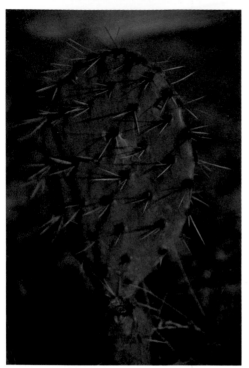

2.8 An image bracketed at -2 EV

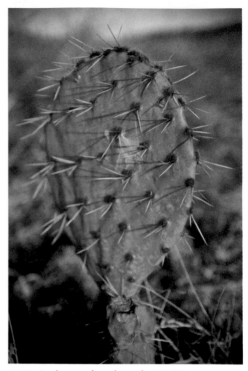

2.10 An image bracketed at 0 EV.

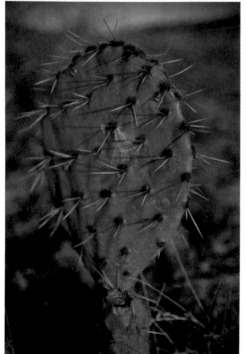

2.9 An image bracketed at -1 EV

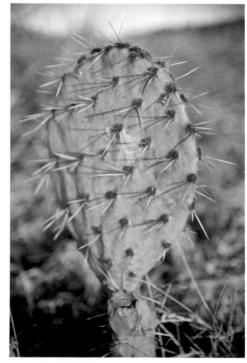

2.11 An image bracketed at +1 EV

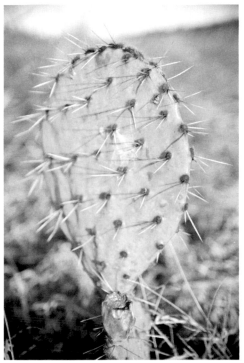

2.12 An image bracketed at +2 EV

Focus Modes

The Nikon D60 has four focus modes: Continuous AF, Single AF, Auto, and Manual. Each mode is useful for different types of shooting conditions, from sports to images to still-life photographs. These modes can be set using the Quick settings menu or by accessing the Custom Settings menu (CSM-2).

Continuous AF

When the camera is set to Continuous AF (AF-C), as long as the Shutter Release button is halfway pressed, the camera continues to focus. If the subject moves, the camera activates Predictive Focus Tracking. With Predictive Focus Tracking on, the camera tracks the subject to maintain focus and attempts to predict where the subject will

be when the Shutter Release button is pressed completely. When in Continuous AF mode, by camera default, the camera fires when the Shutter Release button is pressed, whether or not the subject is in focus (this is known as *release priority*). This is the AF mode you want to use when shooting sports or any subject that may be moving erratically.

Single AF

In Single AF (AF-S) mode, the camera focuses when the Shutter Release button is pressed halfway. When the camera achieves focus, the focus locks. The focus remains locked until you release the shutter or the Shutter Release button is no longer pressed. By default, the camera does not fire unless focus has been achieved (this is known as *focus priority*). This is the AF mode to use when shooting portraits, landscapes, or other photos where the subject is relatively static.

Auto

When the camera is set to this mode, it automatically chooses between AF-C and AF-S depending on the subject. If the camera determines that your subject is not moving, it sets the focus mode to AF-S. When the camera detects a moving subject, it sets the focus mode to AF-C.

Manual

When set to the Manual mode, the D60 AF system is off. You can only focus the camera by rotating the focus ring of the lens. The focus indicator light in the viewfinder display appears when the camera is in focus. You can use Manual mode when shooting still-life photographs or other nonmoving subjects, and when you want total control of the focus.

AF Area Modes

With the D60, Nikon uses the Multi-CAM530 AF module. The D60 focusing system has a three-point AF system. You can use the three AF points individually in Single-area AF mode, or you can set them to use in a group when in Dynamic-area AF mode. You can also set the camera to use the focus point that contains the closet subject to the camera.

The D60 also has Predictive Focus Tracking, which enables the camera to switch focus points as a moving subject crosses the frame. Focus tracking is made possible by the camera recognizing color and light information and using this to track the subject.

Single-area AF

Single-area AF mode is the easiest mode to use when you're shooting slow-moving or completely still subjects. You use the multi-selector to choose one of the three AF points. The camera only focuses on the subject if it is in the selected AF area. When selecting the AF point, the point used will be lit up in the viewfinder while the camera is attempting to achieve focus.

Dynamic-area AF

Dynamic-area AF mode also allows you to select the AF point manually, but unlike Single-area AF the remaining unselected points remain active so just in case the subject moves out of the selected focus area, the camera's AF can track it across the frame.

Closest subject AF

This mode is exactly what it sounds like: the camera automatically determines the closest subject and chooses one or more AF points to lock focus. This is a good mode to use when shooting close-up or macro pictures, or if you're shooting close-up portraits.

Release Modes

The release modes control how (or if) the Shutter Release button controls the actual shooting. You can set the release mode to take only one shot when the button is pressed or you can set it to shoot continuously as long as the Shutter Release button is pressed there are also options for adding a delay and for using a optional wireless remote. The release mode settings can be changed using the Quick Settings display or in the Custom Settings menu (CSM-04).

Single

When set to single mode the camera takes one picture each time the Shutter Release button is pressed. This is the best mode to use when shooting subjects that aren't moving or when shooting portraits.

Continuous

When the camera is set to Continuous release mode the camera takes photographs at up to three frames per second as long as the Shutter Release button is pressed and held down. The actual frame rate can vary depending on the shutter speed and shooting mode selected. To get the fastest frame rate using Shutter Priority mode with a shutter speed of 1/250 is recommended. Using Active D-lighting results in a slower frame rate. This is a good mode to use when shooting moderate to fast action such as sports.

Self-timer

Using this option gives the camera a time delay after the Shutter Release button is pressed before the camera takes the shot. This allows you be able to be in your own pictures. You can also use this option to reduce blur from camera shake that is caused from pressing the Shutter Release button when the camera is on a tripod. The delay allows the tripod and camera to stop shaking before the shutter is released giving you a sharper image especially when using long shutter speeds. By default the camera gives you a 10-second delay. You can change the delay time in the Custom Settings menu (CSM-16). The options are 2, 5, 10, or 20 seconds.

Delayed remote

This release mode can be used only with the optional ML-L3 Wireless Remote Control. When using this mode the shutter is released 2 seconds after the camera has achieved focus.

Quick response remote

This option can also only be used with the optional ML-L3 Wireless Remote Control. When using this release mode the camera takes a picture as soon as the camera is in focus after pressing the Release button on the remote.

ISO Sensitivity

ISO, which stands for International Organization for Standardization, is a rating for the speed of film. In digital terms that translates to the sensitivity of the sensor to light. The ISO numbers are standardized, which allows you to be sure that when you

shoot at ISO 100 you get the same exposure no matter what camera you are using. Because the ISO you choose determines how sensitive the image sensor is to the light that is reaching it through the lens opening, increasing or reducing the ISO affects the exposure by allowing you to use faster shutter speeds or smaller apertures (raising the ISO), or using a slower shutter speed or wider aperture (lowering the ISO).

The D60 has an ISO range of 100 to 1600. In addition to these standard ISO settings, the D60 also offers a setting that extends the available range of the ISO so you can shoot in very dark situations. This setting is labeled as H1 (high speed) and gives you an equivalent ISO sensitivity of 3200.

 Caution *Using the H1 setting does not produce optimal results. The H1 setting can cause your images to have a high amount of digital noise, which are artifacts caused by amplifying the camera's sensor signal to achieve more light sensitivity.*

Auto ISO

The D60 also offers a feature where the camera adjusts the ISO automatically for you when there isn't enough light to make a proper exposure. Auto ISO is meant to free you up from making decisions about when to raise the ISO. The Auto ISO can be set in the Shooting menu under the ISO sensitivity settings option.

 Cross-Reference *For more information on the Shooting menu see Chapter 3.*

By default, when Auto ISO is on, the camera chooses an ISO setting from 100 up to 1600 whenever the shutter speed falls below 1/30 second. You can also limit how high the ISO can be set so you can keep control of the noise created when a higher ISO is used.

Note Auto ISO is automatically selected when shooting in one of the Digital Vari-Program modes, such as Portrait or Child.

Be sure to set the following options in the Shooting menu/ISO sensitivity settings:

✦ **Maximum Sensitivity.** Choose an ISO setting that allows you to get an acceptable amount of noise in your image. If you're not concerned about noisy images then you can set the ISO all the way up to 1600. If you need your images to have less noise you can choose a lower ISO.

✦ **Minimum Shutter Speed.** This setting determines when the camera adjusts the ISO to a higher level. At the default, the camera bumps up the ISO when the shutter speed falls below 1/30 second. If you're using a longer lens or you're photographing moving subjects you may need a faster shutter speed. In that case, you can set the minimum shutter speed up to 1/250. On the other hand, if you're not concerned about camera shake, or if you're using a tripod, you can set a shutter speed as slow as 1 second.

Note The minimum shutter speed is only taken into account when using Programmed Auto or Shutter Priority modes.

Noise reduction

Since the inception of digital cameras, they've been plagued with what is known as *digital noise*. This, simply put, is randomly colored dots that appear in your image giving it a grainy appearance. It is basically caused by extraneous electrons that are produced when your image is being recorded. When light strikes the image sensor in your D60, electrons are produced. These electrons create an analog signal that is converted into a digital image by the Analog to Digital (A/D) converter in your camera.

There are two specific causes of noise.

✦ **The first cause of digital noise is *heat generated* or *thermal noise*.** While the shutter is open and your camera is recording an image, the sensor starts to generate a small amount of heat. This heat can free electrons from the sensor, which in turn contaminate the electrons that have been created as a result of the light striking the photocells on your sensor. This contamination shows up as noise.

✦ **The second cause of digital noise is known as *high ISO noise*.** In any type of electronic device there is background electrical noise. For the most part it's very miniscule and you never notice it. Cranking up the ISO amplifies the signals (photons of light) your sensor is receiving. Unfortunately, as these signals are amplified so is the background electrical noise. The higher your ISO, the more the background noise is amplified until it shows up as randomly colored specks.

Digital noise is composed of two different elements, *chrominance* and *luminance*. Chrominance refers to the colored specks and luminance refers mainly to the size and shape of the noise.

Fortunately, with every new camera released, the technology gets better and better, and the D60 is no exception. You can shoot at ISO 800 and not worry about excessive noise. In previous cameras, shooting at ISO 800 sometimes produced a very noisy image that was not suitable for large prints.

Although very low in noise, there is noise there, especially when shooting at or above ISO 1600 (the Hi setting) or when using long exposure times. For this reason most camera manufacturers have built-in noise reduction (NR) features.

When this setting is turned on (in the Shooting menu), the camera runs a NR algorithm to any shot taken with a long exposure (8 seconds or more). Basically, how this works is that the camera takes another exposure, this time with the shutter closed, and compares the noise from this dark image to the original one. The camera then applies the NR. The NR takes about the same amount of time to process as the length of the initial exposure; therefore, expect to double the time it takes to make one exposure. While the camera is applying NR, the LCD panel blinks a message that says "Job nr." No additional images can be taken until this process is finished. If you switch the camera off before the NR is finished, no noise reduction is applied.

(When the noise reduction is set to on, any image shot at ISO 400 or higher is run through the NR algorithm.) This NR feature works by reducing the coloring in the chrominance of the noise and combining that with a bit of softening of the image to reduce the luminance noise. Even when the NR is turned off, the camera applies a small amount of NR to all images that are shot at ISO 800 or higher.

You can turn NR off in the Shooting menu.

 Note *When shooting in RAW no actual noise reduction is applied to the image.*

For the most part, I choose not to use in-camera NR features. In my opinion, even at the lowest setting, the camera is very aggressive in the NR, and for that reason, there is a loss of detail. For most people, this is a minor quibble and not very noticeable, but for me, I'd rather keep all of the available detail in my images and apply NR in post-processing. This way I can decide for myself how much to reduce the chrominance and luminance rather than letting the camera do it. The camera doesn't know whether you're going to print the image at a large size or just display it on-screen.

Tip *NR can be applied in Capture NX, or by using Photoshop's Adobe Camera Raw or other image-editing software.*

White Balance

Various types of light, whether from sunlight, a light bulb, fluorescent lighting, or a flash, have their own specific color. This color is measured using the Kelvin scale. This measurement is also known as *color temperature*. The white balance allows you to adjust the camera so that your images can look natural no matter what the light source. Because white is the color that is most dramatically affected by the color temperature of the light source, it is what you base your settings on; hence the term *white balance*. You can change the white balance in the Shooting menu or by pressing the WB button on the top of the camera and rotating the Command dial.

The term color temperature may sound strange to you. "How can a color have a temperature?" you might think. Once you know about the Kelvin scale, things make a little more sense.

What is Kelvin?

Kelvin is a temperature scale, normally used in the fields of physics and astronomy, where absolute zero (0K) denotes the absence of all heat energy. The concept is based on a mythical object called a *black body radiator*. Theoretically, as this black body radiator is heated, it starts to glow. As it is heated to a certain temperature, it glows a specific color. It is akin to heating a bar of iron with a torch. As the iron gets hotter, it turns red, then yellow, and then eventually white before it reaches its melting point (although the theoretical black body does not have a melting point).

The concept of Kelvin and color temperature is tricky as it is the opposite of what you likely think of as "warm" and "cool" colors. For example, on the Kelvin scale, red is the lowest temperature, with it increasing through orange, yellow, white, and to shades of blue, which are the highest temperatures. Humans tend to perceive reds, oranges, and yellows as warmer and white and bluish colors as colder. However, physically speaking, the opposite is true as defined by the Kelvin scale.

White balance settings

Now that you know a little about the Kelvin scale, you can begin to explore the white balance settings. The reason that white balance is so important is to ensure that your images have a natural look. When dealing with different lighting sources, the color temperature of the source can have a drastic effect on the coloring of the subject. For example, a standard light bulb casts a very yellow light; if the color temperature of the light bulb is not compensated for by introducing a bluish cast, the subject can look overly yellow and not quite right.

To adjust for the colorcast of the light source, the camera introduces a colorcast of the complete opposite color temperature. For example, to combat the green color cast of a fluorescent lamp, the camera introduces a slight magenta cast to neutralize the green.

The D60 has eight white balance settings:

AUTO   **Auto.** This setting is best for most circumstances. The camera takes a reading of the ambient light and makes an automatic adjustment. This setting also works well when using a Nikon-compatible Speedlight because the color temperature is calculated to match the flash output. I actually recommend using this setting as opposed to the Flash WB setting.

    Incandescent. This setting is best when the lighting is from a standard household light bulb.

    Fluorescent. This setting is best when the lighting is coming from a fluorescent-type lamp. You can also adjust for different types of fluorescent lamps, including high-pressure sodium and mercury vapor lamps. To make this adjustment, go to the Shooting menu and choose White Balance, and then fluorescent. From there, use the multiselector to choose one of the seven types of lamps.

Direct sunlight. This setting is best when shooting outdoors in daylight. 5500K.

 Flash. This setting is best when using the built-in Speedlight, a hot-shoe Speedlight, or external strobes. 5500K

 Cloudy. This setting is best when shooting under overcast skies. 6500K

 Shade. This setting is best when you're in the shade of a tree or a building or even under an overhang or a bridge — anyplace where the sun is out but is being blocked. 7500K

PRE **PRE.** This setting allows you to choose a neutral object to measure for the white balance. It's best to choose an object that is either white or light gray. There are some accessories that you can use to set the white balance from. One accessory is a gray card, which is fairly inexpensive. Simply put the gray card in the scene and balance off of it. Another accessory is the Expodisc. This attaches to the front of your lens like a filter; you then point the lens at the light source and set your white balance. PRE is best used under difficult lighting situations, such as when there are two different light sources lighting the scene (mixed lighting). I usually use this setting when photographing with my studio strobes. To preset a white balance:

1. **Press the Shooting info button twice to enter the Quick Settings menu.**

2. **Use the multiselector to highlight the white balance option then press the OK button.**

3. **Use the multiselector up/down to scroll thorough the WB options until you get to PRE, and then press the OK button.**

4. **Press and hold the OK button until PRE starts flashing on the Shooting info display (PRE also flashes in the viewfinder display).**

5. **Point your camera at an object that is white or gray, and then release the shutter.** The subject does not have to be in focus.

6. **If the Shooting info display flashes Gd, your WB has been recorded; if the info display flashes no Gd, try again.**

Tip *By keeping your digital camera set to the Automatic WB setting, you can reduce the amount of images taken with incorrect color temperatures. In most lighting situations, the Automatic WB setting is very accurate. You may discover that your camera's ability to evaluate the correct white balance is more accurate than setting white balance manually.*

Figures 2.13 to 2.19 show the different looks of the white balance settings.

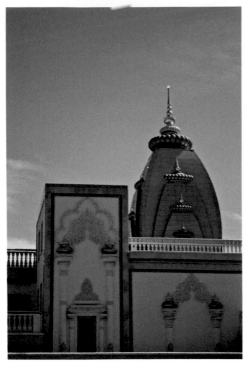

2.13 Auto, 5050K

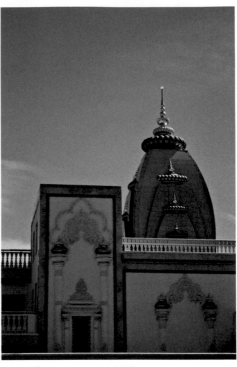

2.15 Fluorescent, 3800K

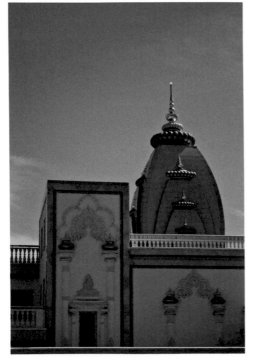

2.14 Incandescent, 2850K

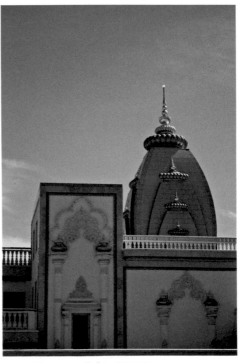

2.16 Direct sunlight, 5500K

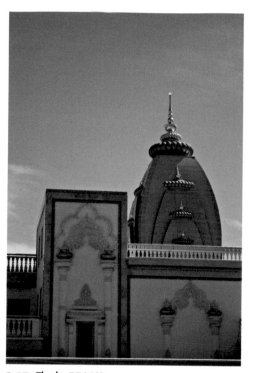

2.17 Flash, 5500K

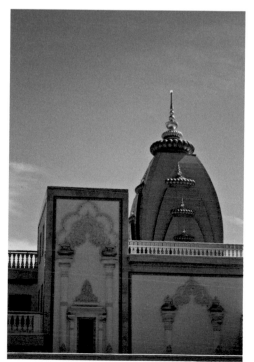

2.18 Cloudy, 6500K

2.19 Shade, 7500K

Image Size and Quality

The Nikon D60 allows you to choose from two different file formats when saving your images: RAW or JPEG. In addition you can also to choose to store a RAW file and a JPEG file at the same time.

The file format you choose depends on how much control you want over the final output of your images and how much post-processing you're willing to do. RAW files allow you a little more flexibility in how your final image turns out because none of the data is actually fixed when you record it. JPEG images work best when you just want to print straight out of the camera and you don't necessarily plan to spend a lot of time editing your images using software. Of course you can easily edit JPEG files using software as well, but as I said before RAW files offer much more flexibility and often yield better results.

RAW

A RAW file is a file format that preserves all of the original image data that was recorded by your camera's sensor. You can manipulate this image data after you have saved the image, which allows you greater control over your images. You can adjust the exposure, white balance, and image size among other things. For the most part, you do these RAW conversions on a computer, using image-processing software such as Nikon Capture NX or Adobe Camera Raw (available in Photoshop).

The Nikon D60 also allows you to make some changes to your RAW files in-camera too. Since RAW files are usually not supported by most print services and cannot be printed using a direct USB connection the NEF (RAW) processing feature in the Retouch menu allows you to make adjustments in camera then save as a JPEG so you can print directly from your camera or memory card.

Cross-Reference *For more information on in-camera RAW processing and the Retouch menu see Chapter 8.*

JPEG

The second option for saving images on the D60 is JPEG. When an image is saved as JPEG, the camera processes the image information and applies any custom settings that you may have chosen in the Optimize image

option, such as sharpening, contrast adjustments, or color adjustments. JPEG images can be processed using image-processing software, but they leave you with less flexibility than RAW files when it comes to making adjustments. JPEG files are also compressed when saved, which gives you a smaller file size, allowing you to fit more images on your memory card.

Cross-Reference *For more information on Optimize image, see the Shooting menu section of Chapter 3.*

Image size and compression

When saving to JPEG format, the D60 allows you to choose an image size. Reducing the image size is like reducing the resolution on your camera: It allows you to fit more images on your card. What size you choose depends on what your output is going to be. If you know you will be printing your images at a large size, then you definitely want to record large JPEGs. If you're going to print at a smaller size (8 × 10 or 5 × 7), you can get away with recording at the medium or small setting.

Image size is expressed in pixel dimensions. The large setting records your images at 3872 × 2592 pixels; this gives you a file that is equivalent to 10.2 megapixels. Medium size gives you an image of 2896 × 1944 pixels, which is in effect the same as a 5.6-megapixel camera. The small size gives you a dimension of 1936 × 1296 pixels, which gives you about a 2.5-megapixel image.

Other than the size setting, which changes the pixel dimension, you have the compression settings Fine, Normal, and Basic. There is considerable controversy regarding whether compressing a JPEG to a smaller size reduces the actual resolution. This controversy stems from the fact that when a JPEG file is closed, it compresses to a smaller size discarding some of the image information to save space. This is known as lossy compression because image data is lost. When set to Basic or Normal, more information is discarded, supposedly resulting in less image detail. Some photographers say that using the Fine setting is the only way to go while others profess that the Normal setting is perfectly good for print use.

I don't want to choose sides in this controversy. The advice that I offer is this: Set up a shot and take one at each of the settings, make a print of each, and decide for yourself whether or not you can see an appreciable difference.

Setting up the Nikon D60

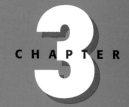

T he first few sections of the book covered how to change the main settings of your D60. In this chapter, I delve deep into the menu options. In the menus, you can customize the D60 options to fit your shooting style, help refine your workflow, or make adjustments to refine the camera settings to fit different shooting scenarios.

Some of these options are the same as those you can access and adjust by pushing a button and/or rotating the Command dial. However, in the menus, you can access other options that don't need to be changed very often or quickly.

After pressing the Menu button, use the multiselector to scroll through the toolbar on the left side of the LCD. When the desired menu is highlighted, press the OK button or turn the multiselector right to enter the menu. Pressing the Menu button again or tapping the Shutter Release button exits the Menu mode screen and readies the camera for shooting.

Note Pressing the Menu button on the back of the camera accesses all of the menus, with the exception of the Quick Settings display.

Quick Settings Display

The Quick Settings display is arguably the most important menu, and you'll probably find yourself accessing this quite often. This is where you can quickly change most of the principal settings: flash mode, Exposure compensation, Flash exposure compensation, Active D-Lighting, metering, AF-area mode, focus mode, release mode, ISO, white balance, and image quality.

Accessing this menu is a very simple process. When the camera is turned on and the shooting information is automatically displayed, press the Info/Zoom in button to enter the Quick Settings display. If the LCD monitor is off you need to press the button twice, first to display the shooting information and then to show the Quick Settings.

Note *Some settings are not available in certain DVP modes. These options are grayed out and not accessible.*

When the Quick Settings menu is displayed use the multiselector left/right or up/down to highlight the setting you want to change. Press the OK button to display the options for the specific setting. Use the multiselector up/down to highlight the setting option. Press the OK button or multiselector right to change the setting. Press the multiselector left to return to the Quick Settings display without changing the setting. To exit the Quick Settings display, press the Information/Zoom-in button or tap the Shutter Release button.

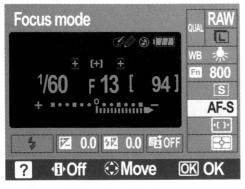

3.1 The Quick Settings display

Playback Menu

The Playback menu is where you manage the images stored on your flash card. The Playback menu is also where you control how the images are displayed and what image information and is displayed during review. There are 6 options available from the Playback menu.

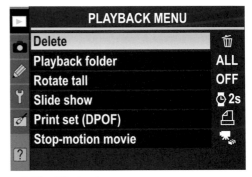

3.2 The Playback menu

Delete

This option allows you to delete selected images from your memory card or to delete all of the images at once.

To delete selected images:

1. **Press the multiselector right, highlight Selected (default) from the Delete menu, and press the multiselector to the right again.** You can now select the image you want to delete.

2. **Use the multiselector left/right to choose the image.** You can also use the Zoom in button to review the image close up before deleting. Press the multiselector up or down to set the image for deletion; more than one image can be selected. When the image is selected for deletion it shows a small trashcan icon in the right-hand corner.

3. **Press the OK button to erase the selected image(s).** The camera asks you for confirmation before deleting the image(s).

4. **Select Yes, and then press the OK button to delete.** To cancel the deletion, highlight No (default), and then press the OK button.

To delete all images:

1. **Use the multiselector down to highlight All from the Delete menu, and then press the OK button.** The camera asks you for confirmation before deleting the images.

2. **Select Yes, and then press the OK button to delete.** To cancel deletion, highlight No (default), and then press the OK button.

Playback folder

This menu allows you to choose the folder from which to display images for review. The default setting is NCD60, which displays images from the default folder created by the D60, which is named NCD60. Selecting All displays images from all folders. Selecting Current displays images only from the folder to which the camera is actively saving at the time.

Changing the active folder is covered later in this chapter.

Rotate tall

This rotates images that are shot in portrait orientation to be displayed upright on the LCD screen. I usually turn this option off because the portrait orientation image appears substantially smaller when displayed upright on the LCD.

The options are:

✦ **On.** The camera automatically rotates the image to be viewed while holding the camera in the standard upright position.

✦ **Off (default).** When the auto-rotating function is turned off, images taken in portrait orientation are displayed on the LCD sideways in landscape orientation.

Slide show

This allows you to display a slide show of images from the current active folder. You can choose an interval of 2, 3, 5, or 10 seconds.

While the slide show is in progress, you can use the multiselector to skip forward or back (left or right), and view shooting information or histograms (up or down). You can also press the Menu button to return to the Playback menu, press the Playback button to end the slide show, or press the Shutter Release button halfway to return to the Shooting mode.

Print set (DPOF)

DPOF stands for Digital Print Order Format. This option allows you to select images to be printed directly from the camera. This can be used with Pict-bridge-compatible printers or DPOF-compatible devices such as a photo kiosk at your local photo printing shop. This is a pretty handy feature if you don't have a printer at home and want to get some prints made quickly, or if you do have a printer and want to print your photos without downloading them to your computer.

To create a print set:

1. **Use the multiselector to choose the Print set (DPOF) option, and then press the multiselector right to enter the menu.**

2. **Use the multiselector to highlight Select/set, and then press the multiselector right to view thumbnails.** Press the Zoom in button to view a larger preview of the selected image.

3. **Use the multiselector right/left to highlight an image to print.** When the desired image is highlighted, press the multiselector up/down to set the image and choose the number of prints you want of that specific image. You can choose from 1 to 99. The number of prints and a small printer icon appear on the thumbnail. Continue this procedure until you have selected all of the images that you want to print. If you want to reduce the number of prints you have set, or to completely remove it from the print set, press the multiselector down.

4. **Press the OK button.** A menu appears with three options:

   • **Done (default).** Press the OK button to save and print the images as they are.

   • **Data imprint.** Press the multiselector right to set. A small check appears in the box next to the menu option. When this option is set, the shutter speed and aperture setting appear on the print.

   • **Date imprint.** Press the multi-selector right to set. A small check appears in the box next to the menu option. When this option is set, the date the image was taken appears on the print

5. **If you choose to set the imprint options, be sure to return to the Done option and press the OK button to complete the print set.**

Stop-motion movie

The Nikon D60 allows you create stop-motion movies through the Retouch menu using images you have stored on your memory card. If you have created a stop-motion movie, you can use this option to playback the movie.

Cross-Reference *See Chapter 8 for an in-depth discussion of the Retouch menu and a look at how to create your own stop-motion movie.*

Shooting Menu

The Shooting menu is where you can change the different options of how the images are stored as well as other settings such as white balance, noise reduction, Active D-Lighting, and JPEG compression.

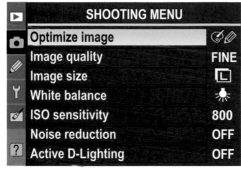

3.3 The Shooting menu

Optimize image

This option allows you to choose different settings to adjust how a JPEG is processed in the camera. These settings apply different amounts of sharpening, contrast, and saturation depending on the setting chosen. The default color space for all of these settings except for Custom is sRGB. The options are:

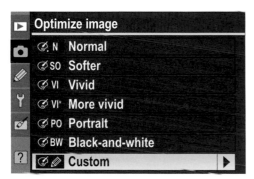

3.4 The Optimize image menu

✦ **Normal.** This is the default setting. This setting is recommended for most shooting situations. The camera automatically applies sharpening and tone compensation as needed.

✦ **Softer.** Using this setting gives your images a softer look. No sharpening is applied. This setting can work well with portraits and images that will be retouched later on with an image-editing program.

✦ **Vivid.** This setting applies a fair amount of sharpening, the saturation is increased, and tone compensation is applied to give the image more contrast. This setting gives you images with bright reds, greens, and blues. This works well for landscapes and night images.

✦ **More vivid.** This setting applies the maximum amount of sharpening, tone compensation, and saturation giving the image intense colors with a lot of contrast and sharpness. This setting is not recommended for shooting images of people as it can give the subject oddly colored skin tones. This setting is best used for landscape images in which the scene lacks contrast.

✦ **Portrait.** This setting gives the image a lower contrast and applies no sharpening to make the subject's skin smoother looking with natural skin tones.

✦ **Black-and-white.** When this setting is chosen the images are converted to black and white. This is a good setting to use when shooting at a very high ISO or to give your images a vintage or retro feel.

✦ **Custom.** This setting allows you to choose your own parameters with which your photos is processed. When choosing the Custom setting a submenu appears that offers you the following options:

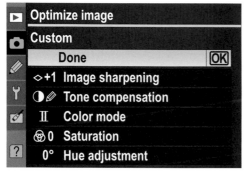

3.5 The Optimize image Custom submenu

- **Image sharpening.** This applies a sharpening algorithm to your images that adds a little contrast between the pixels giving your image the appearance of sharpness. Be careful not to overdo this as it can cause your images to look overprocessed and unnatural. The choices for this setting are: Auto, Normal, Low, Medium low, Medium high, High, and None.

- **Tone compensation.** This controls the amount of contrast in your image. The choices are: Auto, Normal, Less contrast, Medium low, Medium high, More contrast, and Custom. The Custom setting allows you to use a Custom contrast setting that can be uploaded using Nikon's Camera Control Pro 2 software, which is available separately. Use the lower settings when photographing high-contrast scenes to preserve

highlight and shadow detail. When photographing in situations that have low contrast, such as a foggy morning, use the higher settings to add some depth to the image.

- **Color mode.** This allows you to choose which color space your images are saved in. Color space simply describes the range of colors, also known as the gamut, that a device can reproduce. You have two choices of color spaces with the D60: sRBG and Adobe RBG. The color space you choose depends on what the final output of your images will be.

  sRGB is a narrow color space, meaning that it deals with fewer colors and also less-saturated colors than the larger Adobe RGB color space. The sRGB color space is designed to mimic the colors that can be reproduced on most low-end monitors. The D60 offers you two choices in the sRGB color space, I a and III a. The I a option is suitable for most subjects including portraits. The III a option gives bright, highly saturated colors, especially in the green and blue spectrum.

  Adobe RGB has a much broader color spectrum than is available with sRGB. The Adobe gamut was designed for dealing with the color spectrum that can be reproduced with most high-end printing equipment.

- **Saturation.** This allows you to control how vivid the colors in the image appear. The settings are Auto, Moderate, and Enhanced.

Which Color Space Should I Use?

This is a question you have no doubt asked yourself at this point. The color space you use depends on what the final output of your images is going to be. If you take pictures, download them straight to your computer, and typically only view them on your monitor or upload them for viewing on the Web, then sRGB is fine. The sRGB color space is also useful when printing directly from the camera or memory card with no post-processing.

If you are going to have your photos printed professionally or you intend to do a bit of post-processing to your images, using the Adobe RGB color space is recommended. This allows you to have subtler control over the colors than is possible using a narrower color space like sRGB.

For the most part, I capture my images using the Adobe RGB color space. I then do my post-processing and make a decision on the output. Anything that I know I will be posting to the Web I convert to sRGB; anything destined for my printer is saved as Adobe RGB. I usually end up with two identical images saved with two different color spaces. Because most Web browsers don't recognize the Adobe RGB color space, any images saved as Adobe RGB and posted on the Internet usually appear dull and flat.

- **Hue adjustment.** This allows you to adjust the color tone of the images. You can choose ±9° in 3° increments. Choose positive numbers to make reds more orange, greens more blue, and blues more purple and negative numbers to make reds more purple, blues more green, and greens more yellow. I recommend leaving this setting alone as it can cause your images to look strangely colored.

After you adjust the settings to your liking be sure to select Done from the menu list, and press the OK button to save your changes.

Image quality

This menu option allows you to change the image quality of the file. You can choose from these options:

✦ **NEF (RAW).** This option saves the images in RAW format.

✦ **JPEG fine.** This option saves the images in JPEG with minimal compression.

✦ **JPEG normal.** This option saves the images in JPEG with standard compression.

✦ **JPEG basic.** This option saves the images in JPEG with high compression.

✦ **NEF (RAW) + JPEG basic.** This option saves two copies of the same image, one in RAW and one in JPEG with high compression.

These settings can also be changed by using the Quick Settings display.

 Cross-Reference *For more information on image quality, compression, and file formats, see Chapter 2.*

Image size

This menu option allows you to choose the size of the JPEG files. The choices are:

✦ **Large.** This setting gives you a full resolution image of 3872 × 2592 pixels or 10 megapixels.

✦ **Medium.** This setting gives your images a resolution of 2896 × 1944 pixels or 5.6 megapixels.

✦ **Small.** This setting gives your images a resolution of 1936 × 1296 pixels or 2.5 megapixels.

 For more information on image size, see Chapter 2.

White balance

You can change the white balance options using this menu option. Use the multiselector to choose from the different settings. When the white balance is selected from this menu the camera gives you the option to fine-tune before setting it. This option appears as a small colored grid. Use the multiselector to move the spot around the grid if you feel you need to fine-tune the default setting. Press the OK button to set the WB. The Preset manual WB also offers you a couple of different options: Measure and Use photo. Choosing the Measure option allows you to set a custom WB by pointing the camera at a neutral white or gray object and pressing the Shutter Release button allowing the camera to measure the color temperature. The Use photo option allows you to copy the WB balance settings from any photo on your memory card.

 For detailed information on white balance settings, see Chapter 2.

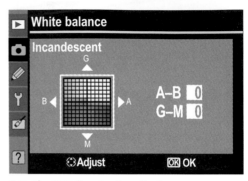

3.6 The WB fine-tuning display

ISO sensitivity settings

This menu option allows you to set the ISO. You can choose from Auto, 100, 200, 400, 800, 1600, and Hi 1. The Auto ISO setting is not available when shooting in the P, S, A, or M mode.

 For more information on ISO settings and noise reduction, see Chapter 2.

Noise reduction

This menu option allows you to turn on noise reduction (NR) for exposures longer than 8 seconds and images taken at ISO 800 and higher. When this option is on, the camera runs a noise-reduction algorithm, which reduces the amount of noise in your image giving you a smoother result.

Active D-Lighting

Active D-Lighting is a setting that is designed to help ensure that you retain highlight detail when shooting in a high-contrast situation, such as shooting a picture in direct bright sunlight, which can cause dark shadows and bright highlight areas. Active D-Lighting basically tells your camera

Fine-Tuning Your White Balance

If you find that your white balance just isn't quite right, it is likely due to the fact that the camera is using generic settings that are made to cover a specific situation, such as direct sunlight or shade. The problem is that even direct sunlight has a different color temperature depending on atmospheric conditions — how high it is in the sky, etc. This is also true for fluorescent lamps and incandescent light bulbs. As these bulbs get older the colors shift a bit, so the white balance setting doesn't exactly match.

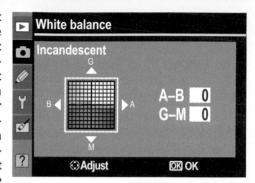

For this reason Nikon has added a feature that allows you to fine tune the pre-existing white balance settings. This feature is accessed by entering the White balance menu in the Shooting menu. Once you have selected a white balance setting a small colored grid appears. This grid allows you to add up to 6 points of green or magenta and amber or blue to the current white balance setting.

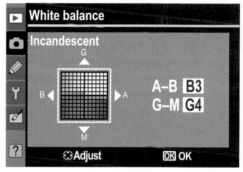

Using the multiselector up adds green, down adds magenta, left adds blue, and right adds amber. Because green and magenta are opposite colors you can only add one at a time, the same with blue and amber. But you can add two colors together, as long as they aren't opposites. For example, you can add 4 points of green and 3 points of blue, which adds a blue-green tint to the existing WB setting. On the opposite side, you can add 4 points of magenta and 3 points of amber, adding a reddish-purple tint to the WB setting.

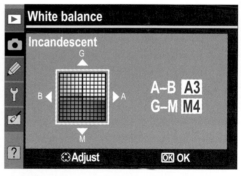

All in all it's actually more complicated to explain than it is to do. The grid gives you a pretty good idea of the color that you can add to the WB setting.

to underexpose the image a bit; this under-exposure helps keep the highlights from becoming blown out and losing detail. The D60 also uses a subtle adjustment to avoid losing any detail in the shadow area that the underexposure may cause.

 Caution *Active D-Lighting is a separate and different setting than the D-Lighting option found in the Retouch menu. For more information on standard D-Lighting, see Chapter 8.*

Custom Settings Menu

The Custom Settings menu (CSM) is where you really start getting into customizing your D60 to shoot to your personal preferences. You can also use this menu to change some of the same settings that are available in the Quick Settings display.

The CSM is an in-depth menu system with a lot of submenus. Here I just give a brief description of what each setting is used for (see the Setup menu information later in the chapter for details on how to set CSM options). The CSM can be changed in the Setup menu to display a simple version with only the most commonly changed settings, or you can choose to display all 19 options. When the Simple view is activated only the first seven options are displayed and accessible.

To enter the CSM, press the Menu button on the rear of the camera. Use the multiselector to highlight the icon that looks like a pencil. This is the CSM. Then use the multi-selector up or down to scroll through the available options. When the desired menu option is highlighted, press the OK button or the multiselector right to access the submenu where you change the settings.

CUSTOM SETTING MENU	
Ⓡ Reset	--
01 Beep	OFF
02 Focus mode	AF-S
03 AF-area mode	[ᴉ ᴉ]
04 Release mode	Ⓢ
05 Metering	▣
06 No memory card?	OK

CUSTOM SETTING MENU	
07 Image review	ON
08 Flash compensation	0.0
09 Af-assist	OFF
10 ISO auto	OFF
11 ⏱/Fn button	ISO
12 AE-L/AF-L	🅰🅴
13 AE lock	OFF

CUSTOM SETTING MENU	
13 AE lock	OFF
14 Built-in flash	M ⚡
15 Auto off timers	⏱ 🖉
16 Self-timer	⏱10s
17 Remote on duration	⏱1ᴍ
18 Date imprint	OFF
19 Rangefinder	ON

3.7 The CSM menu items

✦ **R Reset.** This option allows you to restore all of the Custom settings to Default.

✦ **01 Beep.** This allows you to turn on or off the beep that sounds when the camera achieves focus or when the self-timer or delayed remote is activated.

✦ **02 Focus mode.** This option allows you to change how the camera's focusing system operates. The choices are AF-A, AF-S, AF-C, or MF.

✦ **03 AF-area mode.** This setting allows you to choose how the camera selects the focus point. Your choices are Closest subject, Dynamic area, and Single point.

✦ **04 Release mode.** This allows you to set how the shutter is released. The choices are Single, Continuous, Self-timer, Delayed remote, and Quick-response remote.

✦ **05 Metering.** This is where you choose how the camera determines the settings for exposure. You can choose Matrix, Center-weighted, or Spot metering.

✦ **06 No memory card?** This setting allows you to disable the shutter release when there is no memory card inserted in the camera. Your choices are Release locked, which locks the shutter release; or Release enabled, which allows the shutter to be released.

✦ **07 Image review.** This setting allows you to choose whether your pictures are shown on the LCD monitor immediately after they are taken. When On is selected the camera automatically displays the image after it is taken. When Off is chosen you need to press the Playback button to view your images after they are taken.

✦ **08 Flash compensation.** This allows you to adjust your flash exposure compensation to make the flash brighter or dimmer. The FEC is adjustable in 1/3 stops. The choices are. -3, -2.7, -2.3, -2, -1.7, -1.3, -1, -0.7, -0.3, 0, +0.3, +0.7, +1.

✦ **09 Af-assist.** This allows you to turn off the AF-assist illuminator. The AF-assist illuminator turns on in dim light to give the camera sufficient light to allow the camera to focus. You may want to turn this

off when trying to achieve candid snapshots or when photographing a wedding or similar event where the light may be distracting.

✦ **10 ISO auto.** This is where you choose the ISO auto setting. ISO auto allows the camera to choose the ISO sensitivity for your camera depending on the lighting situation. You can also set the parameters by which the camera chooses the ISO here. By selecting Max. sensitivity from the submenu you can choose how high the camera can set the ISO. The choices are 200, 400, 800, and 1600. This allows you to control how much digital noise your images have because of a high ISO. You can also choose the Min. Shutter speed option from the submenu. This allows you to determine how slow your shutter speed is before the camera starts to boost the ISO. You can choose to set the minimum shutter speed anywhere between 1 second and 1/125 in 1-stop intervals.

✦ **11 Fn button.** This option is used to set a specific function to the Self-timer function button. By default, pressing this button activates the self-timer. You can assign this button to a number of different functions that allow you to change a setting quickly. You can set the button to Self-timer, to change the Release mode from single to continuous, change the Image quality/size, ISO sensitivity, or white balance. I usually set mine to ISO because that is one of the settings that I change the most frequently.

✦ **12 AE-L / AF-L**. This CSM option allows you to control how the AE-L/AF-L button functions. There are five options:

- **AE/AF lock.** When this option is selected the exposure and focus are locked when the button is pressed and held. Releasing the button allows the AE meter and focus to be activated.

- **AE lock only.** This allows you to lock the exposure while pressing and holding the AE-L/AF-L button. The camera still focuses by half-pressing the Shutter Release button.

- **AF lock only.** (This option allows you to lock focus on a subject while still letting the camera's autoexposure metering function.) The focus remains locked as long as the AE-L/AF-L button is pressed and held. Releasing the button allows the camera to focus as normal.

- **AE lock hold.** When this setting is chosen pressing the AE-L/AF-L button locks the exposure in. The exposure remains locked even if you release the button. The exposure is reset when the shutter is released or when the camera goes to Standby mode.

- **AF on.** This option allows you to activate the autofocus by pressing the AE-L/AF-L button.

✦ **13 AE lock.** Turning this option on locks the exposure when the Shutter Release button is half-pressed. This option is useful when you focus on a subject and then recompose the image placing the subject in a different area of the viewfinder.

✦ **14 Built-in flash.** This option allows you to choose how the built-in flash or SB-400 Speedlight operates. You can choose either TTL metering or Manual setting. This CSM option is not available when using the SB-800 or the SB-600 Speedlight. If one of these Speedlights is used, the settings are changed on the Speedlight.

✦ **15 Auto off timers.** This allows you to set how long the LCD monitor and exposure meters remain on before the camera goes to Standby mode. You can choose Short, Normal, Long, or Custom. The custom setting allows you to customize three different options:

- **Playback/menus.** This option allows you to set how long the LCD monitor remains on when in Playback mode or when viewing the menus. You can set this to turn off after 8 seconds, 12 seconds, 20 seconds, 1 minute, or 10 minutes.

- **Image review.** This allows you to choose how long the images are displayed on the monitor after the image has been shot. You can set this to turn off after 4 seconds, 8 seconds, 20 seconds, 1 minute, or 10 minutes.

- **Auto meter off.** This setting allows you to choose how long the camera's meter remains active while no buttons are being pressed. You can set this to turn off after 4 seconds, 8 seconds, 20 seconds, 1 minute, 10 minutes, or 30 minutes.

✦ **16 Self-timer.** This option is used to set the amount of time the camera waits to release the shutter when the self-timer is activated. You can set the amount of delay to 2, 5, 10, or 20 seconds.

✦ **17 Remote on duration.** This allows you to set the amount of time the camera waits for a signal from the optional wireless remote before returning to the camera's default setting. You can choose to set it to 1, 5, 10, or 15 minutes. When the camera is set to Remote the camera stays "awake" regardless of your Auto off timers' settings.

✦ **18 Date imprint.** Turning this option on imprints your images with the date and/or time that they were shot. You can choose to imprint only the date, the time and date, or the date counter, which displays the number of days that have elapsed between the date that the picture was taken and a selected date.

✦ **19 Rangefinder.** This allows you to turn on a display in the viewfinder that indicates the focus distance. This is only displayed when a non-AF-S (MF) lens is attached. The rangefinder display replaces the electronic analog exposure display in all shooting modes except for M.

Setup Menu

This menu contains your basic camera settings, most of which don't need to be changed very often. These options range from setting the time and date to adjusting the LCD brightness and formatting the memory card. You also find the necessary settings for cleaning the image sensor here.

CSM/Setup menu

This menu option allows you to choose which options are displayed in the menus. You can choose to display the Simple version of the CSM, which has only the most fundamental settings or the Full version with all of the available CSM options.

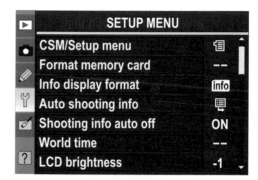

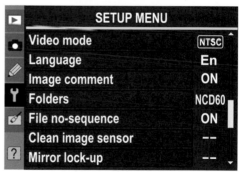

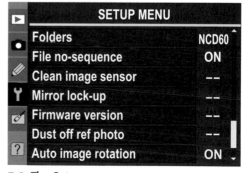

3.8 The Setup menu

This is also where you can choose to set up the My menu options. My menu allows you to build your own custom menus by adding only the settings that you feel are the most important. You can customize all of the menus: the Playback menu, Shooting menu, Custom Settings menu, Setup menu, and the Retouch menu. To customize your menus:

1. **Use the multiselector up/down to highlight the CSM/Setup menu option from the Setup menu, and then press the OK button to enter the submenu.**

2. **Use the multiselector up/down to highlight My menu, and then press the OK button to view the submenu options.**

3. **Use the multiseletor up/down to choose the menu you want to customize.** Choose the Playback menu, Shooting menu, Custom settings menu, Setup menu, or the Retouch menu. Press the OK button to view the available settings.

4. **Select the items you want to display.** Using the multiselector up/down highlight the item you want to show (or not). Next to the menu option is a box with a check mark in it. When the check mark is

displayed the menu option will be displayed. To change the display setting, press the multiselector button to the right. When the option is turned off the check mark is no longer displayed and the menu option is not shown when that specific menu is being viewed. When you have selected the options you want to display, be sure to scroll back up to the top of the menu to the Done option and press the OK button to save your settings. Repeat this with all of the menus until you have set all of the options that you want to be displayed.

Format memory card

This menu option allows you to completely erase everything on your SD card. Formatting your memory card essentially erases all of the data on the card by rewriting the directory structure of the card. It's a good idea to format your card every time you download the images to your computer (just be sure all of the files are successfully transferred before formatting). Formatting the card helps protect against corrupt data. Simply erasing the images leaves fragmented data on the card and allows it to be overwritten; sometimes this older data can corrupt the new data as it is being written. Formatting the card gives your camera a blank slate on which to write.

Information display format

This menu option is how you set the different display options for the LCD shooting information. You can choose between displaying the shooting information in the Classic format or the Graphic format in three

CSM/Setup menu
My menu
Done   OK
Playback menu
Shooting menu
Custom setting menu
Setup menu
Retouch menu

3.9 The My menu submenu display

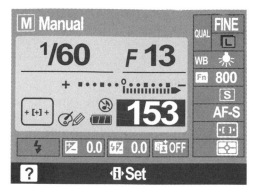

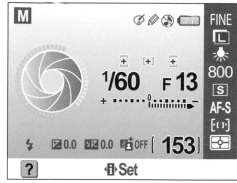

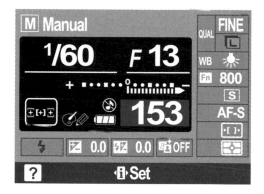

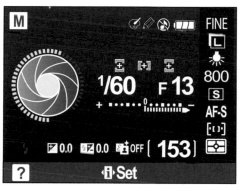

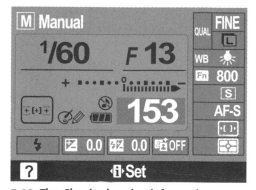

3.10 The Classic shooting information settings: blue, black, and orange

3.11 The Graphic shooting information settings: white, black, and orange

different colors. You can also select an image off of your memory card to display as wallpaper behind the shooting information. Additionally you can also choose for the camera to display the shooting information differently depending on whether you're using the DVP modes or the P, S, A, or M modes.

Auto shooting information

This menu option allows you to choose if the shooting information is displayed on the LCD when the Shutter Release button is half-pressed and then released. This allows you to quickly view your settings. You can set this option differently for the DVP and PSAM modes.

Shooting information auto off

Turning this menu option on activates the eye sensor below the viewfinder and turns off the shooting information display when your eye is at the viewfinder. Turning this option off allows the shooting information to continue to be displayed even when looking through the viewfinder. This can make it difficult to see through the viewfinder, especially in low-light situations. The shooting information will be turned off as long as the Shutter Release button is pressed.

World time

This menu option is used to set the time and date that is added to the EXIF data of your images. You can also set the time zone that you are in as well as adjust for daylight saving time. There is also an option (Date format) that allows you to choose how the date is displayed (year/month/day, month/day/year, or day/month/year).

LCD brightness

This menu option sets the brightness of your LCD screen. You may want to make it brighter when viewing images in bright sunlight or make it dimmer when viewing images indoors or to save battery power. There is also a setting called Auto dim, which reduces the brightness of the LCD monitor when the shooting information is displayed.

Video mode

There are two options in this menu: NTSC and PAL. Without getting into too many specifics, these are types of standards for the resolution of televisions. All of North America, including Canada and Mexico, uses the NTSC standard, while most of Europe and Asia use the PAL standard. Check your television owner's manual for the specific setting if you plan to view your images on a TV directly from the camera.

Language

This menu option is where you set the language that the menus and dialog boxes display. There are 14 languages to choose from. Use the multiselector up/down to highlight the correct language, and then press the OK button to set.

Image comment

You can use this feature to attach a comment to the images taken by your D60. You can enter the text using the Input Comment menu. The comments can be viewed in Nikon's Capture NX or View NX software or can be viewed in the photo information on the camera. Setting the Attach comment option applies the comment to all images taken until this setting is disabled. Some comments you may want to attach are copyright information or your name, or even the location where the photos were taken.

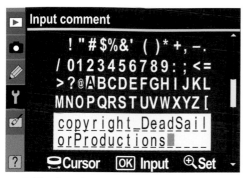

3.12 The Input comment menu

Folders

This menu option allows you to select which folders in your memory card your D60 saves the images to. You can also add new folders or rename existing ones. This is a handy feature when shooting different subjects — for example, when photographing sports car racing events there are often eight or more different groups of cars. By creating different folders and naming them GRP1, GRP2, GRP3, and so on, I am able to keep the groups separate to make it easier for me to locate specific cars by their groups later on.

To create a new folder, simply choose Folders from the Setup menu and then use the multiselector to scroll down to the New option. Pressing OK displays the D60's text entry screen. Use the multiselector and Command dial to enter a name for your new folder. Press OK to save the folder when you finish.

File no. sequence

This menu option determines how the D60 applies sequential file numbering to your images when saving them to the memory card. When this option is set to Off (the default setting), the camera automatically starts the file numbers at 0001 every time you create a new folder, when the memory card is formatted, or when a new memory card is inserted to the camera.

Turning this option On allows the camera to continue sequentially numbering the file numbers until the file numbers reach 9999, at which time the camera resets the number sequence back to 0001.

When the Reset option is selected the camera resets the image numbering to 0001 unless there are images in the current folder. If this occurs, the file numbering starts at the next highest number.

I usually have my file number sequence set to On, which helps to ensure that I don't get any duplicate file numbers.

Clean image sensor

This is one of the best new features on the D60. The camera uses ultrasonic vibration to knock any dust off the filter in front of the sensor. This helps keep most of the dust off of your sensor but is not going to keep it absolutely dust free forever. You may have to have the sensor professionally cleaned periodically. There are two menu options you can choose for cleaning the sensor. You can choose Clean now, which cleans the image sensor immediately, or you can choose for the camera to clean the image sensor whenever the camera is turned on or off or both.

Mirror lock-up

Selecting this menu option locks up the mirror to allow access to the image sensor for inspection or for additional cleaning. The sensor is also powered down to reduce any static charge that may attract dust. Before locking up the mirror to clean your sensor be sure that your batteries are fully charged or the camera is attached to Nikon EH-5a AC power adaptor to ensure that the mirror doesn't close on your cleaning implements.

Although there are many home sensor cleaning kits available, I strongly recommend taking your camera to an authorized Nikon service center for any sensor cleaning.

Firmware version

This menu option displays which firmware version your camera is currently operating under. Firmware is a computer program that is embedded in the camera that tells it how to function. Camera manufacturers routinely update the firmware to correct for any bugs or to make improvements on the camera's functions. Nikon posts firmware updates on its Web site at www.nikonusa.com.

Dust off ref photo

This menu option allows you to take a dust reference photo that shows any dust or debris that may be stuck to your sensor. Capture NX then uses the image to automatically retouch any subsequent photos where the specks appear.

Auto image rotation

Selecting this menu option tells the camera to record the orientation of the camera when the photo is shot (portrait or landscape). This allows image-editing software to show the photo in the proper orientation so you don't have to take the time in post-processing to rotate images shot in portrait orientation.

Retouch Menu

The Retouch menu allows you to make changes and corrections to your images without the use of imaging-editing software. As a matter of fact, you don't even need to download your images. You can make all of the changes in-camera using the LCD preview (or hooked up to a TV if you prefer).

The options in the Retouch menu include D-Lighting, Red-eye correction, Trim, Monochrome, Filter effects, Small picture, Image overlay, NEF (RAW) processing, and Stop-motion movie.

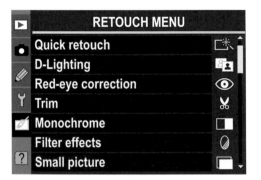

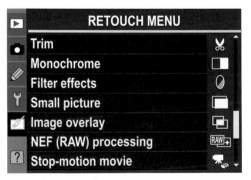

3.13 The Retouch menu

The Retouch menu options are:

✦ **Quick retouch.** Allows you to automatically adjust your photos.

✦ **D-Lighting.** Allows you to bring out shadow detail in contrasty images.

✦ **Red-eye correction.** Automatically fixes red-eye in pictures taken with flash.

✦ **Trim.** Enables you to crop your images.

✦ **Monochrome.** Allows you turn to your photos black and white, sepia, or cyanotype.

✦ **Filter effects.** Applies different photographic filter effects such as color intensifiers and cross screen.

✦ **Small picture.** Saves a small copy of your image for use in e-mailing.

✦ **Image overlay.** Allows you to create a multiple exposure type image using RAW files.

✦ **NEF (RAW) processing.** Enables you to adjust settings on your RAW files and saves the image as a separate JPEG file.

✦ **Stop-motion movie.** This option creates a movie file from selected still images.

Cross-Reference *The Retouch menu is discussed at length in Chapter 8.*

Capturing Great Images with the Nikon D60

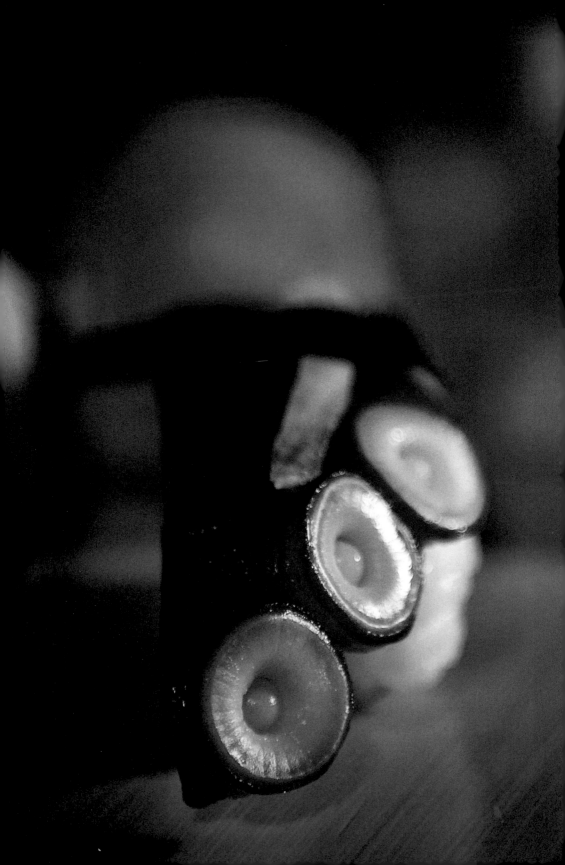

Essential Photography Concepts

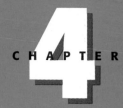
Photography, whether traditional film photography or working with a digital SLR, is built on concepts that are the foundation for every photo you take. This chapter gives you the essential coverage of those items, including information on exposure, the effects the aperture has on depth of field, and some tips and hints on composition techniques.

Understanding Exposure

An exposure is the resulting creation of three elements that are all interrelated. Each depends on the others to create a good exposure. If one of the elements changes, the others must increase or decrease proportionally. The following are the elements you need to consider:

+ **Shutter speed.** The shutter speed determines the length of time the sensor is exposed to light.

+ **ISO sensitivity.** The ISO setting you choose influences your camera's sensitivity to light.

+ **Aperture/f-stop.** How much light reaches the sensor of your camera is controlled by the aperture, or f-stop. Each camera has an adjustable opening on the lens. As you change the aperture (the opening), you allow more or less light to reach the sensor.

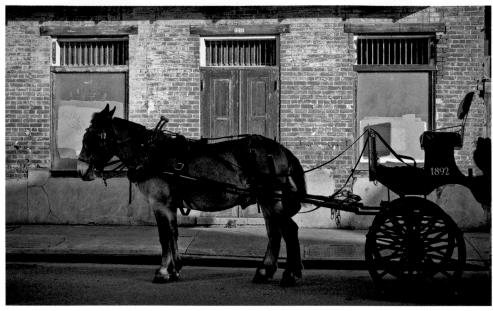

4.1 This image was shot with a shutter speed of 1/640 second, ISO 400 at f/5.6.

Shutter speed

Shutter speed is the amount of time light entering from the lens is allowed to expose the image sensor. Shutter speeds are indicated in fractions of a second. Common shutter speeds (in 1-stop increments) are: 1 second, 1/2, 1/4, 1/8, 1/15, 1/30, 1/60, 1/125, 1/250, 1/500, 1/1000, and so on. Slow shutter speeds mean the shutter is open longer, such as 1/2 second or 1 second. Fast shutter speeds mean the shutter is only open for a very short time, such as 1/1000 second or 1/1500 second. Increasing or decreasing shutter speed by one setting doubles or halves the exposure, respectively. When the shutter speed changes, the amount of light entering the camera changes, so it stands to reason that if you increase or decrease the time that the light is reaching the sensor, you will also have to make an adjustment to other settings to ensure that you still have the proper exposure. This is done in one of two ways.

You can adjust the aperture to increase or decrease the amount of light reaching the sensor, or you can adjust the ISO sensitivity.

The D60 allows you to adjust the shutter speed in 1/3-stops for fine-tuning the exposure (1, 1/1.3, 1/1.6, 1/2, 1/2.5, 1/3, 1/4...). It may seem like math (okay, technically it does involve math), but it is relatively easy to figure out. For example, if you take a picture with a 1/2-second shutter speed and it turns out too dark, logically you want to keep the shutter open longer to let in more light. To do this, you need to adjust the shutter speed to 1 second, the next full stop, which lets in twice as much light.

The shutter speed can also affect the sharpness of your images. When using a longer focal-length lens a faster shutter speed is required to counteract against camera shake, which can cause your image to be blurry. Longer lenses magnify not only your subject but also magnify movement such as camera shake. A good rule of thumb to follow when using a longer lens is to use a shutter speed that is the reciprocal of the focal length of the lens. For example, when using a focal length of 200mm the slowest speed you should use is 1/200, although if you're using a VR lens you can shoot with an even slower shutter speed. When taking photographs in low light, a slow shutter speed is often required, which can also cause blur from camera shake or fast-moving subjects.

> **Cross-Reference** *For more information on lenses and focal length see Chapter 5.*

The shutter speed can also be used to show motion. *Panning*, or moving the camera horizontally with a moving subject while using a slower shutter speed, can cause the background to blur while keeping the subject in focus. This is an effective way to portray motion in a still image as in 4.2. On the opposite end, using a fast shutter speed can freeze action such as the splash of water from a surfer, which can also give the illusion of motion in a still photograph.

ISO

The ISO (International Organization for Standardization) setting is how your camera determines how sensitive your camera is to light. The higher the ISO number is, the less light you need to take a photograph, meaning the more sensitive the sensor is to light. For example, you might choose an ISO of 100 on a bright, sunny day when you are photographing outside because you have plenty of light. However, on a dark, cloudy day you want to consider an ISO of 400 or higher to make sure your camera captures all the available light. This allows you to use a faster shutter speed should it be appropriate to the subject you are photographing. You can also use a higher ISO if you need to use a small aperture to achieve greater depth of field.

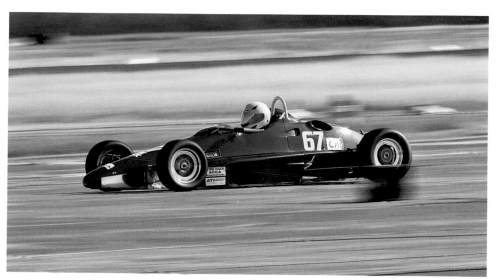

4.2 In this image, a relatively slow shutter speed of 1/80 second was used to create a motion blur. Panning was also employed to keep the subject of the image in sharp focus.

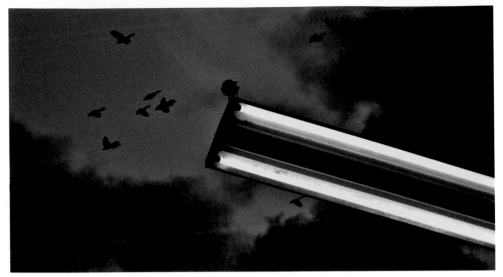

4.3 This image shows digital noise resulting from using a high ISO. Notice that the noise is more prevalent in the darker areas of the image.

It is helpful to know that each ISO setting is twice as sensitive to light as the previous setting. For example, at ISO 400, your camera is twice as sensitive to light as it is at ISO 200. This means it needs only half the light at ISO 400 that it needs at ISO 200 to achieve the same exposure.

Additionally, when in Auto ISO mode the D60 adjusts the ISO in 1/3-stop increments (100, 125, 160, 200...), which enables the camera to fine-tune the ISO to reduce the noise inherent with higher ISO settings.

Aperture

Aperture is the size of the opening in the lens that determines the amount of light that reaches the image sensor. The aperture is controlled by a diaphragm that operates in a similar fashion to the iris of your eye. Aperture is expressed as f-stop numbers, such as f/2.8, f/5.6, f/4 and f/8. Here are a few important things to know about aperture:

✦ **Smaller f-numbers equal wider apertures.** A small f-stop such as f/2.8, for example, opens the lens so more light reaches the sensor. If you have a wide aperture (opening), the amount of time the shutter needs to stay open to let light into the camera decreases.

✦ **Larger f-numbers equal narrower apertures.** A large f-stop such as f/11, for example, closes the lens so less light reaches the sensor. If you have a narrow aperture (opening), the amount of time the shutter needs to stay open to let light into the camera increases.

Deciding what aperture to use depends on what kind of photo you are going to take. If you need a fast shutter speed to freeze action, and you don't want to raise the ISO, you can use a wide aperture to let more available light into the sensor. Conversely, if the scene is very bright, you may want to use a small aperture to avoid overexposure.

Cross-Reference *For an in-depth look at working with light, see Chapter 6.*

Understanding Depth of Field

Depth of field is the distance range in a photograph in which all included portions of an image are at least acceptably sharp. It is heavily affected by aperture, but how far your camera is from the subject can also have an effect.

If you focus your lens on a certain point, everything that lies on the horizontal plane of that same distance is also in focus. This means everything in front of the point and everything behind it is technically not in focus. Because our eyes aren't acute enough to discern the minor blur that occurs directly in front of and directly

behind the point of focus, it still appears sharp to us. This is known as the zone of acceptable sharpness, which we call depth of field.

✦ **Shallow depth of field.** This results in an image where the subject is in sharp focus, but the background has a soft blur. You likely have seen it used frequently in portraits. Using a wide aperture, such as f/2.8, results in a subject that is sharp with a softer background. Using a shallow depth of field is a great way to get rid of distracting elements in the background of an image.

✦ **Deep depth of field.** This results in an image that is reasonably sharp from the foreground to the background. Using a narrow aperture, such as f/11, is ideal to keep photographs of landscapes or groups in focus throughout.

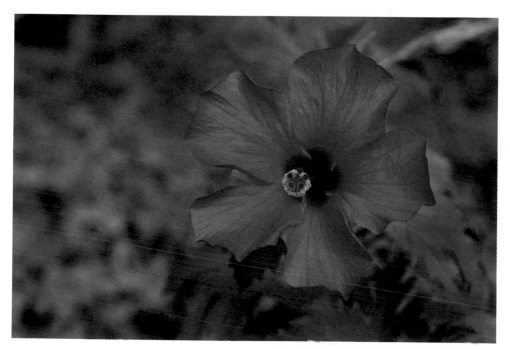

4.4 An image with a shallow depth of field has only the main subject in focus.

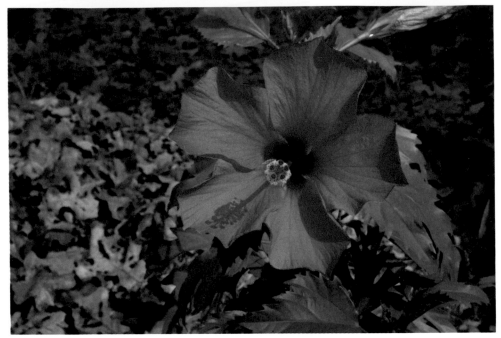

4.5 An image with a deep depth of field has most of the image in focus.

Remember, to enlarge your depth of field, you want a large f-number; to shrink your depth of field, you want a small f-number.

A factor to consider when working with depth of field is your distance from the subject. The farther you are from the subject you are focusing on the greater the depth of field in your photograph. For example, if you stand in your front yard to take a photo of a tree a block away, it has a deep depth of field with the tree, background, and foreground all in relatively sharp focus. If you stand in the same spot and take a picture of your dog that is standing just several feet away, your dog is in focus, but that tree a block away is just a blur of color.

Rules of Composition

Although many of you are likely well versed in these concepts regarding composition, some of you may be coming in cold, so to speak. So this section is intended as a refresher course and a general outline of some of the most commonly used rules of composition.

Photography, like any artistic discipline, has general rules. Although they are called rules, they are really nothing more than guidelines. Some photographers—notably Ansel Adams, who was quoted as saying, "The so-called rules of photographic composition are, in my opinion, invalid, irrelevant, and immaterial" — claim to have eschewed the rules of composition. However, when you look at Adams's photographs, they follow the rules perfectly in most cases.

Another famous photographer, Edward Weston, said, "Consulting the rules of composition before taking a photograph is like consulting the laws of gravity before going for a walk." Again, as with Adams, when you look at his photographs, they tend to follow these very rules.

This isn't to say you need to follow all of the rules every time you take a photograph. As I said, these are really just general guidelines that when followed can make your images more powerful and interesting.

However, when you're starting out in photography, you should pay attention to the rules of composition. Eventually, you become accustomed to following the guidelines and it becomes second nature. At that point you no longer need to consult the rules of composition; you just inherently follow them.

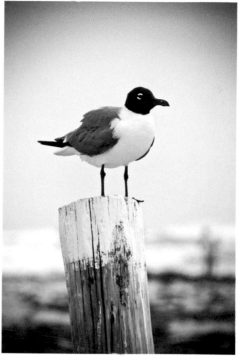

4.7 Getting down and shooting this seagull from a lower angle allowed me to place the sky behind him. Shooting the bird from up high would have placed the distracting elements of the beach behind the main subject of the photo.

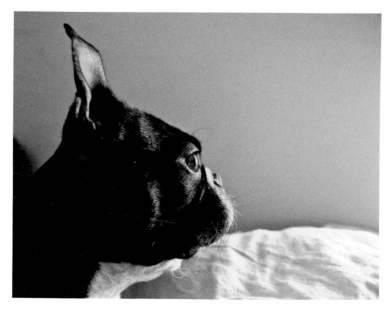

4.6 There's no question as to what the subject is in this photograph.

Keep it simple

Simplicity is arguably the most important rule in creating a good image. In most cases, you want to be sure the viewer can identify what the intended subject of your photograph is. When you have too many competing elements in your image, it can be hard for the viewer to decide what to focus on.

Sometimes changing your perspective to the subject is all you need to do to remove a distracting element from your image. Try walking around and shooting the same subject from different angles.

The Rule of Thirds

Most of the time you are probably tempted to take the main subject of your photograph and stick it right in the middle of the frame. This makes sense, and it often works pretty well for snapshots. However, to create more interesting and dynamic images, it often works better to put the main subject of the image a little off-center.

The Rule of Thirds is a compositional rule that has been in use for hundreds of years, and famous artists throughout the centuries have followed it. With the Rule of Thirds, you divide the image into nine equal parts using two equally spaced horizontal and vertical lines, kind of like a tic-tac-toe pattern. You want to center the main subject of the image at an intersection, as illustrated in figure 4.8. The subject doesn't necessarily

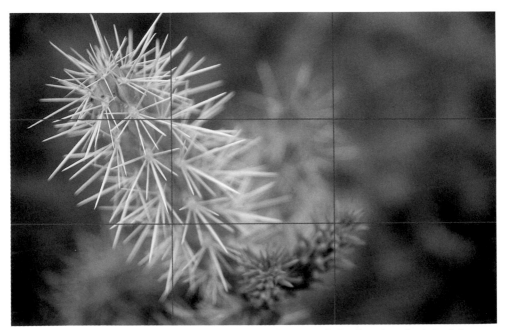

4.8 The cactus, which is the main subject of this photograph, is placed to the left of the frame according to the Rule of Thirds.

have to be right on the intersection of the line, but merely close enough to it to take advantage of the Rule of Thirds.

Another way to use the Rule of Thirds is to place the subject in the center of the frame, but at the bottom or top third of the frame as illustrated in figure 4.9. This part of the rule is especially useful when photographing landscapes. You can place the horizon on or near the top or bottom line; you almost never want to place it in the middle. Notice in figure 4.10 the mountain range is covering the bottom third of the entire frame.

When using the Rule of Thirds with a moving subject, you want to be sure to keep most of the frame in front of the subject to present the illusion that the subject has someplace to go within the frame. You can see the difference the framing makes in figures 4.11 and 4.12.

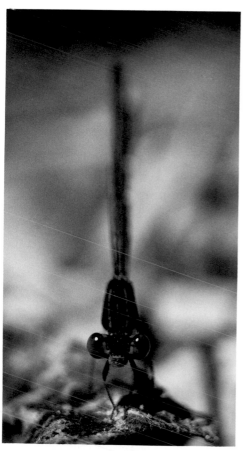

4.9 In this image, the subject is in the center of the frame, but in the bottom third.

4.10 Using the Rule of Thirds in a landscape.

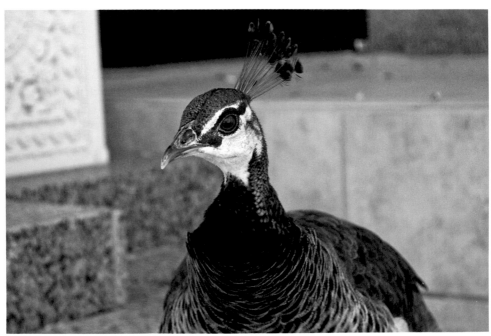

4.11 Placing the peahen directly in the middle of the frame results in a nice picture.

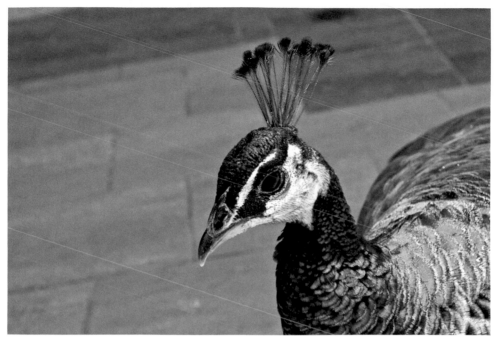

4.12 Recomposing to place the peahen toward the right part of the frame results in a more dramatic image.

Leading lines and S-curves

Another good way to add drama to an image is to use a *leading line* to draw the viewer's eye through the picture. A leading line is an element in a composition that leads the eye toward the subject. A leading line can be a lot of different things: a road, sidewalk, railroad tracks, buildings, or columns, to name a few.

In general, you want your leading line to go in a specific direction. Most commonly, a leading line leads the eye from one corner of the picture to another. A good rule of thumb to follow is to have your line go from the bottom-left corner leading toward the top right.

You can also use leading lines that go from the bottom of the image to the top, and vice versa. Often, leading lines heading in this direction lead to a *vanishing point*. A vanishing point is the point at which parallel lines appear to converge and disappear. Figure 4.13 shows a leading line ending in a vanishing point.

Depending on the subject matter, a variety of directions for leading lines can work equally well.

Another nice way to use a leading line is with an *S-curve*. An S-curve is exactly what it sounds like: It resembles the letter S. The S-curve draws the viewer's eye up from the bottom of the image, through the middle, over to the corner, and back to the other side again.

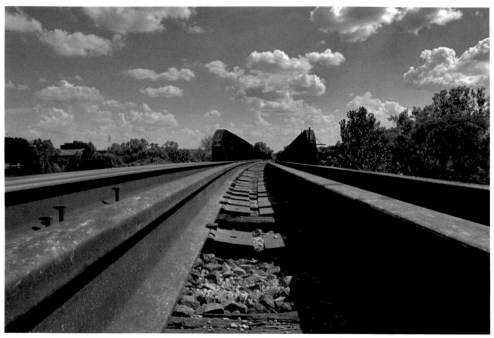

4.13 A leading line ending in a vanishing point

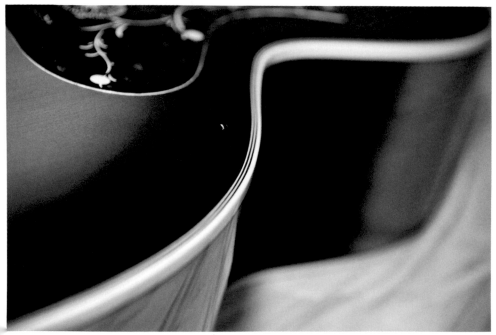

4.14 In this image, the curves of the guitar body form a sort of an S-curve that draws the ye through the whole image.

Helpful hints

Along with the major rules of composition, there are all sorts of other helpful guidelines. Here are just a few that I've found most helpful:

✦ **Frame the subject.** Use elements of the foreground to make a frame around the subject to keep the viewer's eye from wandering.

✦ **Avoid having the subject looking directly out of the side of the frame he or she is closest to.** Having the subject looking out of the photograph can be distracting to the viewer. For example, if your subject is on the left side of the composition having him or her face the right is better, and vice versa.

✦ **Avoid *mergers*.** A merger is when an element from the background appears to be a part of the subject, like the snapshot of granny at the park that looks like she has a tree growing out of the top of her head.

✦ **Try not to cut through the joint of a limb.** When composing or cropping your picture, it's best not to end the frame on a joint, such as an elbow or a knee. This can be unsettling to the viewer.

✦ **Avoid having bright spots or unnecessary details near the edge.** Having anything bright or detailed near the edge of the frame will draw the viewer's eye away from the subject and out of the image.

✦ **Avoid placing the horizon or strong horizontal or vertical lines in the center of the composition.** This cuts the image in half and makes it hard for the viewer to decide which half of the image is important.

✦ **Separate the subject from the background.** Make sure the background doesn't have colors or textures similar to the subject. If necessary, try shooting from different angles, or use a shallow depth of field to achieve separation.

✦ **Fill the frame.** Try to make the subject the most dominant part of the image. Avoid having lots of empty space around the subject unless it's essential to making the photograph work.

✦ **Use odd numbers.** When photographing multiple subjects, odd numbers seem to work best.

These are just a few of the hundreds of guidelines out there. Remember, these are not hard-and-fast rules, just simple pointers that can help you create interesting and amazing images.

Selecting and Using Lenses

 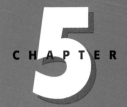

Although your D60 may have come with a kit lens—the 18-55mm f/3.5-5.6G VR— one advantage to owning a digital SLR camera is the ability to change out lenses to fit the specific photographic style or scene that you want to capture. After a while you may find that the kit lens doesn't meet your needs and you want to upgrade. Nikon dSLR owners have quite a few lenses from which to choose, all of which benefit from Nikon's expertise in the field of lens manufacturing.

Arguably the most important part of the camera is the lens, especially when using a camera with a high resolution like the 10-megapixel D60. The high-resolution imaging sensors can magnify any flaws in the lens, such as scratches or chromatic aberration.

If you decide to upgrade your kit lens—or you just want to add to your lens collection—there are literally hundreds of options from which to choose. You have a lot to consider when purchasing a lens; whether it's a zoom or prime lens, a wide-angle or telephoto lens, or any of the numerous other options. This chapter gives you a head start on knowing what kind of lens you want before you actually start looking.

Deciphering Nikon's Lens Codes

When shopping for lenses, you may notice all sorts of strange letter designations in the lens name. For example, the kit lens is the Nikkor 18-55mm f/3.5-5.6G VR AF-S DX. So, what do all those letters mean? Here's a simple list deciphering all of the perplexing designations.

✦ **AI/AIS.** These are auto-indexing lenses that automatically adjust the aperture diaphragm down when the Shutter button is pressed. All lenses made after 1977 are AI lenses. These are all manual focus lenses. The D60 light meter does not function with these lenses.

✦ **E.** These lenses were Nikon's budget series lenses made to go with the lower-end film cameras: the EM, FG, and FG-20. Although these lenses are compact and are often constructed with plastic parts, some of these lenses, especially the 50mm f/1.8, are of quite good quality and can be bought for next to nothing. These lenses are also manual focus only. The D60 light meter does not function with these lenses.

✦ **D.** Lenses with this designation convey distance information to the camera to aid in metering for exposure and flash. Most D lenses do not autofocus with the D60, but all they do allow the D60's meter to function perfectly.

✦ **G.** These are newer lenses that lack a manually adjustable aperture ring. The aperture must be set on the camera body. G lenses also convey distance information.

✦ **AF, AF-D, AF-I, and AF-S.** All of these denote that the lens is an autofocus lens. The D is for distance, the I stands for internal focus, and the S is for Silent Wave (more on this later). AF and AF-D lenses are focused by using a screw type drive motor that is typically found inside the camera body. In order to give the D60 a more compact body size the AF motor drive was left out of the camera.

This means that all standard AF and AF-D lenses must be focused manually. All of Nikon's AF lenses have a *CPU* built in. The CPU allows the lens to communicate directly with the camera body. This allows the camera's light meter to work with these lenses and you can use any of the exposure modes. The AF-S lenses have the AF motor built in to the lenses, focus silently, and work perfectly with the D60 allowing all features to be utilized.

Note *To date, Nikon offers almost 30 AF-S lenses that offer full functionality for your D60. These lenses range from a super-wide 12-24mm zoom lens all the way up to a 600mm super-telephoto lens. Most of the AF-S lenses are zoom lenses, but Nikon does offer a few fixed-focal-length lenses. These fixed-focal–length, or prime, lenses are mostly in the telephoto to super-telephoto range with the one exception being the 60mm macro lens.*

✦ **DX.** This lets you know the lens was designed for use only on a digital camera with an APS-C-sized sensor (all Nikon dSLRs, with the exception of the D3). If you try to use a DX lens on a film camera, severe vignetting in the image area occurs.

✦ **VR.** This code denotes the lens is equipped with Nikon's Vibration Reduction system. VR shifts the lens elements to counteract camera shake when shooting at slower shutter speeds. This technology also helps when shooting with long lenses that can magnify camera shake and cause blurring even at faster shutter speeds.

✦ **ED.** This indicates that some of the glass in the lens is Extra Low Dispersion, which means the lens is less prone to lens flare and chromatic aberrations than lenses without this type of glass.

✦ **Micro.** Even though they are labeled as micro, these are Nikon's macro lenses.

✦ **IF.** IF stands for Internal Focus. The focusing mechanism is inside the lens, so the lens doesn't change length and the front of the lens doesn't rotate when focusing. This feature is useful when you don't want the front of the lens to move; for example, when you use a polarizing filter. The internal focus mechanism also allows for faster focusing.

Tip   *With the D60 you can use almost every Nikon lens made since about 1977, although with most older lenses you have limited functionality. You can also use some of the earlier lenses, known now as pre-AI, but most need some modifications to work with the D60.*

Kit Lenses

The Nikon D60 comes paired with Nikon's new 18-55mm f/3.5-5.6G VR AF-S DX lens. This lens covers the most commonly used focal lengths for everyday photography. The 18mm setting covers the wide-angle range, and zooming all the way out to 55mm gives you a moderate telephoto setting allowing you to get close-up photos of subjects that may not be very close. Nikon also offers a D60 kit with two lenses, the 18-55mm and a 55-200mm f/4-5.6 AF-S DX VR. The 55-200mm lens allows you a good medium-to-long telephoto range to really pull those far-off subjects closer.

For the first time ever, Nikon has added a Vibration Reduction (VR) lens to one of the entry-level camera kits. This feature allows you to handhold the camera at slower shutter speeds without worrying about image blur that can be caused by camera shake.

This lens has received many good reviews. The optics give you sharp images with good contrast when stopped down a bit. When shooting wide open the images can appear a little soft around the corners.

Although Nikon offers many very high-quality professional lenses, the D60 kit lenses are very good performers for their price range and they offer some advantages when paired with the D60 that even some of Nikon's more-expensive lenses don't.

✦ **Low cost.** The 18-55mm VR lens costs less than $200 while the 55-200mm VR lens comes in at just around $250. The 18-200mm VR lens retails for around $750. Buying both the18-55mm and 55-200mm VR lenses can save you around $300!

✦ **Superior image quality.** These lenses are very high quality for the price. They offer aspherical lens elements, which help to eliminate distortion, and Nikon's Super Integrated Coating on the lens helps to ensure accurate color and reduce lens flare. These lenses have been praised by professional and amateur reviewers alike. They are uncommonly sharp for a lens at this price range.

✦ **Compact size.** Being designed specifically for dSLR cameras, these lenses are small in size and super-light. They are great lenses for everyday use or long trips where you don't want a lot or gear weighing you down.

✦ **VR.** Vibration Reduction is a very handy feature especially when working in low-light situations or when using a long focal length. It can allow you to handhold your camera at slower shutter speeds than you can with standard lenses.

 Note Nikon is by no means the only manufacturer of lenses. Many companies make lenses specifically to fit the Nikon, including Tamron, Sigma, and Tokina, to name a few.

Understanding zoom lenses

A zoom lens is a lens that has multiple optical elements that move within the lens body to allow it to change focal length and therefore, field of view, which is how much of the scene you can see at any given focal length.

One of the main advantages of the zoom lens is its versatility. You can attach one lens to your camera and use it in a wide variety of situations. Gone is the need for constantly changing out lenses, which reduces the exposure of your camera's image sensor to dust and debris.

There are a few considerations when buying zoom lenses (or upgrading from one you already have).

Variable aperture

One of the major issues when buying consumer-level lenses such as the 18-55mm VR lens is that it has a variable aperture, which means as you zoom in on something the aperture of the lens gets smaller allowing less light to reach the sensor, thus increasing your shutter speed. In daylight or brightly lit situations this may not be a factor, but when shooting in low light this can be a drawback. Although the VR helps when shooting relatively still subjects, moving subjects in low light will be blurred. If you do a lot of low-light shooting of moving subjects, such as concert photography, you may want to look into getting a zoom lens with a wider aperture such as f/2.8. These are *fast aperture* pro lenses and usually cost quite a bit more than your standard consumer zoom lens. The lens I use most when photographing action in low light is the Nikkor 17-55mm f/2.8, this lens allows me to use an ISO of about 800 (keeping the noise levels low) and relatively fast shutter speeds to freeze the motion of the subject. To keep the same shutter speed while using the 18-55mm VR you would need to boost your ISO up to 3200 (Hi-1), which can add quite a bit of noise to your image. What it boils down to is how much action shooting you may do in low light.

Depth of field

Another consideration when buying a zoom lens is depth of field. For example, the 18-55mm lens gives you more depth of field at all focal lengths than a lens with a wider aperture. If you are shooting landscapes this may not be a problem, but getting into portrait photography you may want a shallower depth of field, therefore a lens with a wider aperture is probably what you want.

Quality

In order to make consumer lenses like the 18-55mm VR and the 55-200mm VR affordable, Nikon makes them mostly out of a composite plastic. Although the build quality is pretty good, the higher-end lenses have metal lens mounts and some have metal alloy lens bodies. This allows them to be a lot more durable in the long run, especially if you are rough on your gear like I sometimes am. Conversely, the plastic bodies of the consumer lenses are much smaller and lighter than their pro-level counterparts. This is a great feature when traveling or if you want to pack light. If I'm going on a trip, more often than not I'll just grab my D60 kit and go. It's more compact and much lighter than my other cameras and lenses and I appreciate the small size.

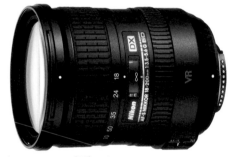

Figure courtesy of Nikon, Inc.
5.1 The Nikkor 18-200mm f/3.5-4.5G ED-IF AF-S DX Super-zoom lens

The range of the zoom lens has vastly improved over the years. Nikon makes an 18-200mm zoom lens, which is an amazing range that almost makes it unnecessary to ever take your lens off. Of course, a zoom range like this comes with a few drawbacks. For example, the lens has a maximum aperture of f/3.5 at the 18mm setting (which is not bad) but a maximum of f/5.6 at the 200mm setting (which is very slow). Nikon makes up for the slow aperture by adding Vibration Reduction, which allows you to handhold the camera at much slower shutter speeds.

Understanding prime lenses

Before zoom lenses were available, the only option a photographer had was using a prime lens, which is also called a fixed-focal-length lens. Because each lens is fixed at a certain focal length, when the photographer wants to change the angle of view, he has to either physically move farther away from or closer to the subject or swap out the lens with one that has a focal length more suited to the range.

One might say, "Well, if I can buy one zoom lens that encompasses the same range as four or five prime lenses, then why bother with prime lenses?" While this may sound logical, there are a lot of reasons why you might choose a prime lens over a zoom lens.

In the past, prime lenses were far superior to zoom lenses. While this is no longer the case, prime lenses can still offer some advantages over zoom lenses. For example, prime lenses don't require as many lens elements (pieces of glass) as zoom lenses do, and this means prime lenses are almost always sharper than zoom lenses. The differences in optical quality are not as noticeable as they were in the past, but with digital camera resolutions getting higher, the differences are definitely becoming more noticeable.

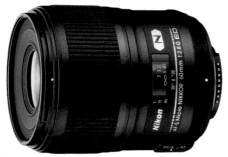

Photo courtesy of Nikon, Inc.
5.2 The Nikkor 60mm f/2.8G AF-S fixed-focal-length macro prime lens

The most important features of the prime lens are the fact that they can have a faster maximum aperture, they are generally far lighter, and cost much less. The standard prime lenses aren't very long, so the maximum aperture can be faster than with zoom lenses. Prime lenses in standard focal lengths also require fewer lens elements and moving parts, so the weight can be kept down considerably; and because there are fewer elements, the overall cost of production is less, therefore you pay less.

One of the most widely sought-after prime lenses is the Nikkor 50mm f/1.8. This lens is a must-have for anyone wanting to delve into the portraiture aspect of photography. The very wide aperture of this lens allows you to blur out the background of the image, making the subject stand out. The most popular portrait lens for the film camera was the 85mm f/1.8, so the 50mm essentially replaces that for the digital DX-format cameras. One great thing about the

Nikkor 50mm f/1.8 is that you can find it new for just over $100 and used for less than $100. The other great thing about this lens is it is one of the sharpest lenses you can buy for your camera, and you can be sure to capture an amazing amount of detail. This lens is not only great for portraits, but for still life and many other types of photography, especially in low light. Unfortunately, due to the D60's lack of a focus motor drive this lens can only be focused manually. If manual focusing isn't a concern this may be a great (and inexpensive) lens to add to your kit.

As discussed earlier in the chapter the Nikon D60 can only autofocus when an AF-S lens is attached to the camera. At this time Nikon only offers a limited number of AF-S prime lenses and they tend to be somewhat expensive and have longer focal-lengths. Currently the AF-S prime lens lineup consists of the 60mm macro lens, the 105mm VR macro, 200mm, 300mm, 400mm, 500mm, and 600mm telephoto lenses.

Third-party lenses

There are a number of different manufacturers that offer lenses to fit Nikon camera bodies, but only one that makes fully functional lenses for the D60. Sigma, a company that manufactures both cameras and lenses, offers some great lenses that can be used with your D60. These lenses are designated as HSM, which stands for Hyper-Sonic Motor. This is similar technology to Nikon's AF-S Silent Wave technology, so the camera retains its ability to autofocus. It offers a 30mm f/1.4 and a 50mm f/1.4 prime lens, which is great for most applications. Sigma also offers a wide selection of zoom lenses that are equipped with the HSM motor. These third-party lenses are often less expensive than the comparable Nikon lenses, many of which are similar in both build and image quality. If you're looking for a good lens on a budget, this is an option worth looking into. Currently, I have a Sigma 17-35mm f/2.8-4 HSM lens that works great with my D60.

Crop Factor

Crop factor is a ratio that describes the size of a camera's imaging area as compared to another format; in the case of SLR cameras the reference format is 35mm film.

SLR camera lenses were designed around the 35mm film format. Photographers use lenses of a certain focal length to provide a specific *field of view*. The field of view, also called the angle of view, is the amount of the scene that is captured in the image. This is usually described in degrees; for example, a 16mm lens when used on a 35mm camera captures almost 180 degrees horizontally of the scene, which is quite a bit. Conversely, when using a 300mm focal length the field of view is reduced to mere 6.5 degrees horizontal, which is a very small part of the scene. Until digital SLRs came along, this field of view was consistent from camera to camera because all SLRs used 35mm film, which had an image area of 24 × 36mm. The sensors on dSLRs can be expensive to manufacture. To keep costs down, the sensor was made smaller than a frame of 35mm film. The lenses that are used with dSLRs have the same focal length as always, but because the sensor doesn't have the same amount of area as the film, the field of view is effectively decreased. This causes the lens to provide the field of view of a longer focal length when compared to 35mm film images.

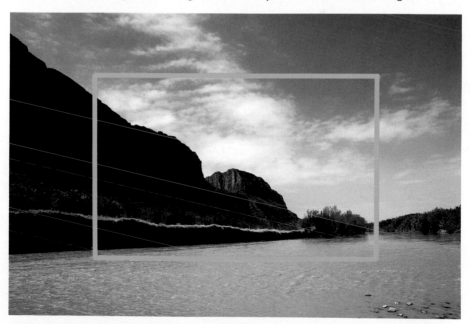

Continued

Continued

Fortunately, the digital sensors in Nikon cameras are a uniform size, supplying a standard you can use to determine how much the field of view is reduced on a dSLR. The digital sensors in Nikon cameras have a 1.5X crop factor, which means that to determine the equivalent focal length of a 35mm camera you simply have to multiply the focal length of the lens by 1.5. Therefore a 28mm lens on a dSLR actually provides an angle of coverage similar to a 42mm lens, a 50mm is equivalent to a75mm, and so on.

When dSLRs were first introduced all lenses were based on 35mm format film. The crop factor effectively reduced the coverage of these lenses, causing ultra-wide-angle lenses to act like wide angles, wide-angle lenses performed like normal lenses, normal lenses provided the same coverage as short telephotos, and so on. Camera and lens manufacturers went to work creating specific lenses for dSLRs with digital sensors. These lenses are known as DX format. The focal lengths of these lenses were shortened to fill the gap so as to allow true super-wide-angle lenses. These DX-format lenses were also redesigned to cast a smaller image inside the camera so that the lenses could actually be made smaller and use less glass than conventional lenses.

There is an upside to this crop factor. Lenses with longer focal lengths now provide a bit of extra reach. A lens set at 200mm now provides the same amount of coverage as a 300mm lens, which can be a great advantage for sports and wildlife photography or when you simply can't get close to your subject.

The figure shows the field of view captured on a frame of film with a 17mm lens. The area inside the green box shows the field of view captured on a digital sensor with the crop factor of 1.5 using the same 17mm lens.

Wide-Angle Lenses

 Cross-Reference *For more information on depth of field, see Chapter 4.*

Wide-angle lenses, as the name implies, provide a very wide angle of view of the scene you are photographing. Wide-angle lenses are great for photographing a variety of subjects, but they really excel in subjects such as landscapes and group portraits where you need to capture a large area.

Wide-angle lenses also provide a greater depth of field than normal and telephoto lenses, so if you are photographing a landscape in which everything needs to be in focus, then you want to use a wide-angle lens.

Another benefit to using wide-angle lenses is they work well for shooting in low light because you can use a longer shutter speed with less worry about camera shake blurring your photos. Wide-angle lenses also come in handy in a tight situation, such as photographing in a small room, because they do capture a wide area so you can get very close to your subject.

Most of the wide-angle lenses commonly available on the market today are wide-angle zoom lenses. The lenses that are available

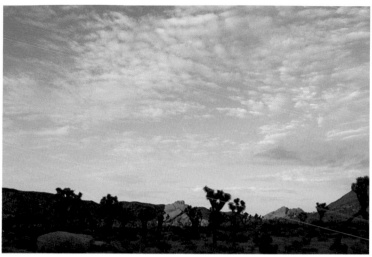

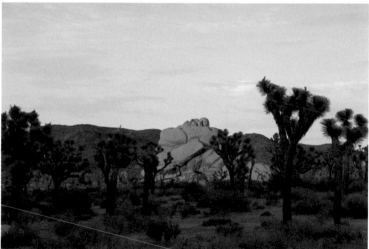

5.3 The image on the top was taken with a wide-angle zoom setting of 17mm, and the image on the bottom used a moderate telephoto zoom setting of 50mm.

with full functionality for the D60 are the Nikkor AF-S 12-24mm f/4, the Sigma 12-24mm f/4.5-5.6 HSM, and the Sigma 10-20mm f/4-5.6 HSM. These lenses are designed to be *rectilinear*, which means additional lens elements are built in to the lens to correct the distortion that is common with wide-angle lenses; this way, the lines near the edges of the frame appear straight.

Some lens manufacturers also offer super-wide-angle *fisheye* lenses. The Nikkor 10.5mm f/2.8 fisheye lens provides an angle

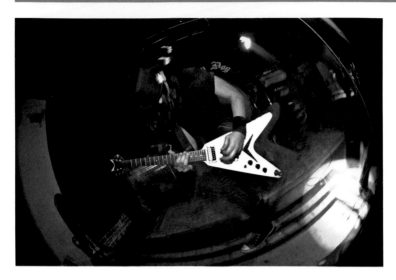

5.4 An image taken with a circular fisheye lens. Note the distortion at the corners of the image.

of coverage of 180 degrees. A fisheye lens is not rectilinear, so the image is distorted (resembling what a fish may see when looking out of a fishbowl), and the lines at the edges of the frame appear bowed out and very exaggerated. Sigma also offers two fisheye lenses that can be used with the D60: the 10mm f/2.8 fisheye and the 4.5mm f/2.8 circular fisheye. The 4.5mm lens provides a complete 180-degree view of the scene, but does not provide full coverage of the camera's sensor. This gives you a circular image with black edges around it.

Some of the drawbacks to wide-angle lenses can be obvious distortion (called barrel distortion) at the edges of the frame, and *vignetting*, or the darkening of the corners of the image. These problems tend to be more pronounced in the lower-priced es, and most of these problems can be d in post-processing using software such dobe Photoshop.

ther possible drawback to using a wide-le lens is the potential for *perspective ortion*. This happens when the lens is close to the subject causing certain

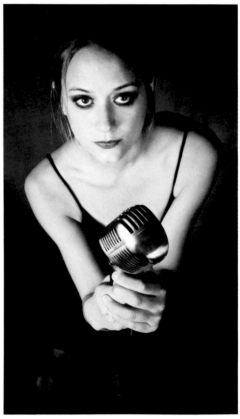

5.5 Wide-angle perspective distortion can also be used creatively.

parts of the image to appear too large while other parts appear too small. This is especially evident with close-up portraits in which the subject's nose can appear huge and the face looks distorted. On the other hand, perspective distortion can be used creatively, allowing you to show an everyday object with a different point of view. Perspective distortion is not limited to wide-angle lenses, but the effect is much more noticeable when using them. Perspective distortion is not caused by the lens, but by the viewpoint.

I don't find the drawbacks to be much of a problem when using wide-angle lenses. I actually like to use them to my advantage. With perspective distortion, I get low and shoot up at a subject, or get up high and shoot down, and I find that a lot of times adding the distortion can make a mundane, everyday subject more interesting. Additionally, the vignetting issue can also be used to your advantage. Sometimes, the darkening of the corners in the image can draw the viewer's eye into the frame, placing emphasis on the subject. I sometimes add a slight vignette to my images in post-processing anyway, so having the camera lens provide it for me actually saves time!

Normal Lenses

A normal lens approximates the field of view of the human eye. In the past, with 35mm film cameras, the normal lens focal length was 50mm. dSLR cameras have a sensor that is smaller than a frame of 35mm film, so the normal lens focal length has shortened to a range from 28 to 35mm to accommodate for the smaller sensor size.

Normal lenses are very versatile and can be used in a variety of shooting situations. Everything from landscapes to portraits can be photographed using a normal lens with very good results.

Most cameras today usually come equipped with a zoom lens that encompasses a wide-angle to short telephoto zoom range (such as the D60's 18-55mm) that has the normal focal length somewhere in between the wide and telephoto settings, but a good 28 or 35mm prime lens can be found relatively inexpensively. And, either of these prime lenses is lighter and usually has a faster aperture than a common zoom lens. Therefore, one of these lenses can be very useful if you need to pack light or if you are shooting in low-light conditions.

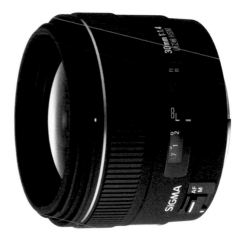

5.6 Sigma 30mm f/1.4 EX DC HSM lens

Telephoto Lenses

Telephoto lenses have very long focal lengths and are used to get close-up photos of distant subjects. These lenses provide a very narrow field of view and are handy when trying to focus on the details of a subject. Telephoto lenses have a much shallower depth of field than wide-angle and normal lenses and can be used effectively to blur out background details to isolate the subject. The telephoto range starts at 50mm (being a short telephoto) all the way up to 600mm on the long telephoto range. The most common focal lengths for consumer telephoto zoom lenses are 50-200mm or 70-300mm.

Telephoto lenses are commonly used for subjects such as sports and wildlife photography to bring the subject closer. The shallow depth of field available makes them one of the top choices for photographing portraits as well.

One important thing to remember about telephoto lenses is that they not only magnify

the subject, they also magnify any movement the camera makes. This means at long focal lengths such as 200mm any small movement you make is more apparent. Even a slight shaking of the hands is noticeable when looking through the viewfinder. For this reason you need to use a faster shutter speed when shooting with a telephoto lens.

As with wide-angle lenses, telephoto lenses have their own set of quirks, such as perspective distortion. As you may have guessed, telephoto perspective distortion is the opposite of the wide-angle variety. Because everything in the photo is so far away with a telephoto lens, the lens tends to *compress* the image. Compression causes the background to look too close to the foreground. Of course, this effect can also be used creatively. For example, compression can flatten out the features of

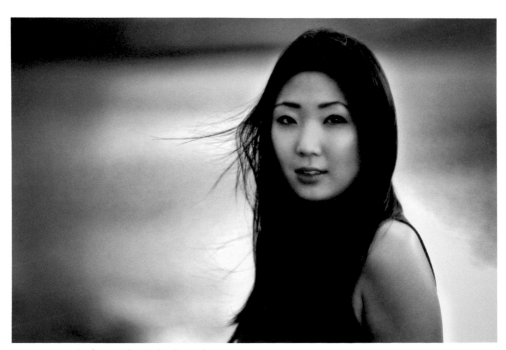

5.7 A portrait shot with a telephoto lens

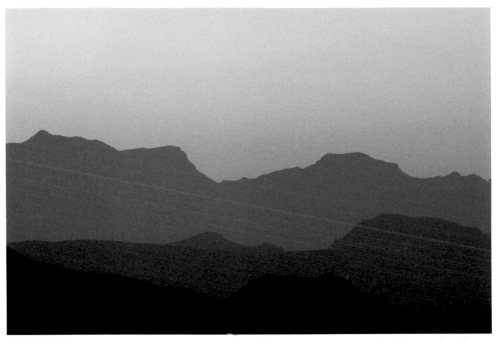

5.8 Although these mountains are miles apart, the compression from the lens makes them look like they are stacked right on top of each other.

a model, resulting in a pleasing effect. Compression is another reason why photographers often use a telephoto lens for portrait photography.

A standard telephoto zoom lens usually has a range of about 70-200mm. If you want to zoom in close to a subject that is very far away, you may need an even longer lens. These super-telephoto lenses can act like telescopes, really bringing the subject in close. These long lenses range from about 300mm up to about 800mm. Almost all super-telephoto lenses are prime lenses, and they are very heavy, bulky, and expensive. A lot of these super-telephoto lenses are a little slower than your normal telephoto zoom lens, usually having a maximum aperture of about f/4 or smaller.

Macro Lenses

A macro lens is a special-purpose lens used in macro and close-up photography. The macro lens allows you to have a closer focusing distance than regular lenses, which in turn allows you get more magnification of your subject, revealing small details that would otherwise be lost. True macro lenses offer a magnification ratio of 1:1; that is, the image projected onto the sensor through the lens is the exact same size as the actual object being photographed. Some lower-priced macro lenses offer a 1:2 magnification ratio, which is half the size of the original object.

Lens Distortion

When dealing with any kind of lenses you eventually have to deal with optical distortion. The lenses you attach to your camera are a complex system of optics with many different lens elements that are used to give a certain field of view. Without getting into the technical details of how a lens works, just know that the lens elements bend or refract the light manipulating it to magnify it (in the case of a telephoto) or making it look farther away (in the case of wide-angle lenses). With all of this light, bending going on, lenses can distort the image-making it look different than the original subject.

Each type of lens has its own different kind of distortion. For example, wide-angle lenses suffer from what is known as *barrel distortion*. Barrel distortion is characterized by the image being sort of rounded out near the edges of the frame. You can see in the following figure that the parallel lines at the edge of the image bulge outward.

Telephoto lenses suffer from the opposite problem, which is referred to as *pincusion distortion.* This type of distortion is characterized by the edges of the frame appearing to be pinched in toward the center, as you can see in the figure with the parallel lines at the edge of the frame bending toward the center.

Both types of distortion are more noticeable near the extreme edges of the frame. Almost all lenses manufactured today are *rectilinear,* which means that there are additional lens elements built into the lens that *rectify,* or fix, the curved lines. In wide-angle lenses these elements are sometimes referred to as aspherical. Although these lens elements are designed to counteract the curvature, no lens design is perfect, so there will always be some lens distortion, although it is usually minimal.

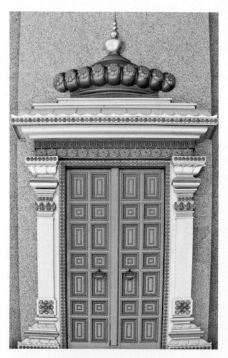 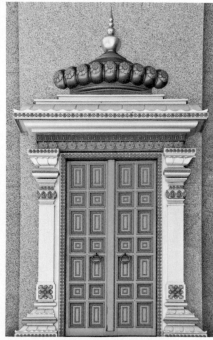

Fisheye lenses are lenses that have not been corrected for any type of distortion and the images appear curved or spherical.

Most lens distortion is only noticeable when photographing subjects that have a lot of straight lines, especially near the edges of the frame, so lens distortion is not always a problem. However for those times when you may be photographing images with a lot of straight lines and distortion may be noticeable, some image-editing programs such as Nikon Capture NX and Photoshop CS3 have tools that allow you to correct for the distortion.

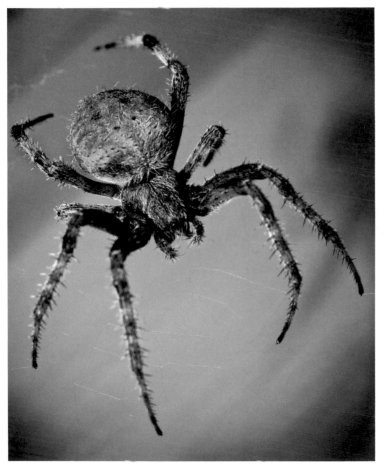

5.9 A shot taken with a 50mm macro lens with a magnification ratio of 4:1 or 4X the original size

Lens Quality and Image Quality

Depending on what the output of your image is, you may want to spend some extra money on quality lenses to be sure your images look as good as they can; otherwise, you may as well be shooting with a lower-resolution camera. Budget-priced lenses such as the Nikkor 16-85mm f/3.5-5.6 VR and the Nikkor 70-300mm f/4-5.6 VR can show a lower image quality due to the lower quality of the lens elements. If you're going to be making large prints with your images you will definitely benefit from the higher-quality glass in the more expensive lenses. On the other hand, if your images are only going to be viewed on a computer monitor or you won't be making prints much larger than 8 × 10, then you may not have the need for the higher-quality pro lenses unless you have a need for the faster apertures.

A major concern with a macro lens is the depth of field. When focusing at such a close distance, the depth of field becomes very shallow. Because of this it is advisable to use a small aperture to maximize your depth of field and ensure everything is in focus. Of course, as with any downside, the shallow depth of field can also be used creatively. For example, you can use it to isolate a detail in the subject.

Macro lenses come in a variety of different focal lengths, with the most common being about 60mm. Some macro lenses have substantially longer focal lengths, which allow more distance to be put between the lens and the subject. This comes in handy when the subject needs to be lit with an additional light source. A lens that is very close to the subject while focusing can get in the way of the light source causing a shadow to be cast on it.

When buying a macro lens, there are a few things you may want to consider: How often are you going to use the lens? Can it be used for other purposes? Do you need auto-

focus? Because newer dedicated macro lenses can be pricey, you may want to consider some cheaper alternatives.

Know is that it's not absolutely necessary to have an AF lens. When shooting very close up, the depth of focus is very small, so all you need to do is move slightly closer or farther away to achieve focus. This makes an AF lens a bit unnecessary. You can find plenty of older Nikon MF macro lenses that are very inexpensive with superb lens quality and sharpness.

Note *Some other manufacturers also make very good-quality MF macro lenses. The lens I use is a 50mm f/4 Macro-Takumar made for early Pentax screw-mount camera bodies. I bought this lens for next to nothing, and I found an inexpensive adapter that allows it to fit the Nikon F-mount. The great thing about this lens is that it's super-sharp and allows me to focus close enough to get a 4:1 magnification ratio, which is 4X life size.*

Using VR Lenses

Nikon has an impressive list of lenses offering Vibration Reduction, including the 18-55mm and 55-200mm kit lenses that are available with the D60. This VR technology is used to combat image blur caused by camera shake that occurs, especially when handholding the camera at long focal lengths. The VR function works by detecting the motion of the lens and shifting the internal lens elements. This allows you to shoot up to 3 stops slower than you would normally. If you're an old hand at photography, you probably know this rule of thumb: To get a reasonably sharp photo when handholding the camera, use a shutter speed that corresponds to the reciprocal of the lens's focal length. In simpler terms, when shooting at a 200mm zoom setting, your shutter speed should be at least 1/200 second. When shooting with a wider setting, such as 28mm, you can safely handhold at around 1/30 second. Of course, this is just a guideline; some people are naturally steadier than others and can get sharp shots at slower speeds. With VR enabled, you should be able to get a reasonably sharp image at a 200mm setting with a shutter speed of around 1/30 second.

Although the VR feature is good for providing some extra latitude when shooting with low light, it's not made to replace a fast shutter speed. To get a good, sharp photo when shooting action, you need to have a fast shutter speed to freeze the action. Remember, when shooting in low light the VR only compensates for camera movement, so if your subject moves even slightly the image will be blurry.

Another thing to consider with the VR feature is that the lens's motion sensor may overcompensate when panning, causing the image to actually be blurrier. So, in situations where you need to pan with the subject, you may need to switch off the VR. The VR function also slows down the AF a bit, so when catching the action is very important, you may want to keep this in mind as well.

While VR is a great advancement in lens technology, few things can replace a good exposure and a solid monopod or tripod for a sharp image.

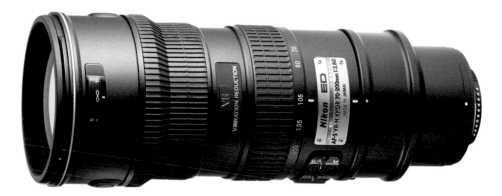

Image courtesy of Nikon, Inc.
5.10 The Nikon 70-200 f/2.8 ED-IF AFS with VR

Extending the Range of Any Lens

There are several ways to extend the range of the lenses you already own — from extending the focal length to focusing closer to magnifying the image. Buying a few of these accessories can effectively add to your lens arsenal without actually adding new lenses.

Teleconverters

In some cases, you may need a lens that has a longer focal length than the lenses you own. You may want a 600mm lens to really get close to a far-away subject, but you don't necessarily want to spend the money on an expensive 600mm prime lens. Fortunately, Nikon, as well as some other lens manufacturers, offer *teleconverters*. A teleconverter attaches to your camera between the lens and the camera body and extends the focal length giving you extra zoom and magnification. There are different sizes of teleconverters; Nikon offers 1.4X, 1.7X, and 2X models. Other manufacturers offer different sizes including and up to 3X.

Teleconverters are a great option for extending the focal length of some of your lenses. Being small in size, they don't take up much room in your camera bag and they aren't nearly as expensive as buying a whole new lens.

There are some drawbacks to using teleconverters. With the extended range you gain in focal length, you lose some light. The teleconverter effectively makes your lens anywhere from 1 to 3 stops slower than

normal. The 1.4X teleconverter causes you to lose 1 stop of light, while using a 3X model causes you to lose a very noticeable 3 stops of light. This causes your f/2.8 lens to function with an effective f/8 aperture. While this may not be a problem during a bright, sunny day, in a low-light condition you could run into some problems.

Additionally, the AF systems on most cameras need a specific amount of light to function. Attaching a teleconverter to a lens with a maximum aperture of less than f/2.8 can cause the AF function to not work properly or to not work at all.

Finally, with the inclusion of additional lens elements and the longer focal length, teleconverters cause you to lose some sharpness in your image. The higher-priced teleconverters like the ones offered by Nikon give you sharper overall images than the lower-priced teleconverters offered by third-party manufacturers. Teleconverters are available in both AF and MF versions.

 Caution *Not all teleconverters work with all lenses and some lenses cannot work with a teleconverter at all. Additionally some teleconverters can cause damage to the lens or camera if used improperly. Check with a reputable camera shop before using a teleconverter.*

Extension tubes

Extension tubes are mounted between the camera and the lens like a teleconverter, but they function completely differently. While the teleconverter allows you to increase the focal length of your lens, an extension tube simply moves the lens farther from the image sensor. Extension tubes give you a closer focusing distance so your lens can get more magnification of the subject, making it possible to take macro photos with a regular lens and giving you increased magnification when used with a macro lens.

Like teleconverters, adding an extension tube effectively reduces your maximum aperture and you lose some light. Unlike teleconverters, extension tubes have no optical elements in them; they are simply open tubes. Additionally, extension tubes are offered in both AF and MF options.

Filters

Filters provide a wide range of effects; some filters add a color tint to the photograph while others neutralize a colorcast (for example, you might use a filter to compensate for the color of a tungsten light bulb). Other filters block certain wavelengths of light or add a special effect, such as a star pattern in the highlight areas of a photograph. Many traditional photo filters can now be replicated using Photoshop or some other image-editing software. However, a few filters cannot be replicated with software, such as the following:

Cross-Reference *For more info on white balance, see Chapter 2.*

✦ **UV (ultraviolet) filters.** This is by far the most common filter found on camera lenses these days. UV filters block UV light resulting in a sharper image. These filters can also reduce the effect of atmospheric haze in landscape photos of distant subjects. Most people also use these filters to protect the front element of the lens from getting scratched or damaged. To be fair, there are those people who doubt the validity of using these filters because, at lower elevations, UV light is not abundant enough to adversely affect the image. In addition, the sensors on dSLR cameras usually already have some sort of UV filter built in. Some people also claim that putting a lower-quality glass filter on an expensive lens lessens the quality of the images. I have a UV filter on almost all of my lenses for protection. Ultimately, the decision is yours.

✦ **ND (neutral density) filters.** This is another commonly used filter. This filter reduces the amount of light that reaches the sensor without changing the color. It is used to prevent blown-out highlights caused by extremely bright lighting conditions, such as when you're at a beach with white sand on a bright sunny day. These filters can also be used to slow down your shutter speed when you need a long exposure, there is too much light on the subject, and reducing the ISO is out of the question. You can also use these filters to increase the shutter speed and use a wider aperture to achieve a shallow depth of field. ND filters normally come in three versions: ND-2, which absorbs 1 stop of light; ND-4, which absorbs 2 stops of light; and ND-8, which absorbs 3 stops of light. You can also find an ND-400 filter, which effectively reduces the amount of light by 9 stops.

✦ **Polarizing filters.** When light is reflected off any surface, it tends to scatter randomly, and the polarizing filter takes these random scattered light rays and makes them directional, thereby reducing or even eliminating the glare from reflective surfaces. Polarizing filters are almost invaluable when photographing landscapes; they can cut down the atmospheric haze and add contrast to the image. Its effect on skies is most evident; the use of a polarizer will increase the contrast between the clouds and the sky. Many people also use the polarizer as a type of ND filter because it reduces the amount of light reaching the sensor by approximately one and a half stops.

When purchasing a polarizer for your camera, be sure to buy a circular polarizer because a linear polarizer may cause your camera's AF and metering not to function properly.

✦ **IR (infrared) filters.** These filters block almost the entire visible light spectrum allowing only infrared light that is invisible to the naked eye to pass through to the sensor. The resulting images are very ethereal, dreamlike, and often surreal. In infrared photography, the skies are very dark and vegetation glows a ghostly white. Because almost all of the light is being blocked, IR photography requires long shutter speeds and a tripod.

For more in-depth information on IR photography, see Chapter 7.

This is just a list of the most common and useful filters. There are many more types of filters available (warming filters, cooling filters, star filters, and so on). A quick search on the Web will yield many more results.

Working with Light

The word photography stems from two Greek words: *photos*, meaning light; and *graphos*, meaning to write or draw, literally *light-drawing*. The most important factor in photography is light; without it, your camera is rendered useless. You need light to make the exposure that results in an image.

Not only is light necessary to make an exposure, it also has different qualities that can impact the outcome of your image. Light can be soft and diffuse, or it can be hard and directional. Light can also have an impact on the color of your images; different light sources emit light at different temperatures, which changes the colorcast of the image.

When there is not enough light to capture the image you're after, or if the available light isn't suitable for your needs, you can employ alternative sources of light, such as flash, to achieve the effect you want.

The ability to control light is a crucial step toward being able to make images that look exactly how you want them to. In this chapter, I explain some of the different types of light and how to modify them to suit your needs.

Lighting Essentials

To get your images to appear exactly as you want them, you need to know a few things about light—how it reacts, its specific properties, and even how to control it to make it suit your needs. This section touches on some of the basic properties of light.

Quality of light

Lighting is the essence of photography. Not only does it create the image, it sets the tone and the mood of the photograph. It can accentuate features and enhance the detail, or it can soften the subject, creating a serene mood. Quality of light can be a misleading term; it not only means good-quality light, but it can also describe some of the unwanted attributes. In the broad scope of things, there are two basic qualities of light: hard light and soft light.

Hard light

Hard light comes from a single bright source and is very directional: for example, photographing in midday open sunlight—the sun is your single, bright source. The shadows are very distinct, and the image has high contrast and a wide tonal range. Using hard light can be effective when you want to highlight textures in your subject. Hard light is also very good at creating a dramatic portrait and is especially effective in black and white.

Because hard light is directional and there is high contrast associated with its use, you want to be very careful with the position of the light source. The placement of the light affects where the shadows fall, and in high-contrast images, shadow placement can make or break an image.

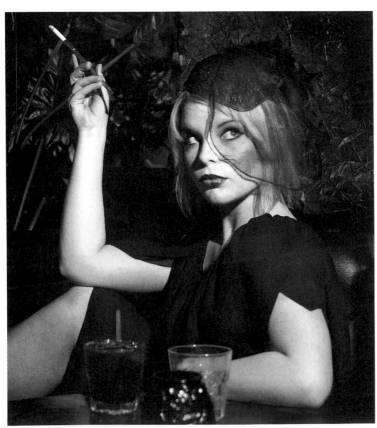

6.1 I used hard light in this image to create a dramatic mood.

Soft light

Soft light is very diffuse and comes from a broad source or is reflected onto the subject. The resulting images are very soft with less-noticeable differences between the shadows and the highlights. With a soft-light image, the lighting seems to be coming from more than one direction, and it is often hard to pinpoint from which direction the light is coming. With soft light, the texture of objects is less apparent and some of the detail is lost.

Soft light is very good for portraits and most everyday subjects. Soft light is also flattering to most subjects, but it can sometimes lack the depth and drama that you may need for your image.

There are quite a few ways to achieve soft light; the most common way is to take your subject out of the direct light by putting it in the shade, such as under trees, a porch, or an overhang when outside. Inside you can create a soft light source by using indirect lighting, bouncing flash of off a ceiling or wall, or the most simple and greatly effective way, to place your subject near a window that allows sunlight to filter in, also known as window lighting.

Metering light

The first thing you need to know before you actually press the Shutter Release button and take the picture is the camera setting necessary to get the proper exposure. Although there are ways to figure the proper exposure in your head, such as using the Sunny 16 Rule (explained later in the chapter), when using the D60 you don't need to figure it out yourself. Fortunately, your D60 is equipped with a very accurate, state-of-the-art light meter built right in.

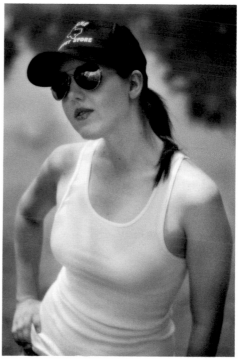

6.2 This soft-light portrait of Melissa was taken by placing her in the shade of a tree to reduce the contrast of the bright afternoon sun – creating soft light in an otherwise hard light situation.

The D60 metering system is what is known as a *TTL* system. TTL is short for *through the lens*, meaning the light measured is actually coming through the lens. The reason this system works so well is the sensor that measures the light is measuring the *exact* amount of light reaching the sensor. This takes into account the amount of light lost traveling down the barrel of the lens and through the glass of the lens.

 For more information on the D60 metering system and the different options, see Chapter 2.

Sunny 16 Rule

The Sunny 16 Rule is a guide to achieving proper exposure outdoors without the aid of a light meter. Since the D60 light meter doesn't function when using older Manual focus lenses, I decided to include this here just in case anyone might want to use these types of lenses as I sometimes do. This is a very tried-and-true method of estimating exposure without the aid of a light meter. The name of the rule is derived from the aperture you should use when photographing outdoors on a sunny day, which is f/16. The shutter speed is equal to the nearest reciprocal of the ISO speed. For example, if you are using ISO 100, your shutter speed should be around 1/125 second at f/16 give or take a 1/3 of a stop. For ISO 200, you change your shutter speed to around 1/250 at f/16.

So, what if the day isn't bright and sunny? In that case, you just open up the aperture. The following is a table showing the settings to use for different outside lighting conditions.

Aperture	Lighting	Shadows
f/16	Sunny	Hard, well-defined shadows
f/11	Slightly overcast	Distinct shadows with soft edges
f/8	Overcast	Very soft, diffused shadows
f/5.6	Dark clouds / heavy overcast	No shadows
f/4	Sunrise / sunset	N/A

In addition to these settings, you can also use equivalent exposures. For example, you can use f/11 on a sunny day by raising your shutter speed by 1 full stop (from 1/125 second to 1/250 second, for example). You can even use f/2.8 at 1/4000 second.

Natural Light

By far the easiest type of light to find, natural light is sometimes the most difficult to work with. Natural light, because it comes from the sun, is often unpredictable and can change from minute to minute. A lot of times I hear people say, "Wow, it's such a nice, sunny day; what a perfect day to take pictures." Unfortunately, this is often not the case. A bright day when the sun is high in the sky presents many obstacles. First, you have serious contrast issues on a sun-drenched day. Oftentimes, the digital sensor doesn't have the latitude to capture the whole scene effectively. For example, it is nearly impossible to capture detail in the shadows of your subject while keeping the highlights from blowing out or going completely white.

Fortunately, if you want to use natural light, it isn't necessary to stand in direct sunlight at noon. You can get desirable lighting effects when working with natural light in many ways. Here are a few examples:

✦ **Use fill flash.** You can use the flash as a secondary light source (not as your main light) to fill in the shadows and reduce contrast.

✦ **Try window lighting.** Believe it or not, one of the best ways to use natural light is to go indoors. Seating your model next to a window provides a beautiful soft light that is very flattering. A lot of professional food photographers also use window light. It can be used to light almost any subject softly and evenly.

✦ **Find some shade.** The shade of a tree or the overhang of an awning or porch can block the bright sunlight while giving you plenty of diffuse light with which to light your subject.

✦ **Take advantage of the clouds.** A cloudy day softens the light, allowing you to take portraits outside without worrying about harsh shadows and too much contrast. Even if it's only partly cloudy, you can wait for a cloud to pass over the sun before taking your shot.

✦ **Use a modifier.** Use a reflector to reduce the shadows or a diffusion panel to block the direct sun from your subject.

Flash Basics

The Nikon D60 not only has a built-in flash for quick use in low-light situations, it is also compatible with additional accessory flashes called Speedlights, which are much more powerful and versatile than the smaller built-in flash. These are *dedicated* flash units, meaning they are built specifically for use with the Nikon camera system and offer much more functionality than a *nondedicated* flash, which is a flash made by a third-party manufacturer. Nikon flashes— both built-in and accessory—use i-TTL flash metering allowing the flash to operate automatically, resulting in a perfect exposure without the user having to do any calculations.

If you are new to using a flash, especially accessory Speedlights, exposure can seem confusing when you first attempt to use it. There are a lot of settings you need to know to get excellent results from your flash, and there are different formulas to use to get the right exposure. If you are using your Speedlight in the i-TTL mode, all of the calculations you would otherwise do manually

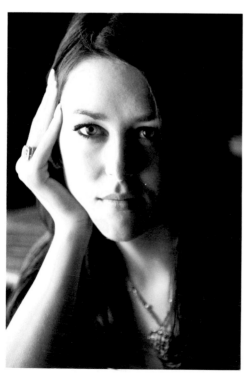

6.3 A portrait using natural light from a window

are done for you. But it's always good to know how to achieve the same results if you didn't have the technology to rely on and so that you understand how the to work with the numbers. When you know these calculations, you can use any flash and get excellent results.

Using the built-in flash

The D60's built-in flash is a handy little flash that's great for taking casual snapshots. Although it lacks the versatility of the bigger external flashes, the built-in flash is always there when you need it and requires no extra batteries because it is powered by the camera's battery. Activate it by pressing the flash pop-up button on the top left of the camera (as you would hold it for shooting) near the built-in flash.

The built-in flash is set to be used in i-TTL mode by default (i-TTL appears as TTL in the menu), although you can choose to set it to be used in Manual mode (you set the output).

It can also be used with all of the different sync modes your camera offers: front curtain sync, rear curtain sync, slow sync, and red-eye reduction. To change the sync mode press the flash pop-up / Flash mode button. Rotate the Command dial while pressing the Flash mode button to change the mode. The selected mode can be seen in the Shooting information display on the LCD.

Pop-up flash diffusers

The best piece of advice that I can offer to you about using the built-in flash is to buy a pop-up flash diffuser. These handy little

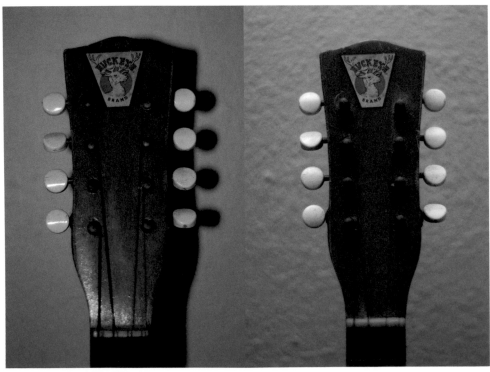

6.4 Shots with and without a pop-up flash diffuser

devices soften the output of the built-in flash giving your images a much more pleasing look. Using one of these diffusers whenever you use the built-in flash will give even random snapshots a more professional look. Pop-up flash diffusers are available from a wide variety of sources and range in price from $5-$20. A popular diffuser is the Gary Fong Puffer, which retails for about $20. This is a very effective model, but you can find diffusers that are very similar on eBay for about one-third of the price of the Gary Fong model. The pop-up flash diffuser that I use is the LumiQuest soft screen, which I picked up at my local camera shop for around $12. The reason I prefer this diffuser is that it folds flat and it fits right in my pocket when I'm not using it. One thing to be aware of when using a flash diffuser is that it will reduce your flash output by about 1 stop. When shooting i-TTL the camera automatically adjusts for it, but when using the flash in Manual mode you will need to add an extra stop of light.

I can honestly say that whenever I have my camera the LumiQuest soft screen is in my pocket. If you plan on doing any amount of photography using the built-in Speedlight, buying a pop-up flash diffuser will be the best money you ever spent. Your images will look much better than if you use straight flash.

Flash exposure modes

Flashes have different modes in which they can operate. These modes determine how the flash receives the information on how to set the exposure.

i-TTL

The D60 determines the proper flash exposure automatically by using Nikon's proprietary i-TTL system. The camera gets most of the metering information from a series of light pulses emitted from the Speedlight; these pulses of light are called preflashes since they fire before that actual flash that is used for the exposure. These preflashes are emitted almost simultaneously with the actual flash so it almost looks as if the flash has only fired once. The camera also uses data from the lens, such as distance information and f-stop values, to help determine the proper flash exposure.

Additionally, there are two separate types of i-TTL flash metering available when using the D60:

✦ **Standard i-TTL flash.** With Standard i-TTL flash the camera determines the exposure for the subject only, not taking the background lighting into account.

✦ **i-TTL Balanced Fill-Flash (BL).** When using the i-TTL Balanced Fill-Flash mode, the camera attempts to *balance* the light from the flash with the ambient light to produce a more natural-looking image.

When using the D60's built-in flash, the default mode is the i-TTL Balanced Fill-Flash mode. To switch the flash to Standard i-TTL, the camera must be switched to Spot metering.

Manual

Setting your Speedlight (either the built-in or accessory) to full Manual mode requires you to adjust the flash output yourself. The best way to figure out the settings is by using a handheld light meter or by using a formula with the Guide Number (GN) of your built-in flash (the D60 has a GN of 43 ft (13 m) at ISO 100), aperture, and distance. If one of these elements changes, another one must be changed proportionally to keep the exposure consistent.

The built-in flash is adjusted manually in the Custom Settings menu (CSM-14). The flash output is set in increments relating to the power of the flash. The settings range from Full power down to 1/32 (Full, 1/2, 1/4, 1/8, 1/16, and 1/32). Each of these settings denotes 1 full stop of light, for example 1/2 is 1 stop less than Full power, 1/4 is 1stop less than 1/2, and so on.

✦ **Guide Number.** This is a numeric value that represents the amount of light emitted by the built-in flash. The GN changes with the ISO sensitivity to which your camera is set, so the GN at ISO 400 is greater than the GN of the same Speedlight when set to ISO 100 (because of the increased sensitivity of the sensor). For a complete listing of the built-in flash's GNs, see Table 6.1.

✦ **Aperture.** This is your f-stop, and as you already know, the wider the aperture is, the more light that falls on the sensor. Using a wider aperture allows you to use a lower power setting (such as 1/4 when in Manual mode) on your flash.

✦ **Distance.** The third element in the flash exposure equation is the distance from the light source to the subject. The closer the light is to your subject, the more light falls on it. Conversely, the farther away the light source is, the less illumination your subject receives. This is important because if you set your built-in flash to a certain output, you can still achieve a proper exposure by moving closer or farther away as needed.

So, your formula is guide number/Distance = Aperture. Once you understand this basic formula, you can change this equation to find out what you want to know specifically: For example, if you were using an accessory Speedlight and you didn't know its GN, use:

$$A \times D = GN$$

Table 6.1
Guide Numbers for the Built-In Flash

Guide Number (ft)	Guide Number (m)	ISO
43	13	100
56	17	200
78	24	400
112	34	800
156	48	160

You multiply your aperture by the distance of the flash from the subject, which gives you the approximate GN of the flash.

If you know your GN and have the approximate distance to the subject, you can find out which aperture would work best:

$$GN / D = A$$

Conversely, if you know what aperture you want to use and the GN, you can use this version of the formula to find out where to place your subject:

$$GN / A = D$$

Flash sync modes

Flash sync modes control how the flash operates in conjunction with your D60. These modes allow you to choose when the flash fires, either at the beginning of the exposure or at the end, and they also allow you to keep the shutter open for longer periods enabling you to capture more ambient light in low-light situations.

Note *If you are using an accessory Speedlight, such as the SB-800, SB-600, and so on, you should use the same flash sync modes.*

Sync speed

Before getting into the different sync modes, you need to understand *sync speed.* The sync speed is the fastest shutter speed that can be used while achieving a full flash exposure. This means if you set your shutter speed at a speed faster than the rated sync speed of the camera, you don't get a full exposure and you end up with a partially underexposed image. With the D60, you can't actually set the shutter speed above the rated sync speed of 1/200 when using the built-in Speedlight because the camera won't let you.

The reason for limited sync speeds is due to the way the shutters in modern cameras work. The shutter controls the amount of time the light is allowed to reach the imaging sensor. All dSLR cameras have what is called a *focal plane shutter.* This term stems from the fact that the shutter is located directly in front of the focal plane, which is essentially on the sensor. The focal plane shutter has two shutter curtains that travel vertically in front of the sensor to control the time the light can enter through the lens. At slower shutter speeds, the front curtain covering the sensor moves away, exposing the sensor to light for a set amount of time. When the exposure has been made, the second curtain then moves in to block the light, thus ending the exposure.

To achieve a faster shutter speed, the second curtain of the shutter starts closing before the first curtain has exposed the sensor completely. This means the sensor is actually exposed by a slit that travels the length of the sensor. This allows your camera to have extremely fast shutter speeds, but limits the flash sync speed to 1/200 because the whole sensor must be exposed to the flash all at once to achieve a full exposure. Because the entire sensor is only fully exposed up to 1/200 this is the *rated sync speed* of the camera. If you were to set your camera to a faster shutter speed when using flash you would see the rear shutter curtain blocking the sensor in your image.

Front-curtain sync

Front-curtain sync is the default sync mode for your camera. With front-curtain sync the flash is fired as soon as the shutter's front curtain has fully opened. This mode works well with most general flash applications.

One thing that needs mentioning about front-curtain sync is that although it works well when using relatively fast shutter speeds, when the shutter is slowed down (also known as *dragging the shutter* when doing flash photography), especially when photographing moving subjects, it causes your images to have an unnatural-looking blur in front of them caused by the ambient light recording the moving subject.

When doing flash photography at slow speeds your camera is actually recording two exposures, the flash exposure and the ambient light. When using a fast shutter speed the ambient light usually isn't bright enough to have an effect on the image. When the shutter speed is slowed down substantially this allows the ambient light to be recorded to the sensor, causing what is known as *ghosting*. Ghosting is a partial exposure that is usually fairly transparent looking on the image.

This ghosting causes a trail to appear in front of the subject because the flash freezes the initial movement of the subject. So, because the subject is still moving, the ambient light records it as a blur which shows in front of the subject creating the illusion that it's moving backward. To counteract this problem there is a setting called rear-curtain sync, which is explained later in this section.

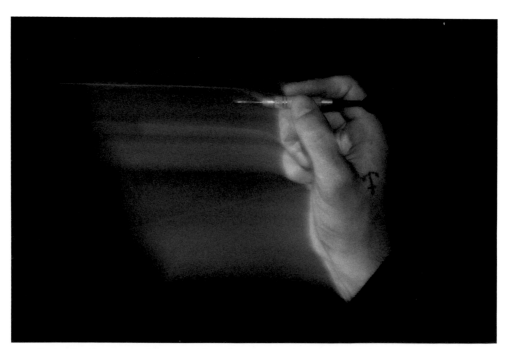

6.5 Shot using front-curtain sync with a shutter speed of 1 second. Notice that the flash freezes the hand at the beginning of the exposure and the trail from the ambient light exposure appears in the front causing the hand to look like it's moving backward.

Red-eye reduction

You've all seen red-eye in a picture at one time or another—that unnatural red glare emanating from a subject's eyes, which is caused by light from the flash reflecting off the retina. Fortunately, the D60 offers a Red-eye reduction flash mode. When this mode is activated, the camera turns on the AF-assist illuminator, which causes the pupils of the subject's eyes to contract. This stops the light from the flash from reflecting off of the retina and reduces or eliminates the red-eye effect. This mode is for use when taking portraits or snapshots of people or pets when there is little light available.

Slow sync

Sometimes when using a flash at night especially when the background is very dark, the subject is lit but appears as if in a black hole. Slow sync helps take care of this problem. When used in slow-sync mode, the camera allows you to set a longer shutter speed (up to 30 seconds) to capture the ambient light of the background. This allows your subject to be lit as well as the background, so you can achieve a more natural-looking photograph.

 Caution *When using slow sync, be sure the subject stays still for the whole exposure to avoid ghosting.*

 Note *Slow sync can be used in conjunction with red-eye reduction for night portraits.*

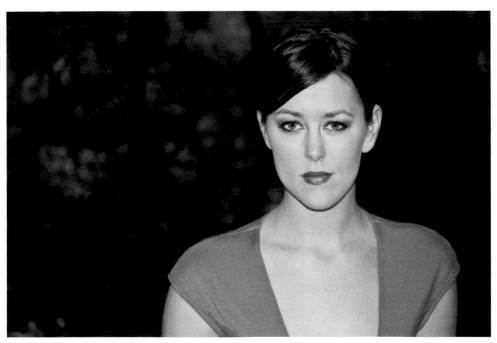

6.6 A picture taken with flash in a dark setting without slow sync. Notice the dark background and the bright subject.

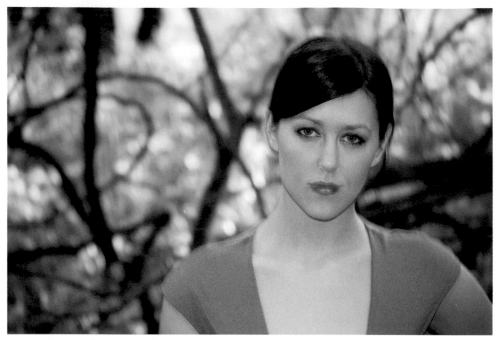

6.7 A picture taken using slow sync flash. Notice how the subject and background are more evenly exposed. There is also slight ghosting from the movement of the model.

Rear-curtain sync

When using rear-curtain sync the camera fires the flash just before the rear curtain of the shutter starts moving. This mode is useful when taking flash photographs of moving subjects. Rear-curtain sync allows you to more accurately portray the motion of the subject by causing a motion blur trail behind the subject rather than out in front, as is the case with front-curtain sync. Rear-curtain sync is most often used in conjunction with slow sync.

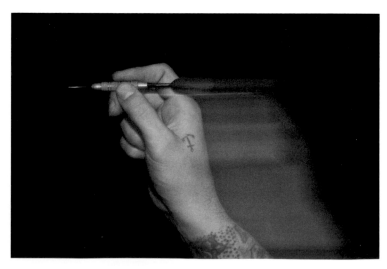

6.8 Shot using rear curtain sync with a shutter speed of 1 second. Notice that the flash freezes the hand at the end of the exposure and the trail from the ambient light exposure appears behind the hand causing it to look like it's moving forward.

Flash Exposure Compensation

When photographing subjects using flash there may be times when the flash causes your principal subject to appear too light or too dark. This usually occurs in difficult lighting situations, especially when using TTL metering, where your camera's meter can get fooled into thinking the subject needs more or less light than it actually does. This can happen when the background is very bright or very dark, or when the subject is off in the distance or very small in the frame.

Flash Exposure Compensation (FEC) allows you to manually adjust the flash output while still retaining TTL readings so your flash exposure is at least in the ballpark. With the D60 you can vary the output of your built-in flash's TTL setting from -3 EV to +1 EV in 1/3 stop settings. This means if your flash exposure is too bright, then you can adjust it down to 3 full stops under the original setting. Or, if the image seems underexposed or too dark, you can adjust it to be brighter by 1 full stop.

The FEC is adjusted on the D60 by simultaneously pressing the Flash button and the Exposure compensation button while rotating the Command dial. Rotating the Command dial to the right gives you less exposure while rotating it to the left gives you more exposure.

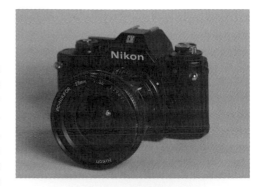

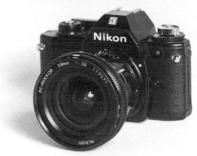

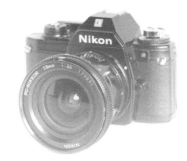

6.9 A series of images using FEC

Fill flash

Fill flash is a handy flash technique that allows you to use your built-in flash as a secondary light source to fill in the shadows rather than as the main light source, hence the term fill flash. Fill flash is used mainly in outdoor photography when the sun is very bright, creating deep shadows and bright highlights that result in an image with very high contrast and a wide tonal range. Using fill flash allows you to reduce the contrast of the image by filling in the dark shadows, thus allowing you to see more detail in the image.

You also may want to use fill flash when your subject is backlit (lit from behind). When the subject is backlit, the camera's meter automatically tries to expose for the brightest part of the image which is behind your subject. This results in a properly exposed background while your subject is underexposed and dark. On the other hand, if you use the spot meter to obtain the proper exposure on your subject, then the background will be overexposed and blown out. The ideal thing is to use fill flash to provide an amount of light on your subject that is just about equal to the ambient light of the background. This brings sufficient detail to both the subject and the background resulting in a properly and evenly exposed image.

All of Nikon's dSLR cameras offer i-TTL BL (Nikon calls this Balanced Fill Flash) or, in laymen's terms, automatic fill flash, with the built-in flash. This is a very handy feature because it allows you to concentrate on composition and not have to worry about your flash settings. If you decide that you don't want to use the i-TTL BL option you can set the camera's metering mode to Spot metering.

Note *i-TTL BL is also available when using an accessory Nikon Speedlight. The camera automatically sets the flash to do fill flash as long as you're not in Spot metering mode.*

Of course, if you'd rather control your flash manually you can still do fill flash. It's actually a pretty simple process that can vastly improve your images when used in the right situations.

To execute a manual fill flash, follow these steps:

1. **Use the camera's light meter to determine the proper exposure for the background or ambient light.** A typical exposure for a sunny day is 1/250 second at f/16 with an ISO of 200. Be sure not to set the shutter speed higher than the rated sync speed of 1/200.

2. **Determine the flash exposure.** Using the GN / D = A formula, find the setting that you need to properly expose the subject with the flash.

3. **Reduce the flash output.** Reducing the flash output by about 1 stop allows the flash exposure to be less noticeable while filling in the shadows or lighting your backlit subject. This makes your images look more natural as if a flash didn't light them, which is the ultimate goal when attempting fill flash.

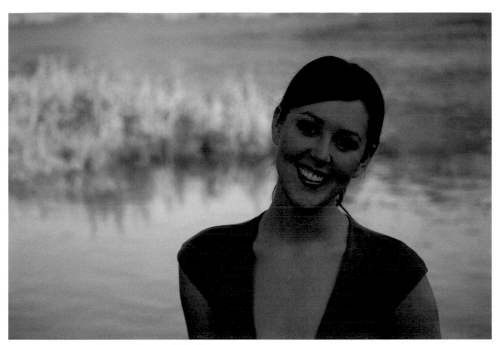

6.10 A picture taken without fill flash

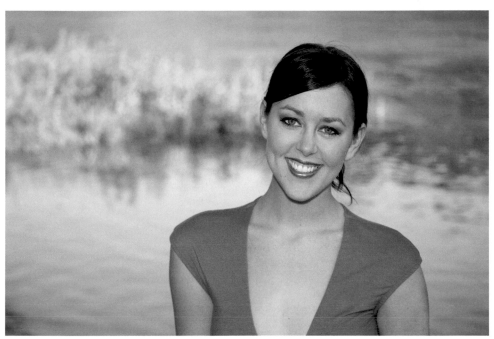

6.11 A picture taken with fill flash

Nikon CLS and Speedlights

Speedlights are Nikon's line of flashes. These flashes are amazing accessories to add to your kit. Most of the new Nikon Speedlights allow full wireless control of the flashes. Currently, Nikon offers three shoe-mounted flashes— the SB-800, SB-600, SB-400—along with two macro lighting ring flash setups—the R1 or R1C1. All current Nikon Speedlights are part of the Nikon Creative Lighting System (CLS).

The CLS is a system designed to enable you to take Nikon Speedlights off of the camera and attach them to stands, so you can position the Speedlights wherever you want and control the direction of light to make the subject appear exactly how you want. The Nikon CLS enables you to achieve more creative lighting scenarios, similar to what a typical professional photographer would do with expensive and much larger studio strobes. All of this can be done wirelessly with the benefit of full i-TTL metering. To take advantage of the Nikon CLS, all you need is the D60 and an SB-800 or SU-800 as a commander and at least one SB-800 or SB-600 for use as a remote flash.

Speedlights

Nikon offers a few dedicated accessory Speedlights. These Speedlights offer more flexibility and power than you can get with just the built-in flash. With these larger accessory flashes you have the option of rotating and tilting the flash heads for more bouncing options and you can even use them off camera with the right combination of equipment. Here is a quick overview of some of the flashes Nikon offers.

Cross-Reference *For more information on Nikon Speedlights and CLS see the Nikon Creative Lighting System Digital Field Guide, also published by Wiley.*

✦ **SB-800 Speedlight.** This is the top-of-the-line Nikon Speedlight. It can be used as a flash and as a commander to control up to three groups of external Speedlights on four channels. You can also set it to work as a remote flash for off-camera applications. The SB-800 has a built-in AF-Illuminator to assist in achieving focus in low light. It has a powerful GN of 174 at ISO 200 and can be used to photograph subjects up to 66 feet away.

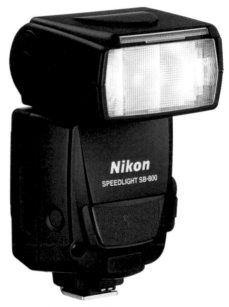

Image courtesy of Nikon, Inc.
6.12 The SB-800

✦ **SB-600 Speedlight.** The SB-600 is the SB-800's little brother. This flash has fewer features than its bigger sibling but has almost everything you need. This Speedlight can be used on the camera as well as off-camera by setting it up for use as a remote. Like the SB-800, the SB-600 also has a built-in AF Illuminator. It cannot, however, be used as a commander to control off-camera flash units. The SB-600 has a GN of 138 at ISO 200 and can be used to photograph subjects up to 60 feet away.

 Note *Speedlight shooting distances are approximate; actual distance depends on the subject, environment, focal length, and aperture.*

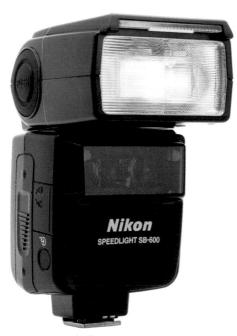

Image courtesy of Nikon, Inc.
6.13 The SB-600

✦ **SB-400 Speedlight.** The SB-400 is Nikon's entry-level Speedlight. It can only be used in the i-TTL/i-TTL BL mode. One nice feature that it does have is a horizontally tilting flash head. For such a small flash the SB-400 has a decent GN of 98 at ISO 200 and can be used to photograph subjects at up to 50 feet away.

Caution *The SB-400 does not work wirelessly with the Creative Lighting System. It only works when connected to the camera hot-shoe or an off-camera hot-shoe cord.*

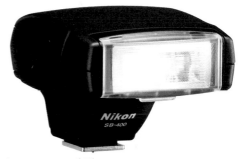

Image courtesy of Nikon, Inc.
6.14 The SB-400

✦ **SU-800 Speedlight commander.** The SU-800 is a wireless Speedlight commander that uses infrared technology to communicate wirelessly with off-camera Speedlights. You can control an unlimited amount of Speedlights set for up to three groups. This allows you to control three different banks of lights adjusting them to different output levels, which gives you greater control of your lighting. The SU-800 can control the groups of Speedlights on four channels in case you are shooting near someone using another SU-800 eliminating the chance of another photographer's SU-800 setting off your remote Speedlights.

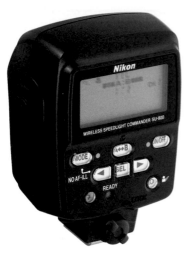
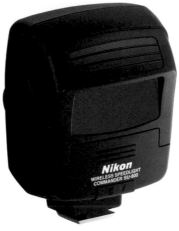

Image courtesy of Nikon, Inc.

6.15 The SU-800 front and back

✦ **R1 / R1C1 Macro flash.** The R1 set consists of a ring that attaches to the lens and SBR-200 Speedlights that attach to the ring. Ring lights are used in close-up and macro photography to provide a light that is direct or on-axis to the subject. This helps to achieve nice, even, shadowless lighting, which can be difficult to do when the lens is close to the subject. The SBR-200 Speedlights can be moved around the ring to provide different lighting patterns to highlight texture. The R1C1 kit comes with an SU-800 wireless commander, which is the only difference between it and the R1.

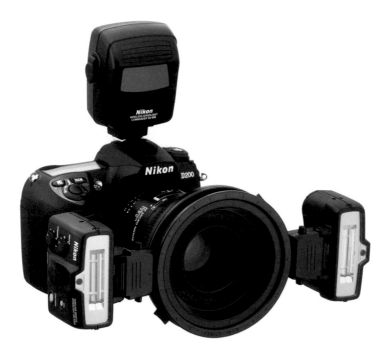

Image courtesy of Nikon, Inc.

6.16 The R1C1 as set up on a D200

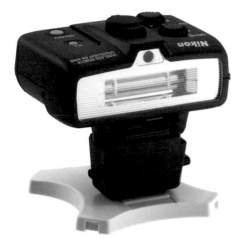

Image courtesy of Nikon, Inc.
6.17 An SBR-200

Understanding the Nikon CLS

The Nikon CLS is basically a communication system that allows the camera, the commander, and the slaves to share information regarding exposure.

A *commander*, which is also called a master, is what controls external Speedlights. The commander can be either the SU-800 wireless Speedlight commander or the SB-800 Speedlight Commander which can be set to Commander mode. *Slaves*, which are sometimes referred to as remote units, are the external flash units controlled remotely by a commander. Communications between the commander and the slaves are accomplished by using *pulse modulation*. Pulse modulation is a term that means the commanding Speedlight fires rapid bursts of light in a specific order. The pulses of light, also known as *monitor* preflashes *or* simply preflashes, are used to convey information to the remote groups of slaves, which interpret the bursts of light as coded information.

Triggering the commander sets off the preflashes, which tell the other Speedlights in the system when and at what power to fire.

This is how CLS happens in a nutshell:

1. The commander unit sends out instructions to the slave groups to fire a series of monitor preflashes to determine the exposure level. The camera's i-TTL metering sensor reads the preflashes from all of the remote groups and also takes a reading of the ambient light.

2. The camera tells the commander unit the proper exposure readings for each group of remote Speedlights. When the shutter is released, the commander, via pulse modulation, relays the information to each group of slave Speedlights.

3. The slaves then fire at the output specified by the camera's i-TTL meter, and the shutter closes.

All of these calculations are done very quickly as soon as you press the Shutter Release button. It almost appears as if the flash just fires once. There is virtually no waiting for the camera and the Speedlights to do the calculations.

Given the ease of use and the portability of the Nikon CLS, I highly recommend purchasing at least one SB-800 or SB-600 Speedlight to add to your camera setup. Adding a commander (either an SU-800 or SB-800) and another Speedlight (or two or three!) can give you the creative freedom of off-camera lighting. With this system you can produce almost any type of lighting pattern you want. It can definitely get you on the road to creating more professional-looking images.

Bounce Flash

One of the easiest ways to improve your flash pictures, especially snapshots, is to employ the use of *bounce flash*. Bounce flash is a technique in which the light from the flash unit is bounced off of the ceiling or off of a wall onto the subject in order to diffuse the light, resulting in a more diffused and evenly lit image. To do this your flash must have a swiveling/tilting head. Most flashes made within the last 10 years have this feature, but some may not.

Bouncing the flash

When you attempt bounce flash you want to get as much light from the flash onto your subject as you can. To do this you need to first look at the placement of the subject and adjust the angle of the flash head appropriately. Consider the height of the ceiling or distance from the surface you intend to bounce the light from to the subject.

Unfortunately, not all ceilings are useful for bouncing flash. For example, the ceiling in my studio is corrugated metal with iron crossbeams. If I attempted to bounce flash from a ceiling like that, it would make little or no difference to the image because the light won't reflect evenly and will scatter in all directions. In a situation where the ceiling is not usable, you can position the subject next to a wall and swivel the flash head in the direction of the wall and bounce it from there. To bounce the flash at the correct angle, remember the angle of incidence equals the angle of reflection.

You want to aim the flash head at such an angle that the flash isn't going to bounce in behind the subject resulting in a poorly lit subject. You want to be sure that the light is bounced so that it falls onto your subject.

When the subject is very close to you, you need to have your flash head positioned at a more obtuse angle than when the subject is farther away. I recommend positioning the subject at least 10 feet away and setting the angle of the flash head at 45 degrees for a typical height ceiling of about 8 to 10 feet.

An important pitfall to be aware of when bouncing flash is that the reflected light picks up and transmits the color of the surface from which it is bounced. This means if you bounce light off of a red surface your subject will have a reddish tint to it. The best way to deal with this is to avoid bouncing light off of surfaces that are brightly colored; your best bet is to stick with bouncing light from a neutral-colored surface. White surfaces tend to work the best because they reflect more light and don't add any color. Neutral gray surfaces also work well although you can lose a little light due to the lessened reflectivity of the darker color.

 Note *Unfortunately, you can't do bounce flash with the D60's built-in flash; you need an external Speedlight such as an SB-800,SB- 600, or SB-400.*

Bounce cards

Sometimes you may find yourself in the situation where you can't use the ceiling or wall to bounce from, you may not be near a wall, the ceiling is just too high, or as in the case of my studio, the ceiling is just not conducive to bouncing. Never fear! There are quite a few options available to you — many companies make devices that attach to your flash to redirect the light, and for mere pennies you can make one for yourself. These gadgets are usually referred to as *bounce cards*, although many of them don't look like cards at all.

The company LumiQuest is the foremost manufacturer of bouncing devices. They've been manufacturing these tools for 20 years and they work quite well. I've been using one for years now and find them to be very good. They have a variety of different products for use in different situations. Most of these products fold up flat and are easy to stow in your camera bag.

Another great product is the Sto-Fen Omnibounce. This product fits right on top of your accessory flash head and diffuses the flash. It's small so it doesn't take up too much room in your camera bag. The Nikon SB-800 Speedlight actually comes with a similar device called the SW-10H diffusion dome.

The SB-800 also has a built-in bounce card that helps redirect some of the bounced back-light into your subject to help give catchlights to a person's eyes and to fill in some shadows that can be caused from bouncing off of the ceiling. This is just a tiny white card that slides out from the top of the SB-800 flash head.

Probably the least-expensive bounce card you can get is one that you make yourself. Take an index card and attach it to the top of your flash head with a rubber band. Voîla! A bounce card that costs almost nothing! This works almost as well as the more-expensive options. Of course there are a lot of other ways to make DIY bounce cards. A quick search on the Internet reveals quite a few ideas, some simple, some more complex.

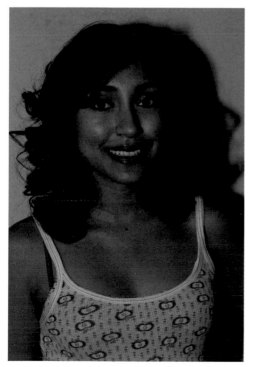

6.18 A picture taken with straight flash

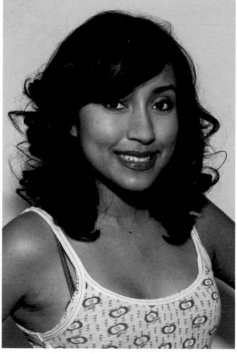

6.19 A picture taken with bounced flash

Studio Strobes

Although the Nikon CLS allows you complete wireless control over lighting, it can be somewhat limited. The Speedlights are small, versatile, and portable, but they are limited in range, power, and options for accessories. Sometimes, there is no other option than to use a studio strobe, especially when lighting large subjects or when you need specific accessories to modify the light in a certain way. A studio strobe has a much higher GN than a shoe-mounted Speedlight, which means more power. Studio strobes run on AC power instead of batteries, which means faster recycle times between flashes. Also, many different accessories and light modifiers are available for studio strobes.

There are two different types of studio strobes: standard pack and head and monolights. Standard pack and head strobes have a separate power pack and flash heads that are controlled centrally from the power pack. Monolights are flash heads that have a power pack built in and are adjusted individually at each head. Mono-lights tend to be lower in power than standard strobes, but they are also more portable and less expensive. For simplicity's sake here on out I refer to both types just as strobes.

One of the downsides to using studio strobes is that you lose the advantage of i-TTL flash metering. Studio strobes are fired from a hot-shoe PC sync device such as the Wein SafeSync or the Nikon AS-15 (or a wireless triggering device such as a Pocket Wizard wireless transmitter), which only tells the flash *when* to fire, not at what output level. All of the strobe settings have to be calculated by you, the photographer. Of course, there are flash meters, which are designed to read the output of the strobe to give you a reading of the proper exposure. And you can always use the handy GN / D = A formula to determine the proper exposure.

One of the plus sides of using studio strobes is the continuous modeling light. Because the strobes are only lit for a fraction of a second, studio strobes are equipped with a constant light source (called a modeling light) that allows you to see where the light is falling on the subject.

Firing Your Studio Strobes

You can't use studio lighting setups completely wirelessly because you have to plug the lights in for power, and in the case of pack and head strobes, you have to not only plug in the power pack, but the flash heads have to be connected to the power pack, also. For the most part studio strobes are fired via a sync cord, which connects to the D60 via a hot-shoe sync device such as the Wein SafeSync. This is the easiest and most affordable way of firing your studio flashes. The SafeSync is a small device that fits into the hot shoe of your camera. On the front of the device is a *PC sync terminal*. No, PC sync doesn't allow you to sync your camera with your personal computer. PC stands for Prontor-Compur, which were companies that built shutters for cameras in the early days of photography. The PC sync terminal allows you to connect your camera to an external flash via a sync cord. When the Shutter Release button is pressed a small amount of voltage is sent through the sync cord telling the flash when to fire. The Wein SafeSync also has built-in electronics that protect your camera from any voltage surges coming from the flash, which could potentially fry your camera's circuitry. Nikon also makes a similar device, the Nikon AS-15 sync terminal adaptor.

Most mono-lights also have a built-in optical slave that allows the flash to be triggered by another flash or even a near invisible infrared triggering device. Most studio strobe power packs can also be fitted with an optical slave. This allows you some freedom from the wires that connect your camera to the main flash unit.

More and more photographers these days are using radio slaves. Radio slaves use a radio signal to trigger the strobes to flash when the shutter is released. Unlike the optical slave, the radio slave is not limited to "seeing" another flash to trigger it to fire. Radio slaves can also fire from a longer distance away and can even work from behind walls and around corners. Radio slave units have two parts: the transmitter and the receiver. The transmitter is attached to the camera and tells the receiver, which is connected to the strobe, to fire when the Shutter button is pressed. Some newer radio units are transceivers, being able to function as a transmitter or a receiver (not at the same time of course), but you still need at least two of them to operate. Radio slaves work very well and free you up from being directly attached to your lights, but they can be very high priced. There are a few different manufacturers of radio slaves but the most well known is Pocket Wizard. They are fairly pricey, but they are built well and are extremely reliable. Recently, there has been a proliferation of radio slave transmitters and receivers on eBay that are priced very low. I can't attest to how well they work, but a lot of folks on the Internet seem to like them. At around $30 for a kit with one receiver and one transmitter, you won't be losing much if they don't work well. Currently, I use the Smith Victor RTK4 radio triggers that I bought for around $80. I bought this set because I am familiar with the Smith Victor product line and I own a few Smith Victor mono-lights. They work well and I feel confident recommending them.

Continuous Lighting

Continuous lighting is just what it sounds like: a light source that is constant. It is by far the easiest type of lighting to work with. Unlike natural lighting, continuous lighting is consistent and predictable. Even when using a strobe with modeling lights, you sometimes have to estimate what the final lighting will look like. Continuous lighting is "what you see is what you get." With continuous lighting, you can see the actual effects the lighting has on your subjects, and you can modify and change the lighting before you even press the Shutter Release button.

Continuous lights, also known as *hot lights* because of the heat they can emit, are an affordable alternative to using studio strobes. Because the light is constant and consistent, the learning curve is also less steep. With strobes, you need to experiment with the exposure or use a flash meter. With continuous lights, the D60's Matrix meter can be used to yield good results.

As with other lighting systems, continuous lights have a lot of different options. Here are a few of the more common types:

✦ **Incandescent.** Incandescent or tungsten lights are the most common type of lights. This is the type of lamp that was invented by Thomas Edison. Your typical light bulb is a tungsten lamp. With tungsten lamps, an electrical current is run through a tungsten filament, heating it and causing it to emit light. This type of continuous lighting is the source of the name "hot lights."

✦ **Halogen.** Halogen lights, which are much brighter than typical tungsten lights, are actually very similar. Halogen lights are considered a type of incandescent light. Halogen lights also employ a tungsten filament, but have a halogen vapor added to the gas inside the lamp. The color temperature of halogen lamps is higher than the color temperature of standard tungsten lamps.

✦ **Fluorescent.** Fluorescent lighting, which most of us are familiar with, is everywhere these days. You find it in most office buildings, stores, and even in your own house. In a fluorescent lamp, electrical energy is used to change a small amount of mercury into a gas. The electrons collide with the mercury gas atoms causing them to release photons, which in turn cause the phosphor coating inside the lamp to glow. Because this reaction doesn't create much heat, fluorescent lamps are much cooler and energy efficient than tungsten and halogen lamps.

✦ **HMI.** HMI, or Hydrargyrum Medium-Arc Iodide lamps, are probably the most expensive type of continuous lighting. This is the type of lamp used by the motion picture industry because of its consistent color temperature and the fact that it runs cooler than a tungsten lamp with the same power rating. These lamps operate by releasing an arc of electricity in an atmosphere of mercury vapor and halogenides.

Incandescent and halogen

Although incandescent and halogen lights have the advantages of making it easier to see what you're dealing with and costing less, there are quite a few drawbacks to using these lights for serious photography work. First, they are hot. When a model has to sit under lamps for any length of time, he will get hot and start to sweat. This is also a problem with food photography. It can cause your food to change consistency or even to sweat; for example, cheese that has been refrigerated. On the other hand, it can help keep hot food looking fresh and hot.

The second drawback to using incandescent lights is that although they appear to be very bright to you and your subject, they actually produce *less* light than a standard flash unit. For example, a 200-watt tungsten light and a 200-watt-second strobe both have a rating of 200 watts so they should be equally bright, right? Wrong. Because the flash discharges all 200 watts of energy in a fraction of a second, the flash is actually much, much brighter. Why does this matter? Because when you need a fast shutter speed or a small aperture, the strobe can give it to you much easier. An SB-600 gives you about 30 watt-seconds of light at full power. To get an equivalent amount of light at the maximum sync speed of 1/200 second from a tungsten light, you would need a 7500-watt lamp! Of course, if you don't need to use a fast shutter speed, then you can use one 30-watt light bulb for a 1-second exposure or a 60-watt lamp for a 1/2-second exposure.

Some other disadvantages of using incandescent lights include the following:

✦ **Color temperature inconsistency.** The color temperature of the lamps changes as your household current varies and as the lamps get more and more use. The color temperature may be inconsistent from manufacturer to manufacturer and may even vary within the same types of bulbs.

✦ **Light modifiers are more expensive.** Because continuous lights are hot, modifiers such as softboxes need to be made to withstand the heat, which makes them more expensive than the standard equipment that are for use with strobes.

✦ **Short lamp life.** Incandescent lights tend to have a shorter life than flash tubes, so you'll have to replace them more often.

Although incandescent lights have quite a few disadvantages, they are by far the most affordable type of lights you can buy. Many photographers who are starting out use inexpensive work lights that can be bought at any hardware store for less than $10. These lights use a standard light bulb and often have a reflector to direct the light; they also come with a clamp you can use to attach them to a stand or anything else you have handy that might be stable.

Halogen work lamps, also readily available at any hardware store, have the advantage of a higher light output than a standard light, generally speaking. The downside is they are very hot, and the larger lights can be a bit unwieldy. You also may have to come up with some creative ways to get the lights in the position you want them. Some halogen work lamps come complete with a tripod stand. If you can afford it, I'd recommend

buying these; they're easier to set up and less of an aggravation in the long run. The single halogen work lamps that are usually designed to sit on a table or some other support are easily available for less than $20; the double halogen work lamps with two 500-watt lights and a 6-foot tripod stand are usually available for less than $40.

If you're really serious about lighting with hot lights, you may want to invest in a photographic hot light kit. These kits are widely available from any photography or video store. They usually come with lights, light stands, and sometimes with light modifiers such as umbrellas or softboxes for diffusing the light for a softer look. The kits can be relatively inexpensive, with two lights, two stands, and two umbrellas for around $100. Or you can buy much more elaborate setups ranging in price up to $2,000. I've searched all over the Internet for these kits and have found the best deals are on eBay.

Fluorescent

Fluorescent lights have a lot of advantages over incandescent lights; they run at much lower temperatures and use much less electricity than standard incandescent lights. Fluorescent lights are also a much softer light source than incandescent lights.

In the past, fluorescent lights weren't considered viable for photographic applications because they cast a sickly green light on the subject. Today, most fluorescent lamps that are made for use in photography are color corrected to match both daylight and incandescent lights. Also, with the white balance being adjustable in the camera or in Photoshop with RAW files, using fluorescents has become much easier because you don't have to worry about color-correcting filters and special films.

These days, because more people are using fluorescent lights, light modifiers are more readily available. They allow you to control the light to make it softer or harder and directional or diffused.

Fluorescent light kits are easily available through most photography stores and online. These kits are a little more expensive than the incandescent light kits — an average kit with two light stands, reflectors, and bulbs costs about $160. Fluorescent kits aren't usually equipped with umbrellas or softboxes because the light is already fairly soft. You can buy these kinds of accessories and there are kits available that come with softboxes and umbrellas, although the kits are significantly higher in price.

Unfortunately there aren't many low-cost alternatives to buying a fluorescent light kit. The only real option is to use the clamp light mentioned in the section about incandescent light and fit it with a fluorescent bulb that has a standard bulb base on it. These types of fluorescent bulbs are easily available at any store that sells light bulbs.

HMI

This type of continuous light is mainly used in the motion picture industry. HMI lamps burn extremely bright and are much more efficient than standard incandescent, halogen, or fluorescent lights. The light emitted is equal in color temperature to that of daylight.

Although I include them here for general information, these kits are usually too cost-prohibitive for use in most average still-photography applications. A one-light kit with a 24-watt light can start at over $1,000. An 18,000-watt kit can cost more than $30,000!

Light Modifiers

Light modifiers do exactly what their name says they do: They modify light. When you set up a photographic shot, in essence, you are building a scene using light. For some images you may want a hard light that is very directional; for others a soft, diffused light works better. Light modifiers allow you to control the light so you can direct it where you need it, give it the quality the image calls for, and even add color or texture to the image.

Umbrellas

The most common type of light modifier is the umbrella. Photographic umbrellas are coated with a material to maximize reflectivity. They are used to diffuse and soften the light emitted from the light source, whether it's continuous or strobe lighting. There are three types of umbrellas to choose from:

✦ **Standard.** The most common type of umbrella has black outside with the inside coated with a reflective material that is usually silver or gold in color. Standard umbrellas are designed so you point the light source into the umbrella and bounce the light onto the subject, resulting in a nondirectional soft light source.

✦ **Shoot-through.** Some umbrellas are manufactured out of a one-piece translucent silvery nylon that enables you to shoot through the umbrella like a softbox. You can also use shoot-through umbrellas to bounce the light as previously mentioned.

✦ **Convertible.** This umbrella has a silver or gold lining on the inside and a removable black cover on the outside. Convertible umbrellas can be used to bounce light or as a shoot-through when the outside covering is removed.

Photographic umbrellas come in various sizes, usually ranging from 27 inches all the way up to 12½ feet. The size you use is dependent on the size of the subject and the degree of coverage you want. For standard headshots, portraits, and small to medium products, umbrellas ranging from 27 inches to about 40 inches supply plenty of coverage. For full-length portraits and larger products, a larger umbrella is generally recommended.

The larger the umbrella is, the softer the light falling on the subject from the light source. It is also the case that the larger the umbrella is, the less light you have falling on your subject. Generally, the small to medium umbrellas lose about a stop and a half to 2 stops of light. Larger umbrellas generally lose 2 or more stops of light because the light is being spread out over a larger area.

Smaller umbrellas tend to have a much more directional light than larger umbrellas. With all umbrellas, the closer your umbrella is to the subject, the more diffuse the light is.

Choosing the right umbrella is a matter of personal preference. Some items to keep in mind when choosing your umbrella include the type, size, and portability. You also want to consider how they work with your light source. For example, regular and convertible umbrellas return more light to the subject when light is bounced from them, which can be advantageous, especially if you are using a Speedlight, which has less power than a studio strobe. Also, the less energy the Speedlight has to output, the more battery power you save. On the other hand, shoot-through umbrellas lose more light through the back when bouncing, but they are generally more affordable than convertible umbrellas.

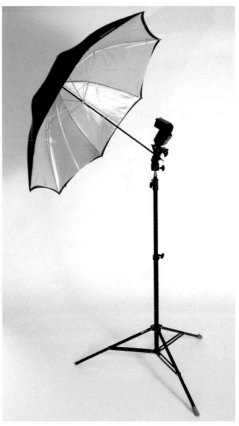

6.20 A Speedlight with a standard umbrella

Softboxes

Softboxes, as with umbrellas, are used to diffuse and soften the light of a strobe or continuous light to create a more pleasing light source. Softboxes range in size from small, 6-inch boxes that you mount directly onto your Speedlight, to large boxes that usually mount directly to a studio strobe.

The reason you may want to invest in a softbox rather than an umbrella for your studio is that softboxes provide a more consistent and controllable light than umbrellas do. Softboxes are closed around the light source, thereby preventing unwanted light from bouncing back onto your subject. The diffusion material makes it so there is less of a chance of creating *hotspots* on your subject. A hotspot is an overly bright spot usually caused by bright or uneven lighting.

Softboxes are generally made for use with studio strobes, although special heat-resistant softboxes are made for use with hot lights. Softboxes attach to the light source with a device called a *speedring*. Speedrings are specific to the type of lights to which they are meant to attach. If you are using a standard hot-shoe flash as your light source, some companies, such as Chimera (www .chimeralighting.com), manufacture a type of speedring that mounts directly to the light stand and allows you to attach one or more Speedlights to the light stand as well. You mount the speedring to the stand, attach the softbox to the speedring, attach the Speedlight with the flash head pointed into the softbox, and you're ready to go.

Softboxes are available in a multitude of shapes and sizes ranging from squares and rectangles to ovals and octagons. Most photographers use the standard square or rectangular softboxes. However, some photographers prefer to use oval or octagonal softboxes for the way they mimic umbrellas and give a more pleasing round shape to the catchlights in the subject's eyes. This is mostly a matter or personal preference. I usually use a medium-sized, rectangular softbox.

As with umbrellas, the size of the softbox you need to use depends on the subject you are photographing. Softboxes can be taken apart and folded up conveniently, and most of them come with a storage bag that can be used to transport them.

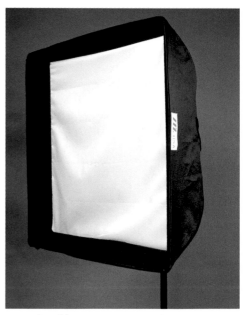

6.21 A softbox

Diffusion panels

A diffusion panel is basically a frame made out of PVC pipe with reflective nylon stretched over it. Diffusion panels function in much the same way as a softbox.

Diffusion panels are usually about 6 feet tall and have a base that allows it to stand up without the need of a light stand. The diffusion panel is placed in front of the subject. Your light source is then placed behind the diffusion panel. You can move the light closer to the diffusion panel for more directional light or farther away for a softer and more even light. For a full-length portrait or a larger subject, you can place two or more lights behind the panel allowing you to achieve greater coverage with your lights.

You can use a diffusion panel as a reflector, bouncing the light from your light source on to the subject. Diffusion panels can be purchased at most major camera stores at a fraction of the price of a good softbox. The PVC frame can be disassembled easily and packed away into a small bag for storage or for transport to and from location.

> **Tip** *If you're feeling crafty, a diffusion panel can be made from items easily found in your local hardware and fabric store. There are numerous sites on the Internet that offer advice on how to construct one.*

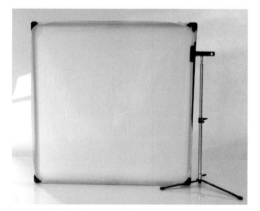

6.22 A diffusion panel

Other light modifiers

There are many different types of light modifiers. The main types — umbrellas, softboxes, and diffusion panels — serve to diffuse the light by effectively increasing the size of the light source, thereby reducing contrast. In addition to softboxes and such, other types of light modifiers are worth your consideration, such as barn doors and snoots. These are also used to control the direction of the light to make it appear stronger or to focus it on a specific area of the subject. The following list includes some of the more-common tools photographers use to direct the light from the light source.

✦ **Parabolic reflectors.** Most light sources come equipped with a parabolic reflector. These reflectors usually range in size from 6 to 10 inches in circumference although you can buy larger ones. Without a reflector, the light from the bare bulb, whether it's a flash tube or an incandescent, would scatter and lack direction resulting in the loss of usable light. The reflector focuses the light into a more specific area actually increasing the amount of usable light by 1 or 2 stops. Parabolic reflectors are commonly used in conjunction with other light modifiers including umbrellas, barn doors, and grids. When using an umbrella, a reflector is always used to direct the light into the umbrella, which diffuses the light. Using only a reflector gives the light a very hard quality that results in a lot of contrast.

✦ **Barn doors.** Barn doors are used to control the direction of light and to block stray light from entering the lens, which can result in lens flare. Blocking the light is also known as *flagging*. Barn doors are normally attached to the reflector and come in two types — 4-leaf and 2-leaf. Barn doors consist of panels that are attached to hinges. These hinges allow you to open and close the doors to let light out or keep it in. Typically, barn doors are used when you want a hard light source to shine on a specific area of the subject but you don't want any stray light striking other parts of the subject or the camera lens.

✦ **Grids.** Grids, also known as grid spots or honeycombs, are used to create a light similar to a spotlight. A grid is a round disc with a honeycomb-shaped screen inside of it. When the light shines through it, it is focused to a particular degree, giving you a tight circle of light with a distinct fall-off at the edges. There are different types of grids that control the spread of light. They run from a 5-degree grid to a 60-degree grid. The 5-degree grid has very small holes and is deep so the light is focused down to a small bright spot. The higher the degree of the grid spot, the more spread out the spot becomes. Grids are great to use as hair lights and to add a spot of light on the background to help the subject stand out.

✦ **Snoots.** A snoot is another device that creates a spotlight-like effect similar to the grid spot. A snoot is shaped like a funnel and it kind of works that way, too, funneling light into a specific area of the scene. The snoot usually has a brighter spot effect than a grid does.

✦ **Reflector.** This type of reflector doesn't directly modify the light coming from the light source, but it is used to reflect light onto the subject. Reflectors are usually white or silver although some can be gold. Professional reflectors are usually round or oval disks with a wire frame that can be easily folded up to a smaller size. You can make your own reflector by using white foam board available at any art supply store and at some photography stores. You can use the board as-is or cover it with silver or gold foil. In a pinch, almost anything white or silver, such as a lid from a styrofoam cooler or even a white T-shirt, will work.

✦ **Gobos.** A gobo can be anything that "goes between" the light source and the subject or background, often to create a pattern or simulate a specific light source, such as a window. They are usually attached to a stand and placed a few feet in front of the light source. A common technique in film noir-type photography is to place Venetian blinds between a light and the background to simulate sunlight shining through the blinds of the office window of a private eye. Gobos can be made or purchased from a photographic supply house.

Real World Applications

This chapter covers a few of the many different types and styles of photography that you might want to try. Each different subject you photograph has certain caveats that you must be aware of.

In each section, I provide different samples of the photographic technique along with some helpful pointers and examples of the types of aperture, shutter speed, ISO settings, and lenses that could be used with the specific subject matter.

If you are not new to photography, this section offers some different insights to old subjects, perhaps inspiring you to create new and more exciting images.

Abstract Photography

For the most part, when you photograph something, you are concerned with showing the subject clearly. When photographing a portrait, you try to represent the face or some revealing aspect of the person; when shooting a landscape, you try to show what's in the environment, be it trees, mountains, or a skyline. However, when shooting abstract photography, you are working with the idea of the subject, rather than an absolute subject.

In abstract photography, the subject is less important than the actual composition. When attempting abstract photography, you want to try to bring out the essence of what you're photographing.

There are no hard-and-fast rules to photography, and this is even truer in abstract photography. With this type of photography, you may be attempting to show the texture or color of something. What the actual object is isn't necessarily important.

An abstract photograph should give the viewer a different perspective of the subject than a normally composed photograph would. There are a few hardliners who say that if you can recognize the subject then it's not truly abstract. To that, I say: Abstract photography (or any abstract art) can be broken down into two types—*objective* and *nonobjective*. Objective abstract art presents something that can be recognized, but it presents it in an unusual way. Nonobjective abstract art takes the subject and breaks it down to a base element such as lines, forms, colors, and texture.

Inspiration

Almost anything can be used to create an abstract photograph. It can be a close-up of the texture of tree bark or the skin of an orange. Look for objects with bright colors or interesting textures.

Many structures have interesting lines and shapes. Cars can have interesting lines. Keep an eye out for patterns. Patterns can be any-where—on the side of a building or the sur-face of a rock. Evening shadows often create dynamic patterns with the added benefit of the rich colors of the sunset.

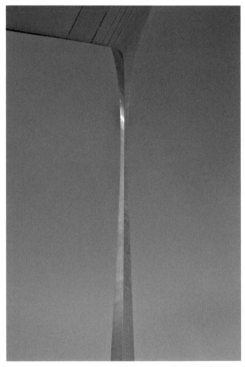

7.1 Bones. This is a photo of an art installation where there were thousands of cow bones suspended from the ceiling. I used a very large aperture to capture the ambient light and to create a shallow depth of field. Shot with a Nikkor 50mm f/1.8 lens, ISO 400 at f/1.8 for 1/80 second.

7.2 Gateway in Blue. This is a photo of the Gateway Arch in St. Louis, Missouri. I specifically stood underneath the arch and shot up at it using the sky as a backdrop to give it an abstract quality. I used a wide-angle setting to maximize perspective distortion. Shot with a Tokina 19-35mm f/3.5-4.5 lens zoomed to 19mm, ISO 200 at f/8 for 1/200 second.

Abstract photography practice

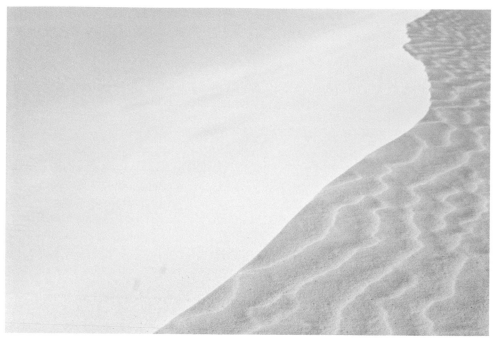

7.3 White Sands photographed at White Sands National Monument in New Mexico

Table 7.1
Taking Abstract Pictures

Setup	**Practice Picture:** Figure 7.3 is a study of a sand dune taken at White Sands National Monument in New Mexico. What caught my eye in this scene was the leading line at the crest of the dune that separated the smooth side of the dune from the side with all of the randomly textured patterns. **On Your Own:** Abstract photo opportunities can exist in even the most mundane subjects; take a closer look at things to find some interesting aspects.
Lighting	**Practice Picture:** I chose to shoot at an angle where the sun was sidelighting the windblown sand dune so that there was a distinct contrast from one side of the ridge to the other. **On Your Own:** Try to find ways to use the lighting to your advantage. Finding the delicate interplay between shadows and highlights can give your images the added dynamic you need.

Continued

Table 7.1 *(continued)*

Lens	**Practice Picture:** Tamron 17-50mm f/2.8 zoomed to 50mm.
	On Your Own: You can use any type of lens to make an abstract image. Using wide angles can add strange distortions, or coming in close can focus on a minute detail.
Camera Settings	**Practice Picture:** I chose Aperture Priority to control the depth of field. I used Spot metering to be sure that some shadow detail was retained. I captured the image in RAW to be able to adjust the white balance in post-processing.
	On Your Own: Controlling your aperture is key in focusing on the details in the image. You may want to use a wide aperture to blur unwanted elements from the background or a small aperture to be sure that the whole scene is in sharp focus.
Exposure	**Practice Picture:** ISO 250 at f/10 for 1.6 seconds. I chose a small aperture to ensure that all of the details were in focus from the front of the frame to the back.
	On Your Own: Your settings can vary widely depending on your subject matter and lighting. With a relatively still subject you can use longer shutter speeds; when your subject is moving, be sure to use a faster shutter speed to freeze any motion.
Accessories	I used a tripod to achieve a sharp focus during the rather long exposure.

Abstract photography tips

✦ **Keep your eyes open.** Always be on the lookout for interesting patterns, repeating lines, or strange textures.

✦ **Don't be afraid to experiment.** Sometimes something as minor as changing the white balance setting can change the whole image. Sometimes the wrong setting may be the right one for the image.

Action and Sports Photography

Action and sports photography is just what it sounds like, although it doesn't necessarily mean your subject is engaging in some type of sport. It can be any activity that involves fast movement, such as your child riding his bike down the street or someone running across the beach. Shooting any type of action can be tricky to even seasoned pros because you need to be sure to shoot at a fast-enough shutter speed to freeze the movement of your subject.

Although the relatively speedy frame rate of 3 fps of the D60 comes in handy when shooting action and sports, often the best approach with shooting action is to get familiar with the movement of the subject, learn when the action is at its peak, and then take your shot.

You can employ a number of different techniques to decrease motion blur on your subject. The most commonly used technique is panning. *Panning* is following the moving subject with your camera lens. With this method, it is as if the subject is not moving at all because your camera is moving with it. When done correctly, the subject should be in sharp focus while the motion blurs the background. This effect is great for creating the illusion of motion. While panning, you can sometimes use a slower shutter speed to exaggerate the effect of the background blur. Panning can be a very difficult technique to master and requires a lot of practice, but the results are worth the effort.

Using flash for action/sports photography is not always necessary or advisable. Sometimes you are so far away from the action your flash won't be effective or you may be in a situation where flash is not allowed. In these cases, just make sure you have a fast-enough shutter speed to freeze the motion. You can either use a wider aperture or higher ISO setting to be sure you get the proper shutter speed.

 Caution *When using the panning technique be sure to switch the VR function on your lens to off. When switched to on, the VR attempts to compensate for the sideways movement of the camera resulting in a blurry image.*

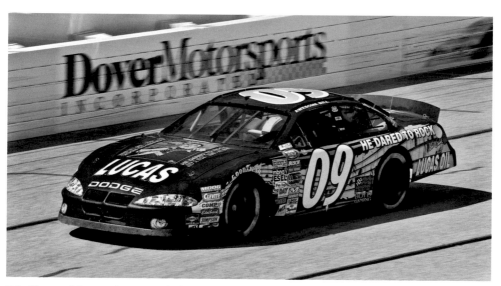

7.4 Along with panning, I used Shutter Priority mode to control the shutter speed to freeze the motion of this car that was racing by at Memphis Motorsports Park while keeping the shutter speed slow enough to catch some motion blur. Shot on a monopod with a Nikkor 80-200mm f/2.8 lens zoomed to 200mm, ISO 100 at f/6.3 for 1/320 second.

Tip *Consider using a monopod, which is a one-legged support, when trying the panning technique. Monopods help keep the camera steady while allowing the photographer more freedom of movement than a tripod.*

Inspiration

When looking for action scenes to shoot, I tend to gravitate toward the more exciting and edgy events. You may find you favor more low-key action events, but regardless of what appeals to you, just keep your eyes open. Nearly everywhere you look there is some kind of action taking place.

Go to the local parks and sporting events. Almost every weekend there is a soccer tournament at the school across the street from my studio. I often go there just to practice getting action shots. Check your local newspapers for sporting events. Often the local skateboard shops and bike shops have contests. I try to take pictures of people having fun doing what they love to do.

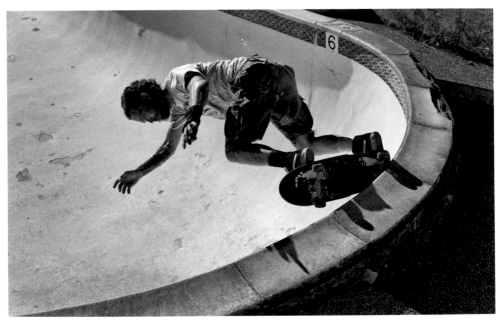

7.5 Skateboarder Joe pulls a backside grind in an abandoned backyard pool. I used a fast shutter speed to freeze the action. Shot with a Sigma 17-35mm f/2.8-4 lens zoomed to 34mm, ISO 100 at f/5.6 for 1/800 second.

Action and sports photography practice

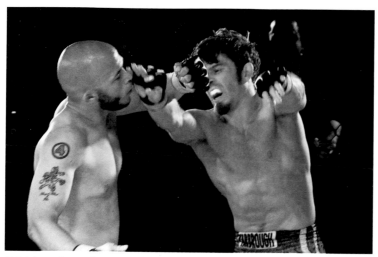

7.6 King of Kombat Mixed Martial Arts tournament

Table 7.2
Taking Action and Sports Pictures

Setup	**Practice Picture:** Figure 7.6 was captured when I was photographing a mixed martial arts tournament. I was always fascinated by the strength and stamina of these fighters. I converted the shot to black and white in Photoshop to give it a nostalgic feel similar to old boxing photos from the 1950s. **On Your Own:** Sporting events are a great place to find exciting action shots. Securing an unobstructed view of the action is one of the hardest parts when photographing sporting events. Try to show up early to stake out the best spot.
Lighting	**Practice Picture:** Because using flash was prohibited at this event, my only source of light was the spotlights lighting up the ring. **On Your Own:** When photographing an outdoor sporting event, if at all possible, try to keep the sun at your back so that your subject is lit from the front. When photographing indoors you may consider investing in a lens with a wider aperture.
Lens	**Practice Picture:** I used a Nikkor 80-200mm f/2.8 zoomed to 86mm. **On Your Own:** Depending on how far you have to be from your subject, you may want to use a telephoto lens in order to get closer to the action. If you can get right up to the action, using a wide-angle lens can also work.

Continued

Table 7.2 *(continued)*

Camera Settings	**Practice Picture:** My camera was set to Aperture Priority mode. The fights took place inside of a caged ring; I needed to be sure to use the widest aperture possible to render the fence nearly invisible by having a shallow depth of field.
	On Your Own: When photographing action, setting your shutter speed is usually the key to capturing the image properly. Whether you want to stop motion by using a fast shutter speed or blur the background using a slower shutter speed and panning with your subject, you want to be able to control the shutter speed in Shutter Priority mode. In some instances, such as this one it was necessary to switch to Aperture Priority. Remember to be flexible because all shooting scenarios are not equal.
Exposure	**Practice Picture:** 1/500 at f/3.5, ISO 800. I used a relatively high ISO to be sure to have a fast-enough shutter speed. I also set the camera to Spot meter because the exposure on the fighters was all I was concerned about.
	On Your Own: Try to use the fastest shutter speed you can to stop motion. If the light is dim, you may need to bump up your ISO in order to achieve a fast shutter speed.
Accessories	Using a monopod can help keep your images sharp when shooting action shots.

Action and sports photography tips

✦ **Practice panning.** Panning can be a difficult technique to master, but practice makes perfect. The more time you spend practicing this, the better you (and your images) will get.

✦ **Pay attention to your surroundings.** Often when concentrating on getting *the* shot, you can forget that there are things going on around you. When photographing sporting events, be sure to remember that there may be balls flying around or athletes on the move. It's better to miss a shot than to get hurt in the process of trying to get the shot.

✦ **Know the sport.** In order to be able to effectively capture a definitive shot, you need to be familiar with the sport, its rules, and the ebb and flow of the action. Being able to predict where the action will peak gets you better shots than hoping that you will luck into a shot.

Architectural Photography

Buildings and structures surround us, and many architects pour their hearts and souls into designing buildings that are interesting to the casual observer. This may be why architectural photography is so popular.

Despite the fact that buildings are such familiar, everyday sights, photographing them can be technically challenging — especially when you're taking pictures of large or extremely tall buildings. A number of different problems can arise, the main one being *perspective distortion*. Perspective distortion is when the closest part of the subject appears irregularly large and the farthest part of the subject appears abnormally small. Think about standing at the bottom of a skyscraper and looking straight up to the top.

Professional architectural photographers have special cameras that allow them to correct for the distortion. Unfortunately, you can't make these types of adjustments in a dSLR camera. You have to either fix the image using software or work with the perspective distortion to make a dynamic and interesting image.

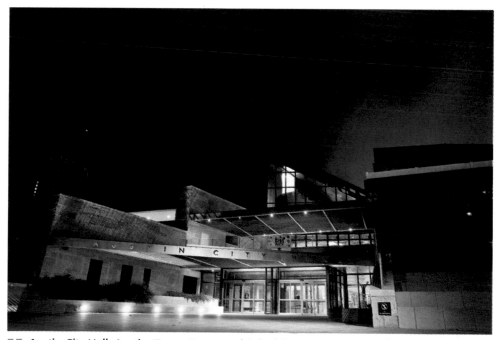

7.7 Austin City Hall, Austin, Texas. Because this building is new and modern looking, I used perspective distortion in my favor to accentuate the converging lines of the building. Using a tripod that sits just a few inches off the ground to shoot up at the building and a fairly wide angle of 18mm gave the image plenty of distortion, which makes it more interesting. A long shutter speed allowed the moving clouds to create a surreal blur in the sky. Shot with a Nikkor 18-55mm VR lens. ISO 200 at f/9 for 10 seconds.

Copyright and Permission

In most places, you don't need permission to photograph a building as long as it's a place to which the public has free access. If you are on private property, you should definitely request permission to photograph before you start. If you are inside a building, it is generally a good idea to ask permission before photographing as well.

Due to recent tightening of security policies, a lot of photographers have been approached by security and/or police, so it's a good idea to check the local laws in the city where you are photographing to know what rights you have as a photographer.

For the most part, copyright laws allow photography of any building on "permanent public display." Although the architect of the structure may own the copyright of the design, it usually does not carry over to photographs of the building. There are exceptions to this, so again, check local laws, especially if you plan on selling your images.

Inspiration

Because buildings and architecture are all around us, there are limitless possibilities to shoot. Try looking for buildings with architectural features that you may enjoy, such as art deco, Gothic, or modern. The building doesn't necessarily have to be in tip-top condition. Sometimes photographing a building in a state of disrepair can give you an excellent image.

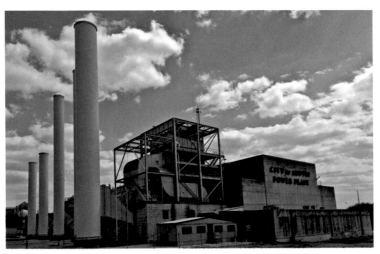

7.8 City of Austin Power Plant, Austin, Texas. I specifically chose a wide-angle setting to fit the building in the frame. I used a Nikkor 18-55mm f/3.5-5.6 VR lens set to 18mm, ISO 100 at f/9 for 1/250 second, Active D-Lighting ON. I used a small aperture to ensure that everything in the photo was sharp.

Architectural photography practice

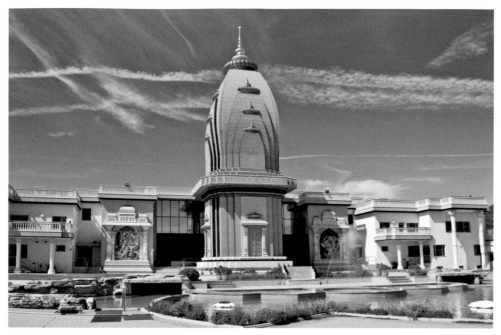

7.9 Barsana Dham

Table 7.3
Taking Architectural Pictures

Setup	**Practice Picture:** For figure 7.9, I photographed the Barsana Dham Hindu temple located near Austin, Texas. I decided to photograph this building because it is so dissimilar from other architecture in Austin.
	On Your Own: Buildings are literally everywhere, but that doesn't mean you have to photograph a huge skyscraper or giant structure. Even a small bungalow can make an interesting architectural photograph.
Lighting	**Practice Picture:** This picture was shot in the afternoon so the building was lit entirely by the sun.
	On Your Own: When shooting during the day, be sure the sun is facing the side of the building you're photographing to ensure a good exposure. Shooting a backlit building can cause the sky to blow out when the building is properly exposed, or when the sky is properly exposed the building will appear too dark. Night is also a fantastic time to take architectural shots because architects and landscape designers often use lighting to create an entirely different look to a building at night.

Continued

Table 7.3 *(continued)*

Lens	**Practice Picture:** For this photo, I used the Nikkor 18-55mm VR kit lens zoomed to 18mm to be able to fit this rather large building in the frame.
	On Your Own: Generally, a wide-angle lens setting is used for close-up architectural shots; when you can put some distance between you and the structure you can zoom in a bit. A good wide-to-short telephoto lens like the 18-55mm is a good choice to cover most architectural shots.
Camera Settings	**Practice Picture:** My camera was set to Aperture Priority and Matrix metering. I chose these settings because I knew the bright sky would fool the meter into underexposing the shadow on the building. Matrix metering takes the whole scene into account and adjusts the exposure so that you have less of a chance for blown-out highlights in a bright sky. I also had the Active D-Lighting on and set to high to reduce some of the contrast caused by the bright midday sun.
	On Your Own: Oftentimes when shooting static objects like buildings you can set up your camera and use the built-in light meter to determine your settings and adjust them as you see fit. Be sure to take into consideration the light source, especially when photographing at night.
Exposure	**Practice Picture:** ISO 100 at f/5 for 1/800 second.
	On Your Own: Achieving a good depth of field is important in architectural photography so using a rather small aperture is usually advisable. Keep your ISO low for the best image quality.
Accessories	A tripod is one of the best tools you can use for architectural photography. Even in fairly bright sunlight, using a small aperture can sometimes make for slow shutter speeds. A tripod keeps your images sharp.

Architectural photography tips

✦ **Shoot from a distance.** When taking pictures of tall buildings and skyscrapers try not to take your photograph too close to the base of the building. The perspective distortion can make the structure look abnormal.

✦ **Avoid backlighting.** If the building you are photographing is backlit you will lose detail in the structure and the background will appear too bright. Try to take your picture when the sun is shining on the part of the building you want to photograph.

✦ **Be aware of lens distortion.**
Different lenses can introduce distortion. Wide-angle lenses often suffer from barrel distortion that can cause the straight lines of the structure that are near the edge of the frame to appear bowed out. Either avoid placing straight lines near the edge of the frame or be sure to correct for the distortion in post-processing.

Child Photography

Kids grow up fast, and having a photographic chronicle of them doing that growing up is great. For a number of people this is one of the main reasons they buy a camera. Most first-time parents buy a compact digital camera, then realizing the limitations, they upgrade to a dSLR, and then before they know it they're hooked not only on photographing their children, but on photography in general.

One of the greatest challenges when photographing children is that they seem to never stop moving, and you have to be on your toes to catch those fleeting moments when they are at their best. Child photography is one-third action photography, one-third portrait photography, and one-third luck!

When trying to set up a shot with children as the subjects, one of the first things you want to consider is the environment. This is very important, as you want the child to be comfortable, and you want to have a nice background that doesn't compete with the subject for attention. Often the child's bedroom can be the perfect place. The child is in his own environment, and there are likely to be toys he can play with and that you can use as props. Another great place is outside, either in the child's own backyard or, even better, at a scenic park where there is playground equipment to explore.

One of the most important things to remember when photographing children is that they are amazingly perceptive to moods and emotions. They can easily tell when you are getting frustrated, so if things aren't exactly working out the way you planned and you're getting a bit irritable, it may be a good time to take a break. The best way to get great pictures is to make sure everyone involved is having fun.

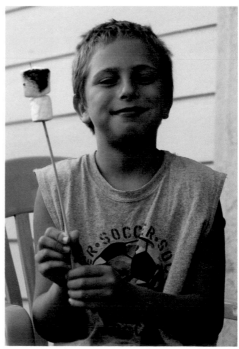

7.10 This shot of Hunter was taken in his aunt's yard; I used a Tamron 17-50 f/2.8 lens, ISO 400 at f/2.8 for 1/100 second.

Inspiration

Having children or grandchildren of your own is inspiration enough to want to take a million photographs of them. However, if you don't have children of your own, maybe you have a niece or nephew or perhaps you just enjoy capturing children's youthful enthusiasm.

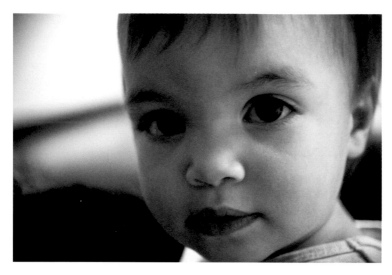

7.11 This is a candid portrait taken using soft evening light shining through a window next to the subject. I used a Nikkor 17-55mm f/2.8 lens. Shot at ISO 800 at f/2.8 for 1/80 second, set to Child portrait DVP mode.

Child photography practice

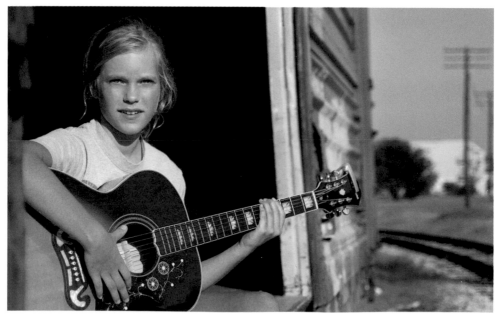

7.12 Aurora

Table 7.4
Taking Children's Pictures

Setup

Practice Picture: A friend and her daughter stopped by my studio one afternoon and we decided to do an impromptu photo shoot at the railroad tracks nearby as shown in figure 7.12.

On Your Own: Try to find an interesting location to add a fun element to your photo. Playgrounds or places where the child can interact with the surroundings can be fun.

Lighting

Practice Picture: The late-afternoon sun provided the lighting for this shot.

On Your Own: Shooting outdoors in the late afternoon or early morning can give your images a nice, golden light. Shooting during the afternoon when the sun is fully bright is not recommended because it can cause images with a lot of contrast and deep shadows. Also try to avoid posing your subject directly facing the sun as this can cause the eyes to squint.

Lens

Practice Picture: Tamron 17-50mm f/2.8 zoomed to 38mm.

On Your Own: Using a longer focal length can help compress the features of the person you're shooting. Shooting with a wide-angle lens can cause the features of your subject to appear distorted especially when used close up.

Camera Settings

Practice Picture: My camera was set to Aperture Priority, Matrix metering, Auto white balance.

On Your Own: As with most portraits you'll want to set your camera to Aperture Priority so you can control how much depth of field you have. Matrix or Center-weighted metering usually works well for children's portraits. Child portrait mode works well, although I prefer to control most of the settings myself.

Exposure

Practice Picture: ISO 100, f/2.8, 1/1000 second.

On Your Own: Expect pretty fast shutter speeds when shooting outdoors while using a wide aperture. You definitely want to use the lowest ISO possible.

Child photography tips

✦ **Have patience.** Sometimes it may take quite a bit of photographing to get the image you're after. Don't get discouraged if it doesn't turn out right away.

✦ **Have some props handy.** A favorite toy or stuffed animal can add a personal touch to the photograph as well as keep the child occupied.

✦ **Bring along some sweets.** Sometimes a little bit of a treat can dry up tears or just keep kids from getting bored.

Concert Photography

Concert photography can be a particularly difficult endeavor, but it's also extremely rewarding, especially if you're a music fan. Getting that quintessential shot of their favorite performer is the reason why many photographers do this type of photography. Unfortunately to get "the" shot, sometimes you have to fight a crowd and risk getting drinks spilled on your camera. Of course, if you're like me, the type of person who likes to get into the fray, this is great fun.

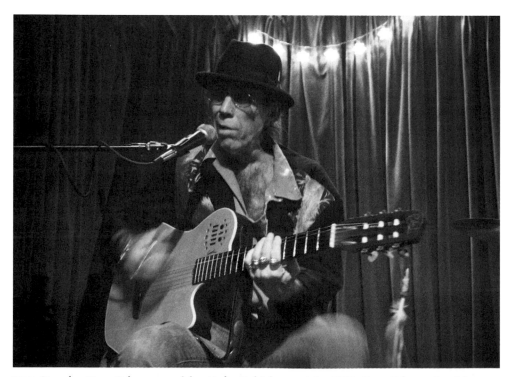

7.13 Popular New Orleans musician Duke Robichaux at the DBA, New Orleans, Louisiana. Shot using a Sigma 17-35mm f/2.8-4 lens zoomed to 35mm, ISO 3200 at f/4 for 1/13 second, Spot metered, Exposure compensation +0.3.

Tip *I strongly suggest that you make sure to keep good earplugs handy if you plan to do much of this type of photography.*

Some photographers are staunchly against using flash at concerts, preferring to shoot with the available light. I like to use some flash at times, as I find that the stage lights can oversaturate the performer, resulting in loss of detail. Another downside to shooting with available light is you need to use high ISO settings to get a shutter speed fast enough to stop action. Typically you need to shoot anywhere from ISO 800 to 3200, which can result in noisy images and the loss of image detail. Fortunately, the D60 excels in high ISO performance so this is not as much of an issue as it was in the past with earlier dSLR cameras.

 Note *Some venues or performers do not allow flash photography at all. In this situation, just try to use the lowest ISO you can while still maintaining a fast-enough shutter speed.*

Inspiration

A good way to get started with concert photography is to find out when a favorite band or performer is playing and bring your camera. Smaller clubs are usually better places to take good close-up photos simply because you are more likely to have closer access to the performers. Most local bands, performers, and regional touring acts don't mind having their photos taken. You can also offer to e-mail the performers some images to use on their Web site. This is beneficial for both them and you, as lots of people will see your photos.

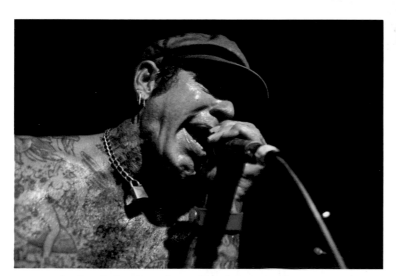

7.14 Professional skateboarder and lead singer of the U.S. Bombs, Duane Peters. I didn't want to use on-camera flash so I opted for a wide aperture and high ISO to get a fast enough shutter speed to freeze the action and counteract against camera shake. Shot with a Nikkor 17-55mm f/2.8 lens zoomed to 50mm. ISO 3200 at f/2.8 for 1/320 second. Spot metered to expose for the singer.

Concert photography practice

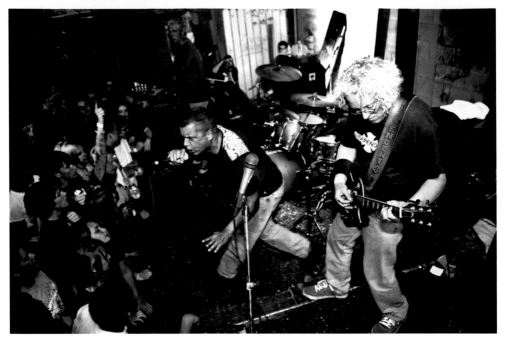

7.15 The JFA at the Red 7 in Austin, Texas

Table 7.5
Taking Concert Pictures

Setup	**Practice Picture:** For figure 7.15, I was photographing the seminal early-1980s skate-rock band JFA playing at a local Austin club, Red 7.
	On Your Own: Smaller venues can offer the most intimate or in-your-face photo ops. Often you can get closer to the stage and the band, giving your images an up-close and personal feel.
Lighting	**Practice Picture:** Because the stage lighting at the venue was dim at best, I used an SB-800 Speedlight to provide most of the lighting for the exposure. The Flash mode was set to Rear/Slow sync to capture some motion blur.
	On Your Own: Concert lighting can be very tricky depending on the venue. Some venues have bright stage lights, while some can be very dim. Make a few test shots to determine if the lighting is bright enough. Sometimes I like to mix it up, taking shots with and without flash.

Lens

Practice Picture: Nikkor 17-55mm f/2.8 zoomed to 17mm. This is my go-to lens for almost everything. It works well for smaller venues allowing you a wide-angle view for close-up shots as well as a small amount of zoom for when you're farther away. The fast, constant f/2.8 aperture allows you to work with available light even when the lighting is quite dim.

On Your Own: For small venues a good wide-angle to short telephoto works well. For larger venues or concerts where you're farther away from the stage you may need to use a longer telephoto lens, but your flash will be of little use. When photographing large concert events I bring both a 17-55mm f/2.8 and an 80-200mm f/2.8 lens with a 2X teleconverter just in case I need some extra reach.

Camera Settings

Practice Picture: I used Aperture Priority mode to ensure that my lens was wide open to capture enough light. I also had the camera set to record the images in JPEG Fine and the camera Optimize image was set to Monochrome Black & White. I chose to use this setting to emulate the early concert photography work of Glen E. Friedman. Friedman covered the burgeoning California skateboarding and punk rock scene in the late 1970s and early '80s. He shot mainly black and white, and he captured the frenetic energy and reckless abandon of the musicians of that era.

On Your Own: Aperture Priority mode is a good place to start to be sure that you have as much light reaching the sensor as possible. Using Spot metering is often a good choice, especially if the performers are on a dark stage with spotlights shining on them. This prevents the camera from trying to expose for the mostly dark areas behind the performers, which can cause your shutter speed to be too slow. Using flash setting to Matrix metering can help keep the ambient light and the light from the flash balanced.

Exposure

Practice Picture: ISO 800 at f/2.8 for 1/10 second.

On Your Own: Because the lighting is often dark at concert events more often than not you'll have to crank up the ISO. When shooting above 1600, choosing the Black & White option can help your images because much of the noise is chrominance noise (color). Most of the time you'll find yourself shooting wide-open apertures. Using a fast shutter speed is recommended although when using flash you can bring the shutter speed down a bit, allowing the bright flash to freeze your subject while allowing some of the ambient light to fill in the shadow areas.

Accessories

An off-shoe camera cord such as Nikon's SC-29 can help to get your flash off of your camera.

Concert photography tips

✦ **Experiment.** Don't be afraid to try different settings and long exposures. Slow Sync flash enables you to capture much of the ambient light while freezing the subject with the short, bright flash.

✦ **Call the venue before you go.** Be sure to call the venue to ensure that you are able to bring your camera in.

✦ **Bring earplugs.** Protect your hearing. After spending countless hours in clubs without hearing protection, my hearing is less than perfect. You don't want to lose your hearing. Trust me.

✦ **Take your Speedlight off of your camera.** If you're using one of the Nikon accessory flashes, such as the SB-800 or SB-600, invest in an off-camera through-the-lens (TTL) hot-shoe sync cord such as the Nikon SC-29 TTL cord. When you're down in the crowd, your Speedlight is very vulnerable. The shoe mount is not the sturdiest part of the flash. Not only is using the Speedlight off-camera safer, but you also gain more control of the light direction by holding it in your hand. This reinforces my suggestion to experiment — move the Speedlight around; hold it high; hold it low; or bounce it. This is digital, and it doesn't cost a thing to experiment.

Flower and Plant Photography

One of the great things about photographing plants and flowers, as opposed to other living things, is that you have almost unlimited control with them. If they are potted or cut, you can place them wherever you want, trim off any excess foliage, sit them under a hot lighting setup, and you never hear them complain.

Some other great things about photographing plants and flowers are the almost unlimited variety of colors and textures you can find them in. From reds and blues to purples and yellows, the color combinations are almost infinite. Plants and flowers are abundant, whether purchased or wild, so there is no shortage of subjects. Even in the dead of winter, you can find plants to take photos of. They don't have to be in bloom to have an interesting texture or tone. Sometimes the best images of trees are taken after they have shed all of their foliage.

Flower and plant photography also offers a great way to show off your macro skills. Flowers especially seem to look great when photographed close up.

You don't have to limit flower and plant photography to the outdoors. You can easily go to the local florist and pick up a bouquet of flowers, set them up, and take photos of them. After you're done, you can give them to someone special as an added bonus!

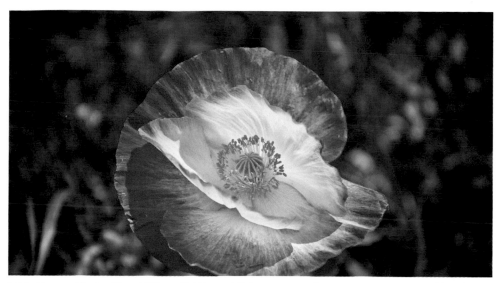

7.16 Poppy. Shot with a Nikkor 18-55mm VR lens zoomed to 55mm, ISO 100 at f/6.5 for 1/1000 second. Close-up DVP mode.

Inspiration

Walk around and look at the interesting colors of the local flora. Pay close attention to the way the light interacts with different plants. A lot of the time, it is undesirable to have a backlit subject, but the light coming through a transparent flower petal can add a different quality of beauty to an already beautiful flower.

It can also be fun to make your own floral arrangements, experimenting with different color combinations and compositions. Taking a trip and talking to a florist can give you some ideas of which plants and flowers work best together.

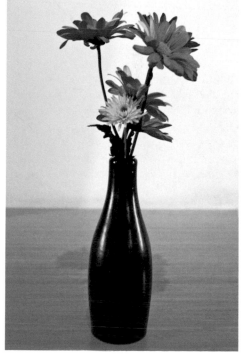

7.17 I was having breakfast at a local coffee shop one morning and decided that this vase full of flowers would make a nice shot. I positioned the vase and myself to eliminate distracting background features. The shot was lit by the ambient light in the room. Shot with a Sigma 17-35mm f/2.8-4 lens set to 30mm, ISO 800 at f/4 for 1/15 second.

Infrared Photography

Infrared photography, commonly known as IR photography, uses invisible (to the naked eye) near infrared light to create the image. Although you can't see infrared light, The CCD sensors in most cameras are very sensitive to this type of light. IR light can have a detrimental effect on the standard images you create using visible light. For that reason Nikon installs an IR blocking filter in front of the sensor. Unfortunately, this means that IR photography with the D60 can be quite difficult. This isn't to say that it's impossible, but it takes very long exposure times and for this reason it's absolutely necessary to use a tripod when attempting IR photography with the D60.

In order to capture an IR image you first need to block visible light from reaching the sensor. An IR filter is used to do this. The most commonly used filter is the Hoya R72, which blocks out all wavelengths of visible light that fall below 720 nanometers (nm). The *nanometer* is the measurement used to determine the wavelength of light. The wavelengths of visible light fall between around 400 and 700nm, so at 720nm the light is just about beyond the reach of our eyes. There are a couple of important things to remember when taking IR photos with your D60:

✦ **Compose the shot with the filter off of the lens.** After you compose the shot you then must focus before placing the filter on the lens. Focusing can be a little tricky. Because IR light doesn't focus at the same point as visible light, you must make some adjustments. The best way to do this is to focus the camera, take a shot, adjust the focus a little, take another shot, and repeat, using the image review to check focus.

✦ **Use the Manual exposure mode.** When using one of the auto exposure modes (P, S, or A), the camera's meter will underexpose, so using manual exposure is necessary. This is another area in which you need to experiment to find the right setting.

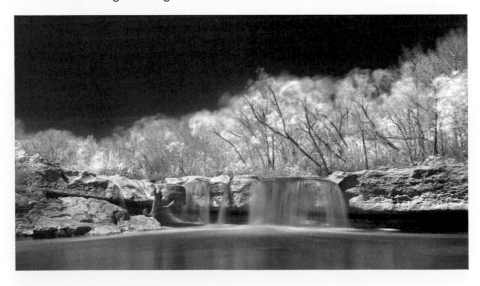

Your infrared image will appear mostly red or deep magenta, so there are some steps that you may need to take to get your image to appear the way you want it. Traditionally, most infrared photography has been done in black and white, but you can also do some post-processing to produce what is known as a false-color infrared image. You can also use the Black and White Optimize image setting with decent results.

Typically, when IR photography is done in black and white the resulting image has vegetation that turns white (living plants reflect a lot of IR) while the sky is usually darkened, sometimes almost black. With false-color infrared you can get a myriad of different colors depending on your post-processing technique.

The bottom line is the D60 is not the ideal camera for attempting IR photography, but it can be done. More information and many tutorials can be found online. If you want to get serious about IR photography your best bet is to purchase a camera that is known to have a relatively weak IR blocking filter such as the D70, or there are companies that will modify a camera by removing the IR blocking filter. However, removing the filter voids the warranty of the camera.

Flower and plant photography practice

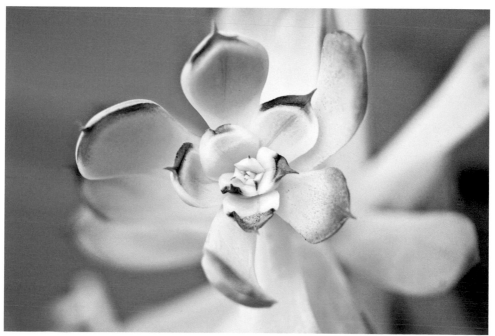

7.18 Succulent with complementary colors

Table 7.6
Taking Flower and Plant Pictures

Setup	**Practice Picture:** While having my morning tea I noticed the colors of this succulent that I bought at a local roadside stand. I thought complementary colors of the plant would work out well, but it wasn't until I previewed the image on the LCD that I noticed the additional complementary colors of blue and orange in the background.
	On Your Own: Using complementary colors such as green/purple and blue/orange can add interest to your images.
Lighting	**Practice Picture:** This picture was taken on the shady side of my house in the morning. The shade provided a nice diffuse light to allow the colors to come through without a lot of contrast.
	On Your Own: Oftentimes, natural light is the best thing for lighting plants and flowers. Even if it's a house plant, you can take it outside and set it in the sun.
Lens	**Practice Picture:** Macro-Takumar 50mm f/4 with a Nikon F-mount adaptor.
	On Your Own: Macro lenses often work well with smaller plants. Additionally a lens with a wide zoom range can offer you quite a bit of compositional leeway, allowing you a wide-angle view or zoomed in to isolate a specific detail.
Camera Settings	**Practice Picture:** I set the camera to Manual because the lens I was using was a manual focus lens. I had to estimate the exposure using the Sunny 16 rule because this was a non-CPU lens and the camera's meter does not work with these types of lenses.
	On Your Own: Be sure to pay attention to the differences between the shadows and the highlights and expose the image so that everything retains detail. You may want Aperture Priority to be able to control your depth of field or use the Close-up DVP mode.
Exposure	**Practice Picture:** ISO 200 at f/5.6 for 1/60 second. The lighting here wasn't very bright so I raised the ISO to 200 to get a fast-enough shutter speed to eliminate any blur from camera shake.
	On Your Own: Keep an eye on your camera exposure settings when shooting and adjust your ISO accordingly if the shutter speed isn't fast enough to get the right exposure.
Accessories	You may not always be shooting in bright sunlight so a tripod can come in handy if the lighting is dim and your shutter speed drops below an acceptable limit for handheld shooting.

Flower and plant photography tips

✦ **Shoot from different angles.**
Shooting straight down on a flower seems like the obvious thing to do, but sometimes shooting from the side or even from below can add a compelling perspective to the image.

✦ **Try different backgrounds.**
Photographing a flower with a dark background can give you an image with a completely different feel than photographing that same flower with a light background.

✦ **Try using complementary colors.**
Adding different flowers with complementary colors to your composition can add a little interest to your image. Adding a splash of yellow into a primarily purple composition can make the image pop.

Landscape Photography

With landscape photography, the intent is to represent a specific scene from a certain viewpoint. For the most part, animals and people aren't included in the composition so the focus is solely on the view.

Landscape photography can incorporate any type of environment – desert scenes, mountains, lakes, forests, skylines, or just about any terrain. You can take landscape photos just about anywhere, and one nice thing about them is that you can return to the same spot, even as little as a couple of hours later, and the scene will look different according to the position of the sun and the quality of the light. You can also return to the same scene months later and find a completely different scene due to the change in seasons.

There are three distinct styles of landscape photography:

✦ **Representational.** This is a straight landscape; the "what you see is what you get" approach. This is not to say that this is a simple snapshot; it requires great attention to details such as composition, lighting, and weather.

✦ **Impressionistic.** With this type of landscape photo, the image looks less real due to filters or special photographic techniques such as long exposures. These techniques can give the image a mysterious or otherworldly quality.

✦ **Abstract.** With this type of landscape photo, the image may or may not resemble the actual subject. The compositional elements of shape and form are more important than an actual representation of the scene.

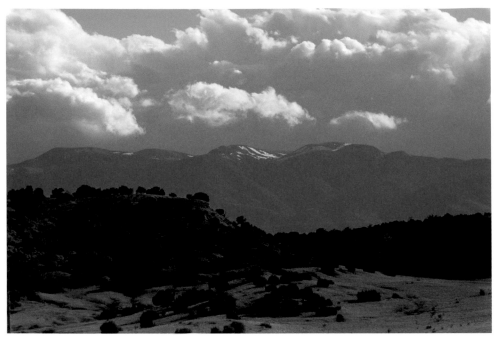

7.19 Rocky Mountains, Colorado. For this shot, I used a small f-stop to get a deep depth of field. I Spot metered a bright spot in the clouds and used Active D-Lighting to avoid a blown-out sky. Shot with a Nikkor 55-200mm f/4-5.6 VR lens zoomed to 155mm, ISO 200 at f/16 for 1/250 second.

One of the most important parts of capturing a good landscape image is knowing about *quality of light.* Simply defined, quality of light is the way the light interacts with the subject. There are many different terms to define the various qualities of light, such as soft or diffused light, hard light, and so on, but for the purposes of landscape photography, the most important part is knowing how the light interacts with the landscape at certain times of day.

For the most part, the best time to photograph a landscape is just after the sun rises and right before the sun sets. The sunlight at those times of day is refracted by the atmosphere and bounces off of low-lying clouds, resulting in a sunlight color that is different, and more pleasing to the eye, than it is at high noon. This time of day is often referred to as the *golden hour* by photographers due to the color and quality of the light at this time.

This isn't to say you can't take a good land-scape photo at high noon; you absolutely can. Sometimes, especially when you're on vacation, you don't have a choice about when to take the photo, so by all means take one. If there is a particularly beautiful location that you have easy access to, spend some time and watch how the light reacts with the terrain.

Inspiration

There are many breathtaking vistas every-where you look. Even in the middle of a large city, you can go to a park and find a suitable subject for a landscape. Remember that a landscape doesn't have to be a spec-tacular scene with awesome natural forces like mountains; it can be a pond, or a small waterfall. Even a simple wheat field can make a great landscape photo.

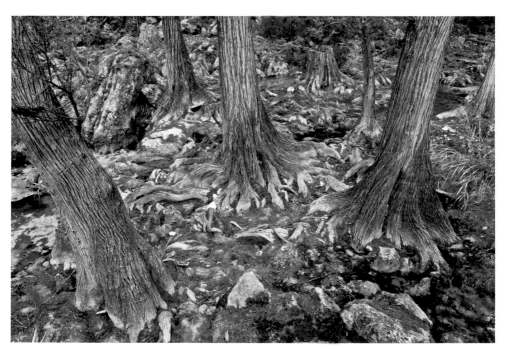

7.20 This landscape shot is actually a detail of the roots of some great trees growing near Hamilton pool, just outside Austin, Texas. Shot with a Sigma 17-35mm f/2.8-4 lens zoomed to 17mm. ISO f/10 for 1/40 second.

Landscape photography practice

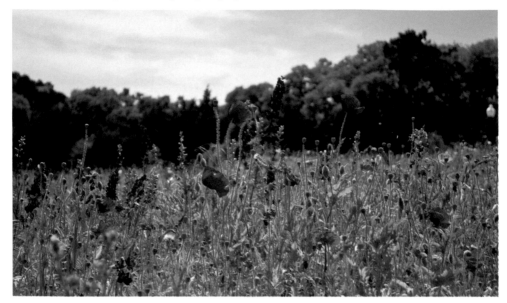

7.21 A field of wildflowers

Table 7.7
Taking Landscape Pictures

Setup	**Practice Picture:** For figure 7.21, I was taking a stroll through a nature preserve just south of Austin. I came across this field of wildflowers and wanted to capture the vivid colors of the flowers in the scene.
	On Your Own: Landscapes are all around you. You can find some fantastic scenery at a nearby park or nature preserve. Find a compelling sight and shoot it.
Lighting	**Practice Picture:** This photo was shot at high noon, which is not usually the best time for shooting landscapes. I got down low and shot up at the scene to capture the darker undersides of the flowers and to make the overhead sunlight appear more directional.
	On Your Own: Lighting can make or break a landscape photograph. If the lighting is flat it can make the photo seem uninteresting and without character. Often, the best time to shoot a landscape is early morning or evening. When not shooting sunset or sunrise landscapes keep your back to the sun to avoid overexposed skies and underexposed land areas.

Lens	**Practice Picture:** Nikon 18-55mm f/3.5-5.6 VR zoomed to 55mm.
	On Your Own: The general rule of thumb when shooting landscapes is the wider the better. More often than not you want to catch a large area in your photograph; however, you can mix it up as I did in figure 7.21 making it more focused on the details of the scene. Keep an open mind and a keen eye when setting up landscape shots.
Camera Settings	**Practice Picture:** My camera was set to Aperture Priority because I wanted to use a medium aperture to keep most of the flowers in the scene in focus while allowing the tree line in the back to appear softer. I chose Spot metering and I metered on the brightest part of the sky to ensure I would capture all of the colors of the sky without blowing out the highlights.
	On Your Own: For landscapes, you want to be in control of the aperture to keep a deep focus so Aperture Priority works great. When photographing directly into the sun like this, spot metering is preferable, but when the lighting is more even, Matrix metering works great. Landscape DVP mode works great on most subjects, but in a low-light scene like this the meter can be fooled causing you to get blown-out highlights instead of capturing the color of the sunset.
Exposure	**Practice Picture:** ISO 100 at f/5.6 for 1/400 second. Exposure compensation set to +0.3 to capture detail in the tree.
	On Your Own: As usual, use a low ISO for better resolution. Use smaller apertures to increase depth of field (here I was shooting at a relatively wide setting due to the decreasing light). Often, shutter speeds will be longer due to the smaller f-stops.
Accessories	A tripod can be a great help when those shutter speeds get really long.

Landscape photography tips

✦ **Bring a tripod.** When you're photographing landscapes, especially early in the morning or at sunset, the exposure time may be quite long. A tripod can help keep your landscapes in sharp focus.

✦ **Scout out locations.** Keep your eyes open; even when you're driving around you may see something interesting.

✦ **Be prepared.** If you're out hiking looking for landscape shots don't forget to bring the essentials such as water and a couple of snacks. It's also a good idea to be familiar with the area you're in, or at the very least bring a map.

Light Trail and Fireworks Photography

One of the most fun types of photography is capturing light trails. You can capture some amazing and surreal images. Fireworks photography is exciting, and while it is simple in theory, getting the timing right can be a big challenge. You need a sharp eye and a good ear to know when the fireworks have been launched so you can be sure to have the camera shutter open before the fireworks explode with a burst of color.

Light trail photography, while different than fireworks photography, shares the same type of camera settings. You need a very slow shutter speed and usually a fairly small aperture. I find that shooting in Aperture Priority mode usually gives long enough shutter speeds to capture a light trail as long as the scene is fairly dark.

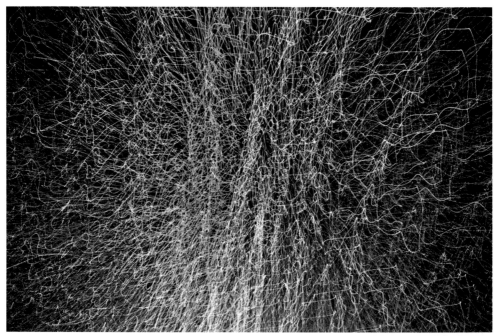

7.22 For this shot, I snapped a long exposure while simply holding the camera in my hand. Shot with a Nikkor 17-55mm f/2.8 lens zoomed to 17mm, ISO 200 at f/8 for 3 seconds.

Inspiration

A tripod is the one thing that is almost essential when you're doing any photography using long shutter speeds. If you try to hand-hold your camera with an 8-second exposure, your image will be nothing but a blurry mess. Of course, sometimes a handheld blur is exactly the effect you're looking for.

When photographing fireworks, I find that using the *Bulb* setting in Manual mode works the best. The Bulb setting opens the shutter when the Shutter Release button is pressed and the shutter remains open as long as the button remains pressed. When the button is released the shutter closes.

The first thing you want to do is figure out where the fireworks are going to "bloom." Set your camera on the tripod and aim it in the right direction. For the most part, you're going to need a wide-angle lens to be sure to get everything in the frame; unless you are very far away, you shouldn't need to zoom in. When the firework is launched, press the Shutter Release button and hold it down until the firework explodes. When the bloom is over, release the Shutter Release button to close the shutter and end the exposure.

When using the Bulb mode, your best bet is to get some sort of remote shutter release, such as the Nikon ML-L3 remote release.

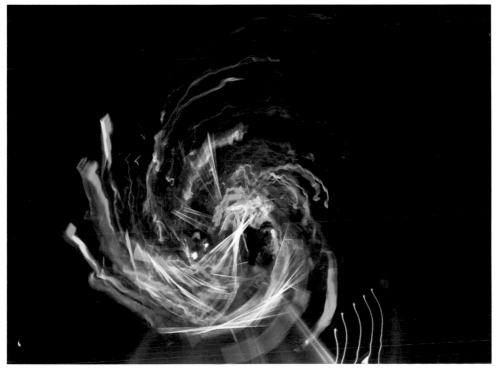

7.23 This long exposure light trail shot was taken of an art installation in the front of the COSI building in Columbus, Ohio. While the shutter was open, I rotated the camera to create the light trails. Taken with a Nikkor 12-24mm f/4 lens zoomed to 12mm. ISO 200 at f/10 for 2 seconds.

Light trail and fireworks photography practice

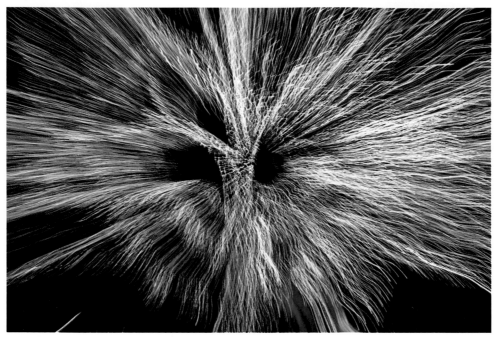

7.24 A tree completely wrapped in lights, with zoom

Table 7.8
Taking Light Trail and Fireworks Pictures

Setup	**Practice Picture:** For figure 7.24, I was hanging around one of the funky neighborhoods in south Austin and I saw this tree that someone had completely wrapped in lights. I thought it would be an interesting effect to zoom in the lens while making a long exposure.
	On Your Own: Of course, the winter holidays are a great time to find displays of lights, but you can also find many types of lights in any downtown area or places that have lots of neon signage, such as Las Vegas or Times Square.
Lighting	**Practice Picture:** The exposure was only 1/2 second, so the lights themselves provided all the lighting in the photo.
	On Your Own: You want to rely on the lights you are photographing; using an outside light source such as flash diminishes the impact and saturation of the lights.

Lens	**Practice Picture:** Nikon 18-55mm f/3.5-5.6. For this shot I started with the zoom set to 17mm and zoomed in while the exposure was being made. This gives the illusion of the lights zooming right at you.
	On Your Own: Almost any type of lens will do, but a nice wide-angle zoom is best. With light trail photography, the blur is the essence of the shot. Moving the camera around and zooming the lens in and out can give you interesting effects.
Camera Settings	**Practice Picture:** I shot this in Aperture Priority mode. I chose this mode because the light levels were varying and when choosing one set shutter speed I reviewed some of my photos in the camera and discovered that some of my photos were underexposed. Using Aperture Priority mode, I adjusted the aperture until I got the desired shutter speed. This way I was assured to have a good exposure. Using Matrix metering allowed the camera to meter for both the light and dark areas of the image. Spot or Center-weighted doesn't generally work well for this type of photo because the lights are very bright and the dark areas are very dark. This causes the camera to severely overexpose or underexpose the lights depending on where the spot is.
	On Your Own: Any one of the modes can work depending on the situation. Programmed Auto can work pretty reliably for this type of photo.
Exposure	**Practice Picture:** ISO 200 at f/3.5 for 1/2 second.
	On Your Own: Low ISO settings and long exposure times are crucial for this type of photography.

Light trail and fireworks photography tips

✦ **Be patient.** Sometimes you will have to take many photos before you get one you like. It can be a trial-and-error process to find the exposure that works.

✦ **Look for multicolored lights.** Bright lights of different colors can add more interest to your images.

✦ **Get there early.** To get a good spot for the fireworks, show up a little early to stake out a spot.

✦ **Use a remote shutter release cord.** Using a remote release can reduce camera shake when the camera is mounted on the tripod for long exposures.

Painting with Light

When doing long exposures in low-light situations you can often use a little bit of external light to add dimension, color, or to bring out some details in your subject. This technique is called painting with light. You can fire a handheld Speedlight or shine a flashlight on dark areas that aren't receiving enough ambient light.

When using this technique you want to be sure to use a low-power light so as not to overlight your subject, thus causing it to look like a flash exposure.

For example, when photographing figure 7.30, the statue was coming out too dark due to the fact there wasn't as much ambient light falling on the subject as there was being captured from the city skyline. To bring out some detail in the stature I brought out an SB-600 set to Manual. I dialed in a flash setting of 1/32. This added a little shine to the statue.

Macro Photography

Macro photography is easily my favorite type of photography. Sometimes you can take the most mundane object and give it a completely different perspective just by moving in close. Ordinary objects can become alien landscapes. Insects take on a new personality when you can see the strange details of their faces, especially their multifaceted eyes.

Technically, macro photography can be difficult. The closer you get to an object, the less depth of field you get, and it can be difficult to maintain focus. When your lens is less than an inch from the face of a bug, just breathing in is sometimes enough to lose focus on the area that you want to capture (or scare the bug off). For this reason, you usually want to use the smallest aperture you can (depending on the lighting situation) and still maintain focus. I say "usually" because a shallow depth of field can also be very useful in bringing attention to a specific detail.

 Caution *When shooting extremely close up, the lens may obscure the light from the built-in flash, resulting in a dark area on the bottom of the images.*

One of the best things about macro photography is that you aren't limited to shooting in one type of location. You can do this type of photography indoors or out. Even on a rainy day, you can find something in your house to photograph. It can be a piece of fruit, a trinket, a coin, or even your dog's nose (if the dog sits still for you).

Macro photography requires special lenses or filters to allow you to get closer to your subject. Most lens manufacturers offer lenses that are designed specifically for this purpose. These macro lenses give you a reproduction ratio of 1:1, which means that the image projected onto the sensor is exactly the same size as the physical subject. Some other lenses that can be used to do macro photography are actually telephoto lenses. Although you can't actually

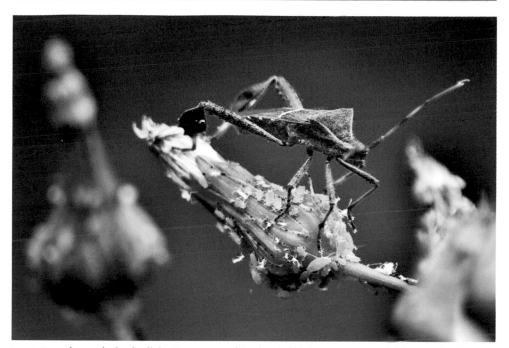

7.25 Acanthocephala declivis. To capture this shot I didn't use any special lens. I simply used my Nikkor 55-200mm f/4-5.6 VR kit lens zoomed all the way out to 200mm. I shot at a higher ISO of 400 to be sure to get a high-enough shutter speed of 1/125 to counteract any camera shake. I also had VR turned on to further stabilize the shot. I used a relatively wide aperture of 5.6 to blur out some distracting elements in the background.

get close to the subject with a telephoto the extra zoom gives you a close-up perspective. Telephoto lenses usually have a reproduction ratio of 1:4, or one-quarter size.

An inexpensive alternative to macro lenses are *close-up filters*. A close-up filter is like a magnifying glass for your lens. It screws onto the end of your lens and allows you to get closer to your subject. There are a variety of different magnifications, and they can be *stacked* or screwed together to increase the magnification even more. Using close-up filters can reduce the sharpness of your images because the quality of the glass isn't quite as good as the glass of the lens elements. This reduction in sharpness becomes more obvious when stacking filters.

Reversing rings are adapters that have a lens mount on one side and filter threads on the other. The filter threads are screwed into the front of a normal lens like a filter, and you attach the lens mount to the camera body. The lens is then mounted to the camera backward. This allows you to closely focus on your subject. One thing to be careful of when using reversing rings is damaging the rear element of your lens; special care should be taken when using one of these. Not all lenses work well with reversing rings. The best lenses to use are fixed focal-length lenses that have aperture rings for adjusting the f-stop. Zoom lenses simply do not work well, nor do lenses that have no aperture control.

A very good alternative to expensive autofocus macro lenses is to find an older manual-focus macro lens. These lenses can be found for much less money than AF lenses. You can also check into lenses from other camera companies. The lens I use for macro photography most often was actually made for older Pentax screw-mount (M42) camera bodies. I found an adapter on eBay that allows you to attach M42 lenses to Nikon F-mount cameras. The lens and adapter together cost me less than $50. The lens allows me to get a 4:1 magnification, which is 4X life size.

Inspiration

My favorite subjects for macro photography are insects. I go to parks and wander around, keeping my eyes open for strange bugs. Parks are also a great place to take macro pictures of flowers. Although flowers are easily the most common subjects for macro photography enthusiasts, by no means are they the only subjects you can take pictures of. Many normal, everyday objects can become interesting when viewed up close.

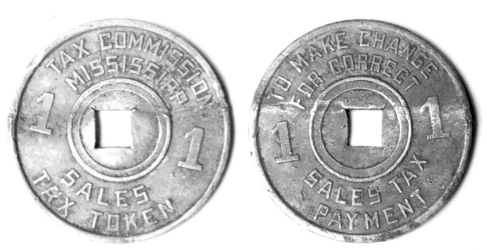

7.26 Mississippi sales tax token. For this composite shot (I shot both sides of the coin and combined them in Photoshop), I used a Nikon SC-29 off-camera TTL cord to get the flash off of the camera to get more even lighting. I used an SB-600 mounted on a light stand with a flash diffuser to soften the light. I aimed the flash directly down at the token at the left side of the camera. The lens was a Macro-Taumar 50mm f/4. I shot ISO 200 at f/11 for 1/60 second. Both the camera and flash were set to Manual mode.

Macro photography practice

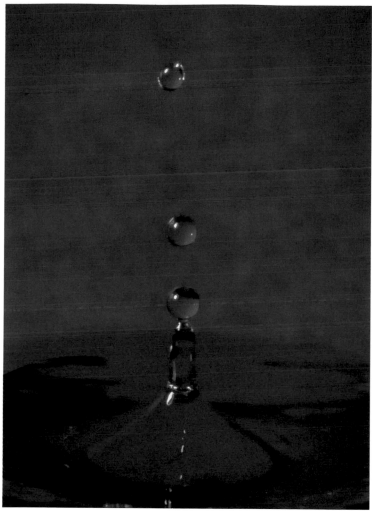

7.27 Water drop

Table 7.9
Taking Macro Pictures

Setup	**Practice Picture:** For the tricky shot in 7.27 I wanted to capture a high-speed exposure of a water drop. Setting the camera to a long shutter speed, I used a flash to freeze the action. The camera was set up on a tripod and the shutter was released using the Nikon ML-L3 wireless remote. All of the lights in my studio were out to cut down on any ambient light exposure. **On Your Own:** You can find plenty of interesting macro subjects; just look around. It's a good idea to always have your macro lens or close-up filters in your camera bag because you never know when you may run across interesting subjects for a macro shot.
Lighting	**Practice Picture:** The lighting was provided by an SB-800 Speedlight with a blue filter attached. After I released the shutter, I used an eyedropper to drop the water into a clear glass cup full of water. When I anticipated the drop hitting the water I pressed the test fire button on the flash to fire it. I was holding the flash in my hand just to the left front of the cup. **On Your Own:** When setting up the lighting for a shot like this I usually start out with the flash in Manual mode at 1/16 power and adjust the exposure accordingly after making a few test shots.
Lens	**Practice Picture:** Nikkor 80-200mm f/2.8. This lens doesn't autofocus with the D60 which is precisely why I chose it. I manually focused on the edge of the glass and used a small aperture to achieve enough depth of field to get the drop in focus. **On Your Own:** A good macro lens can be invaluable to get nice, sharp images. Using close-up filters or extension tubes can also be a good option.
Camera Settings	**Practice Picture:** I used Manual exposure settings because I needed to set a long shutter speed to perform all of the necessary maneuvers of using the eyedropper and firing the flash by hand. The flash was also set manually using trial and error; the final setting ended up being 1/16 power at the ISO 100 f/16 setting. **On Your Own:** If you are using an AF lens, it's best to set it to the Manual focus setting to avoid the camera refocusing on the wrong area. Using Manual settings allows you more control over the exposure.

Exposure **Practice Picture:** ISO 200 at f/13 for 4 seconds. I used a long shutter speed with a small aperture. The long shutter speed allowed me to drop the water and fire the flash; the small aperture gave me enough depth of field to keep the drop in sharp focus and also allowed me to keep the ambient light exposure to a minimum. The short duration of the flash in the dim light allows the flash to act as a fast shutter speed freezing the water droplet in midair.

On Your Own: Your exposure may vary depending on the lighting situation. Using a small f-stop is recommended for maximum depth of field and keeping out ambient light.

Accessories Close-up filters or a telephoto lens can be used instead of a dedicated macro lens. A tripod can be a good tool to have when photographing macro subjects because focusing close up to a subject tends to exaggerate camera shake.

Macro photography tips

✦ **Use the self-timer.** When using a tripod, use the self-timer to make sure the camera isn't shaking from pressing the Shutter Release button.

✦ **Use a low ISO.** Because macro and close-up photography focuses on details, use a low ISO to get the best resolution.

✦ **Use a remote shutter release.** If using a tripod, using a remote shutter release can also help reduce blur from camera shake.

Night Photography

Taking photographs at night brings a whole different set of challenges that are not present when you take pictures during the day. The exposures become significantly longer, making it difficult to handhold your camera and get sharp images. Your first instinct may be to use the flash to add light to the scene, but as soon as you do this, the image loses its nighttime charm. It ends up looking like a photograph taken with a flash in the dark. In other words, it looks like a snapshot.

When taking photos at night, you want to strive to capture the glowing lights and the delicate interplay between light and dark.

The best way to achieve this is to use a tripod and a longer exposure. This allows you to capture the image keeping your subjects in sharp focus even with the long exposures that are often necessary.

Flash can be used effectively at night for portraits. You don't necessarily want to use it as your main light; as a matter of fact you almost never want to use it as your main light. Ideally, you want a good balance of flash and ambient light. To get this effect, set your flash to the Slow Sync or the Rear/Slow Sync setting. This allows longer exposures so the ambient light is sufficiently recorded while the flash adds a nice bright "pop" to freeze the subject for sharp focus.

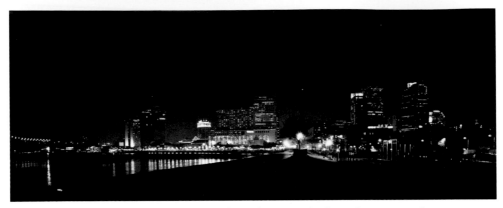

7.28 New Orleans skyline from the French Market. I used a long shutter speed to get a glass-like appearance to the water. Shot with a Nikkor 18-55mm f/3.5-5.6 VR lens zoomed to 18mm, ISO 100 at f/2.5 for 2 seconds.

Inspiration

When I look for scenes to photograph at night, I try to think of subjects that have a lot of color that can be accented by the long exposures. City skylines, downtown areas, and other places with lots of neon or other brightly colored lights are very good subject matter for this type of photography.

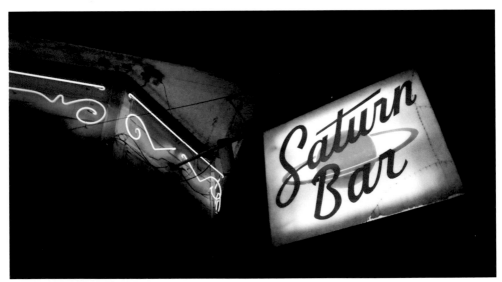

7.29 I took this shot of a sign for an interesting New Orleans bar. I liked the funky colors and the retro feel of the photo. Taken with a Sigma 17-35 f/2.8-4 lens set to 17mm, ISO 3200 at f/2.8 for 1/1000 second.

Night photography practice

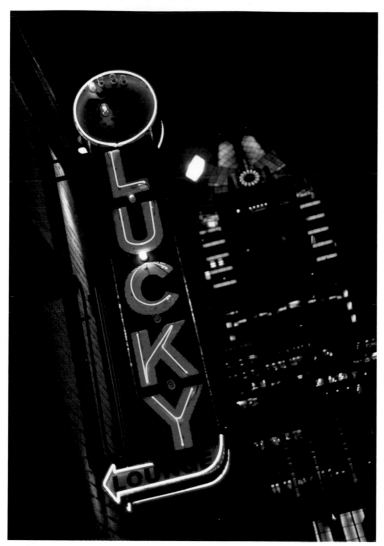

7.30 The Lucky Lounge and the Frost Bank building

Table 7.10
Taking Night Pictures

Setup	**Practice Picture:** Figure 7.30 is a photo of the sign outside the Lucky Lounge night club in downtown Austin, behind the sign is one of Austin's most well-known buildings, the Frost Bank building. **On Your Own:** Skylines and neon lights make great night pictures. The lights at night are often brightly colored and long exposures can make them super-saturated.
Lighting	**Practice Picture:** For this shot the lighting is ambient. **On Your Own:** For the most part, ambient lighting is all you need. If there are some details in the foreground you want to bring out, you can use a low-powered flash pop to paint some light into the scene.
Lens	**Practice Picture:** Nikkor 18-55mm f/3.5-5.6 VR zoomed to 17mm. **On Your Own:** Any lens will do for night photography. It just depends on your subject matter. Sometimes a lens with a wider aperture can give a little bit more light allowing for a faster shutter in case it's necessary to handhold your camera. A VR lens is great for night shots with still subjects.
Camera Settings	**Practice Picture:** To get this shot I used the Aperture Priority mode. Because there are many different light sources in this shot I recorded the image in RAW mode so I could adjust the white balance manually in post-processing until I got the effect that I liked the most. The camera white balance was set to Auto. **On Your Own:** When photographing a scene with multiple light sources it's best to shoot RAW so you can adjust the white balance in post-processing to suit your particular taste.
Exposure	**Practice Picture:** ISO 3200 at f/2.8 for 1/6 second. For this particular image, I chose a wide aperture to get a fast-enough shutter speed to handhold the camera while using VR and to get a shallow depth of field to throw the building in the background slightly out of focus. **On Your Own**: For night shots, long exposures are the norm. Extremely long exposures can sometimes bring unexpected results (like motion blur). These results may not always be desired, so open your f-stop to get a faster shutter speed if you need it.
Accessories	A tripod is a great tool for shooting photos at night. The ML-L3 wireless remote can also be handy for reducing camera shake when using long shutter speeds and a tripod.

Night photography tips

✦ **Bring a tripod.** Without a tripod, the long exposure times will cause your photos to be blurry.

✦ **Use the self-timer.** Pressing the Shutter Release button when the camera is on the tripod often causes the camera to shake enough to blur your image. Using the self-timer gives the camera and tripod enough time to steady so your images come out sharp.

✦ **Try using slow sync flash.** If using flash is an absolute must, try using slow sync to capture some of the ambient light in the background.

Pet Photography

Photographing pets is something every pet owner likes to do (I've got hundreds of pictures of my dog on my hard drive). The most difficult aspect about pet photography is getting the animal to sit or stand still. Whether you're creating an animal portrait or just taking some snapshots of your pet playing, patience is a good trait to have.

If your pet is fairly calm and well trained, using a studio-type setting is entirely possible. If you have trained your pet to sit and wait for a treat it can be easy to snap a formal portrait. Some pets such as snakes or

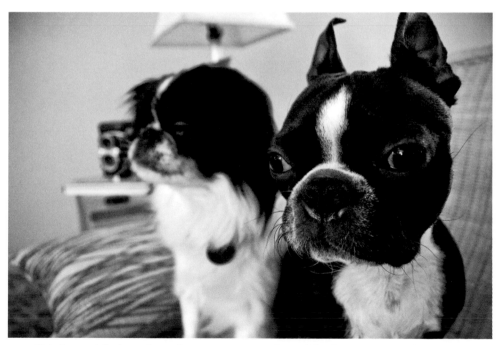

7.31 This is a quick shot of Henrietta, a Boston terrier, while she was visiting her friend Migs (the Japanese Chin in the background). I specifically used a wide-angle setting on the lens to get a distorted look. Because the lighting was very low, even using ISO 3200, I used a slow shutter speed, switched on the VR, and was able to capture a good sharp shot. Shot using the Nikkor 18-55 VR lens set to 18mm, ISO 3200 at f/4.5 for 1/10 second.

rodents may be more difficult to pose. In these types of situations it's good to have someone on hand to help you out.

Some of my most popular pictures are the ones I have taken of my dog just doing her normal dog things: sitting and waiting for a treat, yawning, or jumping around. The best photos of pets often are those that capture their personality, and this isn't necessarily achieved by sitting them in front of studio lights.

Inspiration

Animals and pets are an inspiration in and of themselves. If you don't have a pet yourself, you likely have friends or relatives who have one they would be happy to let you photograph. Go to the park and find people playing with their dogs. Lots of people have pets so it shouldn't be hard to find one.

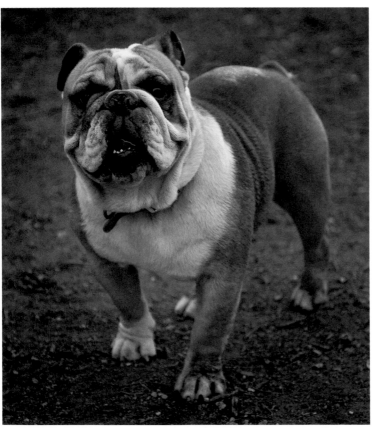

7.32 I shot a photo of this great English bulldog while at one of the many dog parks in Austin, Texas. It took a few shots and some coaxing to get him to look directly at me as there were a lot of dogs around distracting him. I got down fairly low in order to show him more on his level rather than looking down at him. Shot with a Nikkor 17-55mm f/2.8 lens set to 55mm, ISO 400 at f/2.8 for 1/500 second.

Pet photography practice

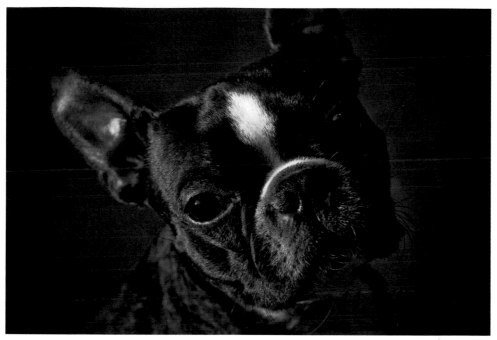

7.33 Henrietta posing for a portrait

Table 7.11 Taking Pet Pictures	
Setup	**Practice Picture:** For figure 7.33, I wanted to do a studio-type shot of Henrietta, but I wasn't at my studio with my backgrounds so I decided to use my stained concrete floors as a pseudo backdrop.
	On Your Own: Odd or unusual angles often make the most interesting shots. Keep an eye on your background. Distracting elements can take the focus off of your subject.
Lighting	**Practice Picture:** I was going more for a studio look for this shot so I used an SB-800 Speedlight to trigger an off-camera SB-600 that I had set on a chair. I used the Nikon SW-10H diffusion dome that came with the SB-800 to soften the light.
	On Your Own: Using off-camera flash can give your pet portraits a professional look, although using natural light is also great for shooting pets. Using natural light allows you to concentrate on the composition without worrying about your lighting setup.

Continued

Table 7.11 *(continued)*

Lens	**Practice Picture:** Nikkor 28-70 f/2.8 set to 70mm.
	On Your Own: Although the 28-70 works fine for these types of shots, a good wide-angle to short telephoto lens like the 18-55mm is invaluable for pet photography. This type of lens allows you the freedom to try many different compositions, from wide-angle shots to close-ups.
Camera Settings	**Practice Picture:** I chose Aperture Priority for this shot to use a relatively wide aperture to throw the background out of focus a bit. I used the Matrix metering to be sure that both the subject and the background were both nicely exposed.
	On Your Own: Programmed Auto can work fine when photographing pets. It frees you from worrying about the exposure and allows you to concentrate on dealing with the animal.
Exposure	**Practice Picture:** ISO 100 at f/5.6 for 1/60 second.
	On Your Own: Your exposures may vary depending on the setting that your subject is in. Using a wide aperture can help blur out distracting background details. A fast shutter speed can also help to keep your subject sharp in case of any movement.

Pet photography tips

✦ **Be patient.** Animals aren't always the best subjects; they can be unpredictable and uncooperative. Have patience and shoot plenty of pictures. You never know what you're going to get.

✦ **Bring some treats.** Sometimes animals can be coaxed to do things with a little bribe.

✦ **Get low.** Because we're used to looking down at most animals, we tend to shoot down at them. Get down low and shoot from the animal's perspective. This can make your picture much more interesting.

✦ **Use Red-Eye Reduction.** If you are going to use the flash, using Red-Eye Reduction is a must, although sometimes it doesn't completely remove the glare. Using off-camera flash or a flash diffuser can often help reduce the red-eye effect.

Portrait Photography

Portrait photography can be one of the easiest or one of the most challenging types of photography. Almost anyone with a camera can do it, yet it can be a complicated endeavor. Sometimes simply pointing a camera at someone and snapping a picture can create an interesting portrait; other times elaborate lighting setups may be needed to create a mood or to add drama to your subject.

A *portrait*, simply stated, is the likeness of a person — usually the subject's face — whether it is a drawing, a painting, or a photograph. A good portrait should go further than that. It should go beyond simply showing your subject's likeness and delve a bit deeper, hopefully revealing some of your subject's character or emotion also.

You have lots of things to think about when you set out to do a portrait. The first thing to ponder (after you've found your subject, of course) is the setting. The setting is the background and surroundings, the place where you shoot the photograph. You need to decide what kind of mood you want to evoke. For example, if you're looking to create a somber mood with a serious model, you may want to try a dark background. For something more festive, you may need a background with a bright color or multiple colors. Your subject may also have some ideas about how they want the image to turn out. Keep an open mind and be ready to try some other ideas that you may have not considered.

There are many different ways to evoke a certain mood or ambiance in a portrait image. Lighting and background are the principal ways to achieve an effect, but there are other ways. Shooting the image in black and white can give your portrait an evocative feel to it. You can shoot your image so that the colors are more vivid giving your photo a live, vibrant feeling, or you can tone the colors down for a more ethereal look.

Studio considerations

Studio portraits are essentially indoor portraits, except that with studio portraits the lighting and background are controlled to a much greater extent. The studio portrait is entirely dependent on the lighting and background to set the tone of the image.

The most important part of a studio setting is the lighting setup. Directionality and tone are a big part of studio lighting, and close attention must be paid to both. There are quite a few things to keep in mind when setting up for a studio portrait. A few things to consider:

✦ **What kind of tone are you looking for?** Do you want the portrait to be bright and playful or somber and moody? These elements must be considered, and the appropriate lighting and background must be set up.

✦ **Do you want to use props?** Sometimes having a prop in the shot can add interest to an otherwise bland portrait.

✦ **What kind of background is best for your shot?** The background is crucial to the mood and/or setting of the shot. For example, when shooting a high-key portrait you must have a bright, colored background. You can also use props in the background to evoke a feeling or specific place. One photographer I know went so far as to build walls, complete with windows, inside his studio. He then set up a couch, end tables, and lamps to create a 1970s-style motel room for a series of photographs he was shooting for assignment.

✦ **What type of lighting will achieve your mood?** Do you want hard or soft light? Do you need to light the background?

Studio portraits require the most thought and planning of all the different types of portraits. This type of photography also requires the most equipment; lights, stands, reflectors, backgrounds, and props are just a few of the things you may need.

For more information on lighting and accessories, see Chapter 4.

Candid

Sometimes the best portraits can be taken in available light when the subject isn't necessarily aware of the photographer. This is known as candid portrait photography. Many photojournalists use this approach to portraiture.

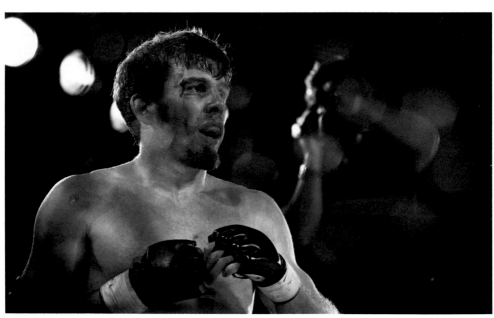

7.34 I shot this candid portrait of mixed martial arts fighter Lane Yarborough during a break in the action. Shot with a Nikkor 70-200mm f/2.8 VR lens set to 80mm, ISO 800 at f/3.5 for 1/180 second.

The main difference between candid portrait photography and standard portraits is control. Candid portraits are most often shot in available light with little interaction between the subject and photographer. You must be on your toes and ready for anything. Portraits in the studio are usually carefully planned with the photographer using certain settings to achieve an effect. Candid portrait photographers often have to "shoot from the hip," figuratively speaking.

Although you can use a flash when doing candid photography you run the risk of attracting the attention of your subject, therefore ruining the spontaneity of the moment. So if you're going to use a flash you better get it right the first time for the opportunity probably won't be there again.

Using an automatic setting such as Programmed Auto can help you focus on getting the shot rather than worrying about the settings.

Indoor

When shooting portraits indoors, more often than not there isn't enough light to make a correct exposure without using flash or some sort of other additional lighting. Although the built-in flash on the D60 sometimes works very well, especially outdoors, I find that when I try to use it for an indoor portrait, the person ends up looking like a deer caught in headlights. This type of lighting is very unnatural looking and doesn't lend itself well for portraiture. It works fine for snapshots, but your goal here is to get beyond taking snapshots and move up to making quality images. If you absolutely must use the built-in flash, using a flash diffuser greatly improves your images.

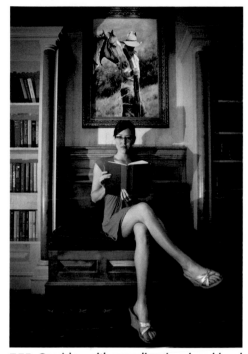

7.35 Cassiday with very directional and hard light. I placed an SB-800 Speedlight off to camera left aimed directly at her with no diffuser. When I was setting up this shot I realized that I only brought one SB-800 Speedlight (the D60 built-in flash does not function as a wireless commander). The SB-800 can be triggered by another flash (SU-4 mode). I set the built-in flash to Manual mode at the lowest power setting. I blocked the light just allowing enough flash to trigger the off camera SB-800, achieving a sort of wireless flash with the D60's built-in flash after all.

The easiest way to achieve a more natural-looking portrait indoors is to move your subject close to a window. This gives you more light to work with and the window acts as a diffuser, softening the light and giving your subject a nice glow.

Another easy way to get nice portrait lighting indoors is to use an additional light source, as I did for figure 7.35. A good source of additional lighting is one of the Nikon Speedlights. As with the built-in flash, photographing your subject with the Speedlight pointed straight at him or her is unadvisable. When using one of the shoe-mounted Speedlights, the best bet is to bounce the flash off the ceiling or a nearby wall to soften the flash. Ideally, use the flash off-camera, utilizing the wireless capabilities of the Nikon's Speedlights or simply using a SC-29 off-camera TTL flash cord.

Outdoor

When you shoot portraits outdoors, the problems that you encounter are usually the exact opposite of the problems you have when you shoot indoors. The light tends to be too bright, causing the shadows on your subject to be too dark. This results in an image with too much contrast.

In order to combat this contrast problem, you can use your flash. I know that this sounds counterintuitive; you're probably thinking, "If I have too much light, why should I add more?" Using the flash in the bright sunlight fills in the dark shadows, resulting in a more evenly exposed image. This technique is known as *fill-flash*.

Another way to combat images that have too much contrast when you're shooting outdoors is to have someone hold a diffusion panel over your model or move your model into a shaded area such as under a tree or a porch. This helps block the direct sunlight, providing you with a nice soft light for your portrait. Using a reflector to direct some light into the shadow areas of the face works really well also.

 Cross-Reference *For more information on fill-flash see Chapter 4. For more information on diffusion panels see Chapter 6.*

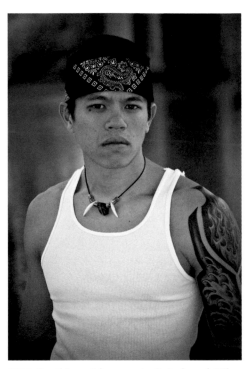

7.36 For this outdoor portrait, I placed Mike under the shadow of a nearby bridge to block the harsh afternoon sun. I used an SB-600 set to iTTL-BL to provide fill-flash to give an even exposure between the background and the subject. The combination of wide aperture and longer focal length makes the background a nice soft indistinct blur of color. Shot with a Nikkor 28-70mm f/2.8 lens zoomed to 70mm, ISO 100 at f/2.8 for 1/640 second.

Portrait photography practice

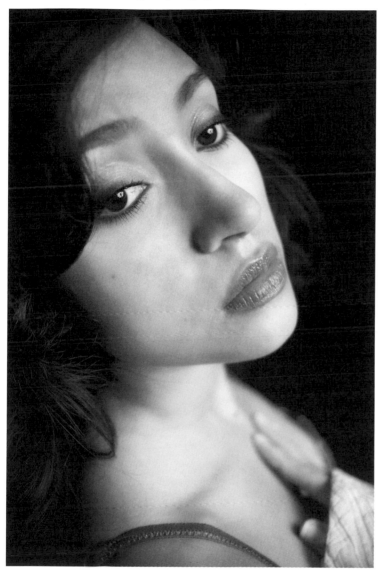

7.37 Inne in a 1940s-style Hollywood pose

Table 7.12
Taking Portrait Pictures

Setup	**Practice Picture:** For figure 7.37, my model Inne and I wanted to do a shoot reminiscent of a 1940s Hollywood starlet. **On Your Own:** You can find inspiration in many different areas; look into the past for some interesting ideas. Portraits can portray many different moods from somber to happy. Try to bring out some of your subject's personality.
Lighting	**Practice Picture:** For this shot, I used a 200-watt-second studio strobe set up to the right of the camera. The strobe was bounced into a 36-inch standard umbrella to soften the light. **On Your Own:** There are a lot of different studio lighting techniques. I find that using softboxes and umbrellas gives softer lighting causing the subject's skin to appear smoother. This allows me to spend less time on post-process retouching. The Internet has many different resources for learning about studio lighting.
Lens	**Practice Picture:** Nikkor 17-55mm f/2.8 zoomed to 26mm. I used a wider angle than I normally would to add a different perspective to this shot. **On Your Own:** When shooting portraits, it's generally advisable to use a longer focal length to avoid the perspective distortion common with wide-angle lenses. Wide-angle lenses, especially when used close up, can cause the subject's features to appear distorted. For example, the nose can appear too large while the ears will seem too small.
Camera Settings	**Practice Picture:** I used Manual exposure mode for this and all of the shots that I take using studio strobes. I preset the camera's white balance using a grey. **On Your Own:** When shooting natural light portraits, Aperture Priority mode is the preferred setting. This gives you the option to control the depth of field. Be sure to set your white balance to the proper light source. When using external studio strobes use Manual exposure to set your shutter speed to the sync speed of the camera and to choose your aperture. It is also a good idea to set a custom white balance to match the strobes.
Exposure	**Practice Picture:** ISO 100 at f/2.8 for 1/125 second. **On Your Own**: When using studio strobes, shooting at or near the sync speed is recommended. Using a wide aperture is common to draw attention to the subject and blur out the background, but be sure that your aperture is small enough to get your whole subject's face in focus.
Accessories	I used a Wein Safe-Sync hot shoe PC terminal to trigger the strobes. Using a reflector can help bounce some light into shadow areas.

Portrait photography tips

✦ **Plan some poses.** Take a look at some photos in fashion magazines or even on the Internet and find some poses that you like. Have these in mind when photographing your models.

✦ **Have some extra outfits.** Ask your model to bring a variety of clothes. This way you can get some different looks during one shoot.

Still-life and Product Photography

In still-life and product photography, lighting is the key to making the image work. You can set a tone using creative lighting to convey the feeling of the subject. You can also use lighting to show texture, color, and form to turn a dull image into a great one.

When practicing for product shots or experimenting with a still life, you obviously need to locate something to photograph. It can be one object or a collection of objects. Remember, if you are shooting a collection try to keep within a particular theme so the image has a feeling of continuity. Start by deciding which object you want to have as the main subject, and then place the other objects around it, paying close attention to the balance of the composition.

The background is another important consideration when photographing products or still-life scenes. Having an uncluttered background that showcases your subject is often best, although you may want to show the particular item in a scene, such as photographing a piece of fruit on a cutting board with a knife in a kitchen.

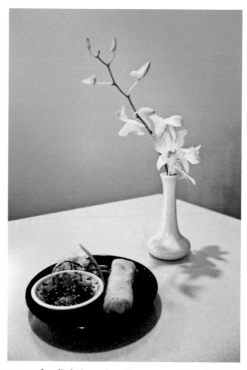

7.38 The lighting situation was difficult with two distinct color temperatures, one from the tungsten lights of the room, the other from the daylight filtering in through the windows, so I shot the image in RAW so I could manipulate the white balance in post-processing. At ISO 1600 my shutter speed was relatively slow so I used the VR feature. Shot with a Nikkor 18-55mm f/3.5-5.6 VR lens set to 20mm, ISO 1600 at f/3.8 for 1/5 second Exposure compensation +0.7.

Diffused lighting is often the best in this type of photography. You don't want harsh shadows to make your image look like you shot it with a flash. The idea is to light it so it doesn't look as if it was lit. You can use hard directional lighting to highlight any texture that your subject may have, but you want the lighting to come from off-camera. If you use on-camera flash using a diffuser is almost absolutely necessary.

Even with diffusion, the shadow areas need some filling in. You can do this by using a second light as fill or by using a fill card. A *fill card* is a piece of white foam board or poster board used to bounce some light from the main light back into the shadows, lightening them a bit. When using two or more lights, be sure that your fill light isn't too bright, or it can cause you to have two shadows. Remember, the key to good lighting is to emulate the natural lighting of the sun.

Inspiration

When searching for subjects for a still-life shot, try using some personal items. Some ideas are objects such as jewelry or watches, a collection of trinkets you bought on vacation, or even seashells you brought home from the beach. If you're interested in cooking, try photographing some dishes you have prepared. Fruits and vegetables are always good subjects, especially when they have vivid colors or interesting textures.

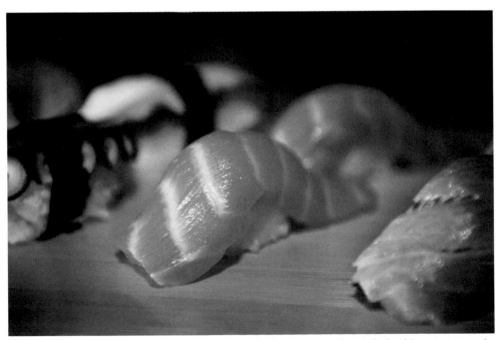

7.39 Sushi is one of my favorite subjects for still-life photography. To light this setup I used an SB-600 connected to the camera using a Nikon SC-29 off-camera TTL cord. I held the flash above the sushi slightly to the left to give the shot some texture and shadows. I specifically chose a wide-open aperture to draw attention to the centerpiece of sushi allowing the others to go out of focus while retaining some color and definition to add interest to the shot. Shot with a Nikkor 17-55mm f/2.8 lens set to 55mm. Spot metered, ISO 200 at f/2.8 for 1/60 second.

Still-life and product photography practice

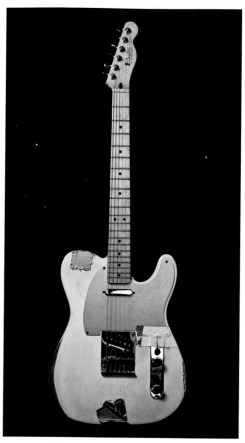

7.40 Fender Telecaster

Table 7.13
Taking Still-life Pictures

Setup	**Practice Picture:** For figure 7.40, I set out to take a picture of my road-worn Fender Telecaster. Its battle-scarred appearance makes it an interesting subject for a still life. I chose to photograph this on a black background in order to allow the guitar to stand out.
	On Your Own: Simple arrangements work best for still-life photos. Cramming too many objects into the composition can leave it looking cluttered. Keep it simple.

Continued

Table 7.13 *(continued)*

Lighting	**Practice Picture:** For this shot, I used two older SB-26 Speedlights at camera left that were mounted on stands and fired through shoot-through umbrellas to soften the light. One flash was positioned low to light the body of the guitar and the other was set up a little higher to light the neck. I wanted to keep this a low-key shot to emphasize the guitar so the background was deliberately left unlit. I fired the Speedlights by linking one of the flashes to the camera with a PC sync cord and a Wein Safe-Sync; a built-in optical slave triggered the second flash.
	On Your Own: You don't need expensive studio strobes to achieve professional lighting results. These older Speedlights are a fraction of the cost of studio strobes and work very well when photographing small-to medium-sized setups.
Lens	**Practice Picture:** Nikkor 17-55mm f/2.8 set to 55mm.
	On Your Own: A normal to medium telephoto focal length is recommended to reduce the perspective distortion that can occur when shooting close up. This is a common problem when using wide-angle lenses. For smaller objects, using a macro lens or a telephoto lens can work well.
Camera Settings	**Practice Picture:** Once again, as with most of my studio shots, I used Manual exposure. When shooting with studio flash the only option is to set the shutter speed and aperture and adjust the lights to fit my chosen settings. When using Nikon CLS (SB-800 commander and SB-600 remotes) I use Aperture Priority to control my depth of field.
	On Your Own: Be sure to adjust your white balance settings to match your light source. Shooting in RAW can also help you to fine-tune your white balance and exposure in post-processing.
Exposure	**Practice Picture:** ISO 200 at f/7.1 for 1/60 second. For this shot, I first set the shutter speed to 1/60 (the normal flash-sync speed). I then set aperture to f/8 so I would be sure to carry enough depth of field; the shot was then a little dark so I opened up the aperture a little more to get just the right exposure.
	On Your Own: Manual exposure is the best choice if using studio strobes, but if you're taking advantage of the Nikon CLS using a Nikon Speedlight setup you can just as easily shoot in one of the auto modes such as Programmed Auto, Shutter Priority, or Aperture Priority.

Still-life and product photography tips

✦ **Keep it simple.** Don't try to pack too many objects into your composition. Having too many objects for the eye to focus on can lead to a confusing image.

✦ **Use items with bold colors and dynamic shapes.** Bright colors and shapes can be eye-catching and add interest to your composition.

✦ **Vary your light output.** When using more than one light on the subject, You can also use one as a fill light with lower power to add a little depth to the subject by creating subtle shadows and varied tones.

Travel Photography

Traveling can provide you with the opportunity to take some of your most interesting photos. Foreign locations can be truly inspiring. Filled with strange and wonderful people and scenes they can fuel your creativity, but don't forget that there are many travel opportunities right in your own backyard. Domestic travel can be just as compelling as foreign travel.

Travel photography doesn't just include photo-taking. One of the most important aspects about this type of photography starts before you even leave for your trip —

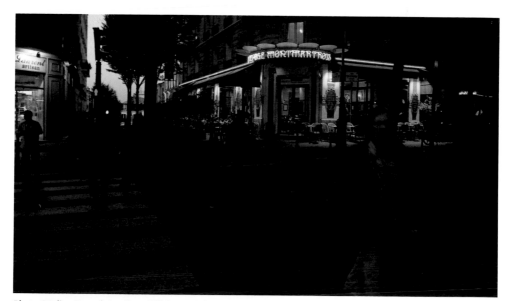

Photo ©Julian Humphries (http://flickr.com/photos/austintexas/)

7.41 Rue Damrémont, Paris, France. This is a perfect example of travel and street photography. This shot shows the Paris nightlife coming alive just after sunset. The rather slow shutter speed blurs the people giving you a sense of motion while the rest of the scene is in sharp focus. Shot with a Nikkor 18-70mm f/3.5-4.5 lens zoomed to 18mm, ISO 800 at f/3.5 for 1/25 second.

packing. Most people who have traveled extensively know that packing light is a must. Lugging around every piece of camera equipment you have can be physically exhausting. Take only what you need, but don't leave any essentials behind. Many times you can cover all of your bases by using smaller pieces of gear. If I'm going on a short hike often I use the smaller 55-200mm f/4-5.6 VR lens rather than bringing along a huge 70-200 f/2.8 VR. I may lose a couple of stops of light, but I save myself some space and weight. It's the small things that can make a big difference. If it's in your budget the 18-200mm VR lens makes an excellent travel lens encompassing a wide range of focal lengths in one compact lens.

Inspiration

Uncommon architecture, people, and landscape features are just a few of the things you may find on your ventures. Most of the topics covered in this chapter can be related to your travel photography, from abstracts to landscapes to wildlife photos. The most important part about travel photography is to use your images to not only remember what the place looked like, but also to convey the feeling of the locale. For example, when in a foreign place a few shots of the local people can remind you of the cultural differences that exist in some areas of the world or even just regional differences.

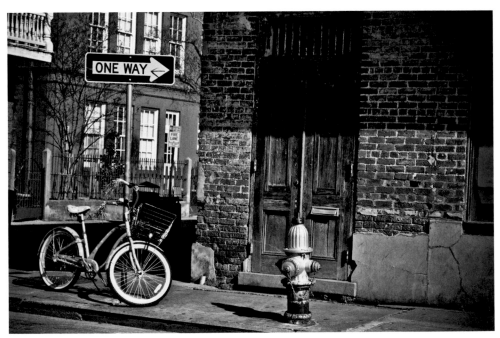

7.42 View from Lafitte's Blacksmith Bar, Bourbon Street, New Orleans, Louisiana. With most of the recent shots of New Orleans centering on the destruction from the hurricane, I wanted to show New Orleans in a different light. This view just struck me as wholly "New Orleanian." Shot with a Nikkor 18-55mm f/3.5-5.6 VR lens zoomed to 55mm, ISO 100 at f/5.6 for 1/800 second.

Travel photography practice

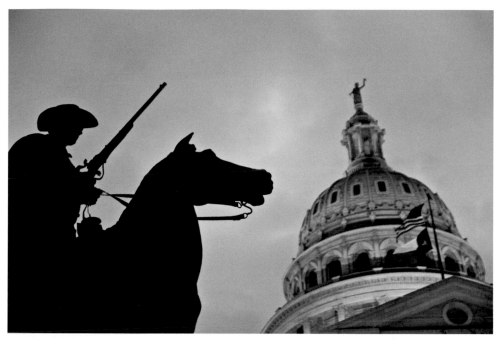

7.43 Texas State Capitol

Table 7.14
Taking Travel Pictures

Setup	**Practice Picture:** Figure 7.43 is a shot of the statue honoring the soldiers who fought for Texas independence. In the background is the rotunda of the capitol building. Although I didn't have to travel far to take this picture, Austin is the capital of Texas and is a travel destination for many people from here and abroad. My attempt was to show a little bit about the spirit of Texas.
	On Your Own: Try to capture the feeling and spirit that exists in different places of the world. You can also take a series of images to tell a story about your travels.

Continued

Table 7.14 *(continued)*

Lighting	**Practice Picture:** This was shot just after sunset, using only the light that was provided by the fading sun. I first metered on the rotunda of the capitol to capture the color of it and the sky allowing the statue to fall mostly in dark shadow for dramatic effect. I locked the exposure then recomposed the shot-locking focus on the statue.
	On Your Own: A lot of the time when traveling you don't have the time to wait for the ideal lighting conditions to come along so you may have to make do with what you have. You can also try to plan your trip so that you arrive at your destination when the lighting is likely to be ideal.
Lens	**Practice Picture:** Nikkor 17-55mm f/2.8 zoomed to 50mm. I used a fairly long setting in order to create a close, frame-filling crop.
	On Your Own: Use a wide-angle setting to capture vistas or you can choose to zoom in to focus on smaller details. Having a zoom lens that goes from a wide-angle to a short telephoto is almost a necessity when traveling. This type of lens is very versatile and can be used to cover almost any type of scene you encounter.
Camera Settings	**Practice Picture:** I used Aperture Priority mode to control the depth of field. The image was shot in RAW so I could be sure to adjust the white balance to my preference later in post-processing.
	On Your Own: Shooting in RAW can give you a little insurance in case your camera doesn't record the white balance or exposure exactly as you want it.
Exposure	**Practice Picture:** ISO 400 at f/2.8 for 1/50 second. I also set the Exposure compensation to −0.7EV in order keep the statue looking dark and giving the background colors more saturation. The aperture was opened wider to give the capitol a softer appearance.
	On Your Own: Underexposing a bit when photographing areas with both light and dark areas can give your colors deeper saturation and can give your image a more dramatic feel.

Travel photography tips

✦ **Keep your gear close.** When traveling, especially abroad, keep a close eye on your gear. Many thieves target camera gear because it's fairly expensive and small enough to grab and make a quick getaway.

✦ **Bring plenty of memory.** There's nothing worse than missing a once-in-a-lifetime shot because you ran out of space on your SD card. It's also a good idea to bring along a few memory cards. It can be better to have four 2GB cards as opposed to one 8GB card in case your card fails or malfunctions. It's best not to have all of your eggs in one basket.

✦ **Do some research on your destination.** Knowing what type of scenery to expect can help you to decide what kind of equipment to pack. For example, if you know you'll be shooting mostly landscapes, a wide-angle lens will be needed. If you're going to be shooting a lot of indoor subjects you may need a fast lens or a tripod.

Wildlife Photography

Photographing wildlife is a fun and rewarding pastime that can also be intensely frustrating. If you know what you want to photograph, it can mean standing out in the freezing cold or blazing heat for hours on end, waiting for the right animal to show up. But when you get that one shot you've been waiting for, it's well worth it.

Wildlife can be found at many different places: zoos, wildlife preserves, and animal sanctuaries, as well as out in the wild. One of the easiest ways to capture wildlife photos is to be where you know the animals are.

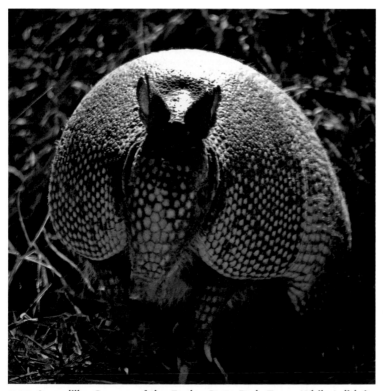

7.44 Armadillo, Canyon of the Eagles State Park, Texas. While I didn't see any eagles this day, I did spot this armadillo foraging for food. When he saw me he popped up his head just log enough to snap this picture. Shot with a Nikkor 55-200mm f/4-5.6 VR lens set to 92mm, ISO 400 at f/5.6 at 1/60 second, VR on.

Wildlife photography is another one of those areas of photography where people's opinions differ on whether or not you should use flash. I tend not to use flash to avoid scaring off the animals. But, as with any type of photography, there are circumstances in which you might want to use a flash, such as if the animal is backlit and you want to bring out some detail.

Opportunities to take wildlife pictures can occur when you're hiking in the wilderness, or maybe when you're sitting out on your back porch enjoying the sunset. With a little perseverance and luck, you can get some great wildlife images, just like the ones you see in *National Geographic*.

Inspiration

You can go to wildlife reserves, a zoo, or even your backyard to find wildlife. I tend to go the easy route, focusing on places where I'm pretty sure to find what I'm looking for. For example, while driving through Louisiana, I saw a sign that advertised an alligator swamp tour. I was pretty sure I'd see some alligators if I went. And even though I'd missed the last tour, there were still plenty of alligators there.

Even in the city or urban areas, you may be able to find wildlife, such as songbirds perched on a power line or hawks in trees near roadsides. A lot of cities have larger parks where you can find squirrels or other smaller animals as well. For example, I've photographed the animals at a park near my studio where you can see peacocks and armadillos running around.

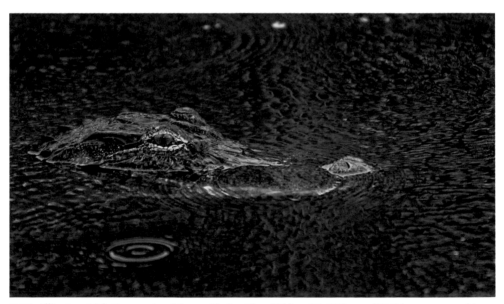

7.45 Alligator, Irish Bayou, Louisiana. Shot with a Nikkor 80-200mm f/2.8 lens zoomed to 200mm. ISO 200 at f/2.8 for 1/500 second.

Wildlife photography practice

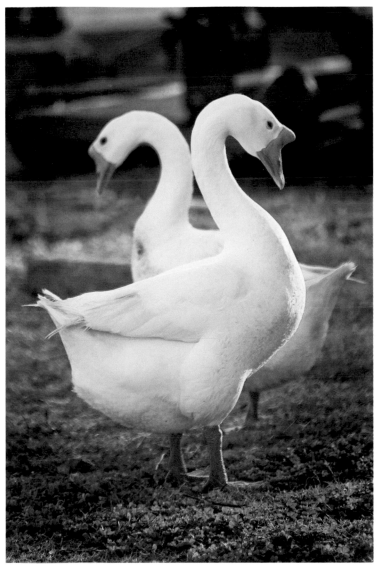

7.46 Geese

Table 7.15
Taking Wildlife Pictures

Setup	**Practice Picture:** I stopped to take a swamp tour in the Atchafalaya Basin. I missed the tour but I continued to wander around the area hoping to catch a glimpse of some alligators. I happened to see the two geese in Figure 7.46 posturing. I lifted my camera and did some maneuvering to create this symmetrically patterned composition.
	On Your Own: You can go to state parks or wildlife preserves to try your hand at photographing wildlife if you are interested in more than what you might find in an urban backyard. If you aren't successful in your hunt, at least you can enjoy a hike.
Lighting	**Practice Picture:** The golden light that often occurs before sunset lit these birds giving them a bit of a golden glow.
	On Your Own: Wild animals aren't often inclined to cooperate with you by being in the perfect lighting at all times, so you should basically take what you can get. Don't miss out on a shot because the lighting is less than ideal. However, going out in search of wildlife near sunrise or sunset should help you to catch those animals in some nice light.
Lens	**Practice Picture:** Nikkor 70-200mm f/2.8 zoomed to 200mm.
	On Your Own: A long telephoto lens is almost an absolute necessity when it comes to photographing wild animals. Geese are known to be quite aggressive and had I gotten too close I probably wouldn't have been able to capture them in this perfect pose.
Camera Settings	**Practice Picture:** This shot was taken using Aperture Priority. I chose Aperture Priority to select a wide aperture to blur out the distracting elements of the swamp boats in the background. It was captured in RAW, and Matrix metering was used.
	On Your Own: When shooting with a long lens it is often best to use Shutter Priority to be sure that you have a fast-enough shutter speed to counteract any camera shake (remember that longer focal lengths suffer from camera shake due to the extreme magnification). You may want to choose Aperture Priority to control your depth of field. Spot metering can also be a good choice, allowing you to be sure that the subject is properly exposed. Shooting in RAW can give you a little latitude in post-processing if the lighting isn't exactly right.
Exposure	**Practice Picture:** ISO 200 at f/2.8 for 1/400 second.
	On Your Own: Because the sun was just starting to go down, there wasn't quite enough light so I adjusted the ISO up a bit. A shutter speed of 1/250 second is just about the minimum you can get away with when handholding the camera at this focal length.

Wildlife photography tips

✦ **Use a telephoto lens.** This allows you to remain inconspicuous to the animal, enabling you to catch it acting naturally.

✦ **Seize an opportunity.** Even if you don't have the lens zoomed to the right focal length for capturing wildlife, snap a few shots anyhow. You can always crop them later if they aren't perfect. It's better to get the shot than not.

✦ **Be patient.** It may take a few hours, or even a few trips, to the outdoors before you have the chance to see any wild animals. Keep the faith; it will happen eventually.

✦ **Keep an eye on the background.** When photographing animals at a zoo, keep an eye out for cages and other things that look man-made — and avoid them. It's best to try to make the animal look like it's in the wild by finding an angle that shows foliage and other natural features.

Viewing, Downloading, and the Retouch Menu

You can use the D60's large, bright 2.5-inch, 230,000-dot VGA LCD monitor to view your images and then, use the in-camera editing features that allow you to save some time in post-processing and give you the option to fine-tune your images for printing without ever having to download your images to a computer. Nikon also offers some new options on the D60 that have not been available on other cameras, such as the ability to make a stop-motion movie that you can view on your computer or share on the Internet via YouTube or the new Flickr video.

Viewing Your Images

The Nikon D60 offers two ways to view your images while the SD card is still inserted in the camera. You can view the images directly on the LCD monitor on the camera or you can hook your camera up to a standard TV using the Nikon EG-D100 video cable that's available separately from Nikon. Nikon used to supply these cables with all of its cameras but for some reason chose not to include it with the D60 kit. You can find the EG-D100 cable at most camera shops or online for around $10.

When viewing through an external device such as a TV, the view is the same as would normally be displayed on the LCD monitor. The camera's buttons and dials function exactly the same.

Before connecting the camera to your television you need to set the Video Out mode. There are two different types of video interface, NTSC and PAL. These modes control how the electronic signal is processed. In NTSC mode, the likely setting if you are in North or South America, 30 frames are transmitted each second with each frame being made up of 525 scan lines. PAL mode, used mainly in Europe and Asia, transmits 25 frames per second with each frame made up of 625 scan lines.

While it may never be important to you, knowing this is important if you travel much because these video modes are used in different parts of the world. If you are located in North America, you want to leave the Video mode set to NTSC. If you happen to be located overseas or you are going to travel overseas, you should set the Video mode to PAL. If you're unsure to whether your TV accepts NTSC or PAL, check the owner's manual of your TV.

To change the Video mode from the default setting:

1. **Turn the camera on.**

2. **Press the Menu button.**

3. **Use the multiselector button to highlight the Setup menu.**

4. **Use the multiselector to highlight Video mode, and then press the OK button.**

5. **Use the multiselector to highlight NTSC (or PAL).**

6. **Press the OK button to save the settings.**

 Cross-Reference *For more information on playing back images, see Chapter 3.*

To connect your camera to a standard TV:

1. **Turn the camera off.** This helps prevent damage to your camera's electronics from static electricity.

2. **Open the connector cover.** The connector cover is on the left side of the camera when the lens is facing away from you.

3. **Plug the EG-D100 video cable into the Video Out jack.** This is the connection at the top. Note that this Nikon cable is available separately.

4. **Connect the EG-D100 video cable to the input jack of your television or VCR.**

5. **Set your TV to the video channel.** This may differ depending on your TV. See the owner's manual if you are unsure.

6. **Turn on the camera and press the Playback button.** Your images appear on the TV screen, beginning with the most recently taken.

Downloading Images

After you finish taking your pictures you're probably going to want to download them to your computer for further image editing and tweaking, or so you can post them to the Web or send them off to your friends and family.

Downloading your images is a fairly simple process, and there are a couple of different ways to this. The most common way is to remove the SD card from the camera and insert it into a card reader that is connected to your computer. The other option is to use the USB cable supplied with the D60 and connect the camera directly to the computer. Either option works just as well as the other, and it's mostly a personal preference.

Using Nikon Transfer

There is a CD included inside the box with your D60. In addition to Nikon Transfer on the CD there is also Nikon's image-editing and viewing software, Nikon View. You can use Nikon View to do most basic editing of your photos such as contrast adjustments and red-eye removal.

After installing Nikon Transfer, as soon as your D60 is connected to the computer and turned on the application launches automatically (some operating systems may differ). By default, Nikon Transfer is set up to create a new folder named Nikon Transfer where your images will be saved. Transfer also automatically creates a numbered subfolder each time new images are downloaded.

There are a number of different tabs in the Nikon Transfer main window that allow you to specify how Nikon Transfer deals with your files.

Source

The first tab is the Source tab. This allows you to set what type of media Nikon Transfer searches for. Clicking the Search For

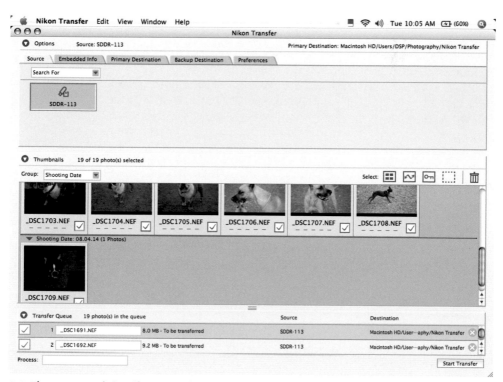

8.1 The source tab in Nikon Transfer

drop-down menu allows you to set the program to recognize when a camera is attached or a removable disk has been connected. Both of these options can also be set at the same time. Choosing the camera option allows the program to recognize only when a camera has been connected. When using an external card reader you want to set the removable disk option.

Embedded Info

This tab allows you to attach text information into the EXIF data of your image. EXIF stands for exchangeable image file. EXIF data is embedded into your image file and has information such as the date and time,

camera make and model, white balance settings, shutter speed and aperture, exposure and flash modes, as well as other information. The EXIF data can be read using programs such as Adobe Bridge as well as other image-editing software. Some photo sharing Web sites, such as Flickr.com, also allow you to view the EXIF data on images that are uploaded.

You can add all sorts of different information using the Embedded Info feature; a description of the photo, a title, your name and address, copyright information, and the location that the image was taken. You can also save a number of presets for saving different information.

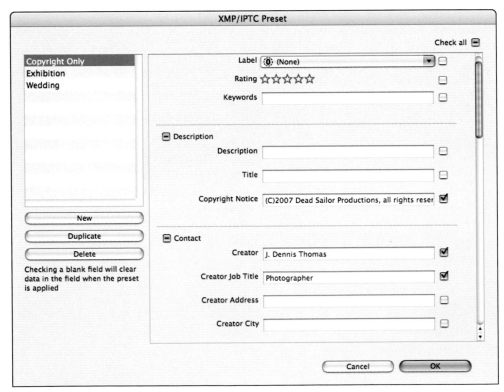

8.2 The Embedded Info editing screen

Primary Destination

This allows you to choose where your images are downloaded. You can browse your hard drive to choose a specific destination or you can leave it at the default. There is also an option that allows you to customize the folder-naming sequence that Nikon Transfer employs.

Backup Destination

This tab allows you to automatically back up your images when transferring them. Backing up your images to an external hard drive is a good idea in case of a computer or hard drive failure. This feature works in much the same way as the Primary Destination tab.

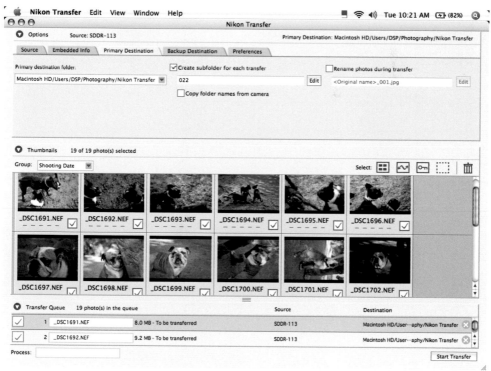

8.3 Primary Destination tab in Nikon Transfer.

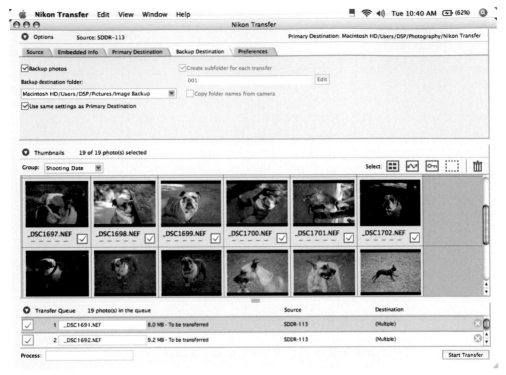

8.4 Backup Destination tab in Nikon Transfer

Preferences

This tab allows you to customize how the program works and what it does with the files after transferring them. You can choose from a number of different options:

✦ Launch automatically when device is attached.

✦ Disconnect automatically after transfer.

✦ Shut down computer automatically after transfer.

✦ Quit Nikon Transfer automatically after transfer.

✦ Synchronize camera date and time to computer when camera is connected.

✦ Transfer new photos only.

✦ Delete original files after transfer.

✦ Open destination folder with other application after transfer.

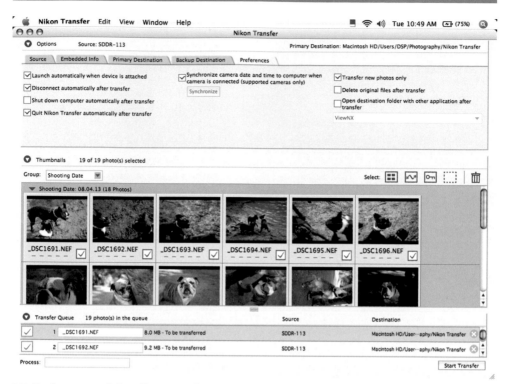

8.5 Preferences tab in Nikon Transfer

Transferring your images

After everything is set the way you want it, transferring your images is a very simple process. All of the images on the memory card are displayed as thumbnails in the Nikon Transfer window. Below the thumbnail is the image filename and a check box that can be checked or unchecked. Simply click in the box to select the image. When the check mark appears in the box, the image is set to be transferred; if the box is empty, the image is not copied. After you select all of the images you want to transfer, simply click Start Transfer, which is located on the bottom right-hand side of the window. The images are copied to the specified destination.

The Retouch Menu

The Nikon D60 has a very handy Retouch menu. These in-camera editing options make it simple for you to print straight from the camera without downloading it to your computer or using any image-editing software.

One great feature of using the Retouch menu is that the camera saves the retouched image as a copy so you don't lose the original image. This can be beneficial if you decide that you would rather edit the photo on your computer or if you simply aren't happy with the outcome. There are two ways to access the Retouch menu.

The first and quickest method:

1. **Press the Play button to enter Playback mode.** Your most recently taken image appears on the LCD screen.

2. **Use the multiselector to review your images.** When you see an image you want to retouch press the OK button to display the Retouch menu options.

3. **Use the multiselector to highlight the Retouch option you want to use.** Depending on the Retouch option you choose, you may have to select additional settings.

4. **Make adjustments if necessary.**

5. **Press the OK button to save.**

The second method:

1. **Press the Menu button to view menu options.**

2. **Use the multiselector to scroll down to the Retouch menu.** It's the fifth menu down and appears as an icon with a paintbrush.

3. **Press the multiselector right, then use the multiselector up/down to highlight the Retouch option you want to use.** Depending on the Retouch option you select, you may have to select additional settings. After you select your option(s), thumbnails appear.

4. **Use the multiselector to select the image to retouch, and then press the OK button.**

5. **Make the necessary adjustments.**

6. **Press the OK button to save.**

There are a few options you can select when using the Retouch menu. The options vary from cropping your image to adjusting the color balance to taking red-eye out of your pictures.

Quick retouch

The Quick retouch option is the easiest option. The camera automatically adjusts the contrast and saturation making your image brighter and more colorful, perfect for printing straight from the camera or memory card. In the event that your image is dark or backlit the camera also automatically applies D-Lighting to help bring out details in the shadow areas of your picture.

Once your image is selected for Quick retouch you can choose how much of the effect is applied: High, Normal, or Low. The LCD monitor displays a side-by-side

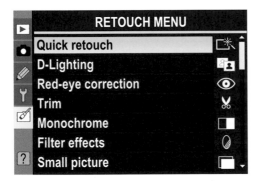

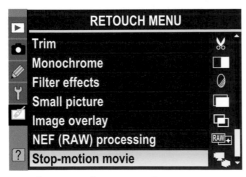

8.6 The Retouch menu options

comparison between the image as shot and retouched to give you a better idea of what the effect looks like.

After you decide how much of the effect you want, press the OK button to save a copy of the retouched image or you can press the Playback button to cancel without making any changes to your picture.

D-Lighting

This allows you to adjust the image by brightening the shadows. This is not the same as Active D-Lighting. D-Lighting uses a curves adjustment to help to bring out details in the shadow areas of an image. This option is for use with backlit subjects or images that may be slightly underexposed.

1. **With the D-Lighting option selected from the Retouch menu, use the multiselector to choose a thumbnail and the Zoom in button to get a closer look at the image.**

2. **Press the OK button to choose the image to retouch.** Two thumbnails are displayed; one is the original image, and the other is the image with D-Lighting applied.

3. **Use the multiselector up or down to select the amount of D-Lighting: Low, Normal, or High.** The results can be viewed in real time and compared with the original before saving.

4. **Press the OK button to save the changes.** You can also press the Playback button to cancel and the Zoom in button to view the full-frame image.

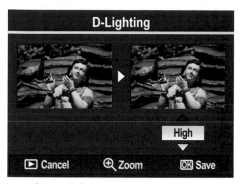

8.7 The D-Lighting option

Red-eye correction

This option enables the camera to automatically correct for the red-eye effect that can sometimes be caused by using the flash on pictures taken of people or animals. This option is only available on photos taken with flash. When choosing images to retouch from the Playback menu by pressing the OK button during preview, this option is grayed out and cannot be selected if the camera detects that a flash was not used. When attempting to choose an image directly from the Retouch menu, a message is displayed stating that this image cannot be used.

Once an image is selected, press the OK button; the camera then automatically corrects the red-eye and saves a copy of the image to your SD card.

If an image is selected that flash was used on but there is no red-eye present, the camera displays a message stating that red-eye is not detected in the image and no retouching is done.

Trim

This option allows you to crop your image to remove distracting elements or to allow you to crop closer to the subject.

1. **With the Trim option selected from the Retouch menu, use the multiselector to choose a thumbnail.**

2. **Press the OK button to choose the image to trim.**

3. **Use the Zoom in and Zoom out buttons to adjust the size of the crop.** This allows you to crop closer in or farther out, depending on your needs.

4. **Use the multiselector to move the crop around the image so you can center the crop on the part of the image that you think is most important.**

5. **When you are happy with the crop you have selected, press the OK button to save a copy of your cropped image.** You can also press the Playback button to return to the main menu without saving.

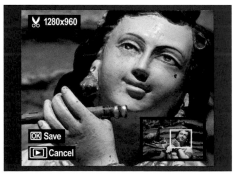

8.8 Using the in-camera crop (Trim) option

Monochrome

This option allows you to make a copy of your color image in a monochrome format. There are three options:

✦ **Black-and-white.** This changes your image to shades of black, white, and gray.

✦ **Sepia.** This gives your image the look of a black-and-white photo that has been sepia toned. Sepia toning is a traditional photographic process that gives the photo a reddish-brown tint.

✦ **Cyanotype.** This option gives your photos a blue or cyan tint. Cyanotypes are a form of processing film-based photographic images.

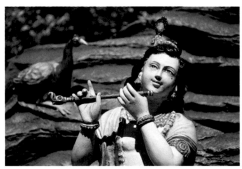

8.9 An image converted to black and white

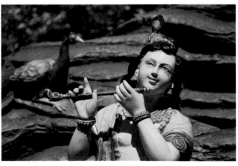

8.10 An image converted to sepia

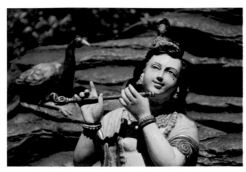

8.11 An image converted to cyanotype

When selecting the Sepia or Cyanotype options you can use the multiselector up and down buttons to adjust the lightness or darkness of the effect. Press the OK button to save a copy of the image or press the Playback button to cancel without saving.

Filter effects

Filter effects allow you to simulate the effects of using certain filters over your lens to subtly modify the colors of your image. There are seven filter effects available:

✦ **Skylight.** A skylight filter is used to absorb some of the UV rays emitted by the sun. The UV rays can give your image a slightly bluish tint. Using the skylight filter effect causes your image to be less blue.

✦ **Warm filter.** A warming filter adds a little orange to your image to give it a warmer hue. This filter effect can sometimes be useful when using flash because flash can sometimes cause your images to feel a little too cool.

✦ **Red intensifier.** This adds a red colorcast to your image. You can use the multiselector up/down to lighten or darken the effect.

✦ **Green intensifier.** This adds a green colorcast to your image. You can use the multiselector up/down to lighten or darken the effect.

✦ **Blue intensifier.** This adds a blue colorcast to your image. You can use the multiselector up/down to lighten or darken the effect.

✦ **Cross screen.** This effect simulates the use of a star filter. A star filter creates a star-shaped pattern on the bright highlights in your image. If your image doesn't have any bright highlights the effect is not apparent. Once an image is selected from the cross screen filter you see a submenu with a few options that you can adjust. You can choose the number of points on the stars: 4, 6, or 8. You can also choose the amount; there are three settings, which give you more or less stars. You can choose three angle settings, which control the angle at which the star is tilted. You also have three settings that control the length of the points on the stars.

✦ **Color balance.** Although this really isn't a filter effect, you can use the Color balance option to create a copy of an image on which you have adjusted the color balance. Using this option, you can use the multiselector to add a color tint to your image. You can use this effect to neutralize an existing color tint or to add a color tint for artistic purposes.

Press the multiselector up to increase the amount of green, down to increase the amount of magenta, left to add blue, and right to add amber.

A color chart and color histograms are displayed along with an image preview so you can see how the color balance affects your image. When you are satisfied with your image, press the OK button to save a copy.

After choosing the desired filter effect, press the OK button to save a copy of your image with the effect added.

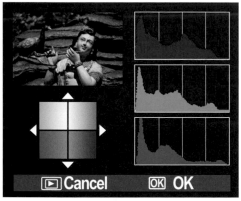

8.12 Color chart and histograms using the Color balance option

Small picture

This is a handy option that allows you to make a copy of your images that are a smaller size. These smaller pictures are more suitable for e-mailing to friends and family.

1. **The first thing you need to do when creating a small picture is to select the Choose size option from the Small picture sub-menu.** You have three sizes to choose from: 640 × 480, 320 × 240, or 160 × 120.

2. **After deciding what size you want your small picture copies to be, go to the Select picture option.** When the Select picture option is selected the LCD displays thumbnails of all of the images in the current folder. Scroll through your images using the multiselector left and right.

3. **Select or deselect images using the multiselector up and down.** You can select as many images as you have on your memory card.

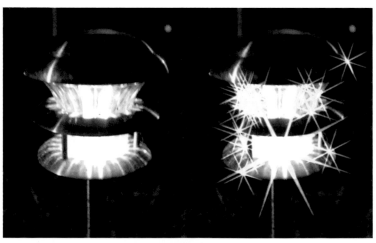

8.13 Cross screen filter before (left) and after (right)

4. **Press the OK button to make the copies when all of the images that you want to make a small copy of are selected.**

Image overlay

This option allows you to combine two RAW images and save them as one. This menu option can only be accessed by entering the Retouch menu using the Menu button (the longer route); you cannot access this option by pressing the OK button when in Playback mode.

Note *To use this option you must have at least two RAW images saved to your memory card. This option is not available for use with JPEG images.*

To use this option, follow these steps:

1. **Press the Menu button to view the menu options.**

2. **Use the multiselector to scroll down to the Retouch menu, and press the multiselector right to enter the Retouch menu.**

3. **Use the multiselector up/down to highlight Image overlay.**

4. **Press the multiselector right.** This displays the Image overlay menu.

5. **Press the OK button to view RAW image thumbnails.** Use the multiselector to highlight the first RAW image to be used in the overlay. Press the OK button to select it.

6. **Adjust the exposure of Image 1 pressing the multiselector up or down.** Press the OK button when the image is adjusted to your liking.

7. **Press the multiselector right to switch to Image 2.**

8. **Press the OK button to view RAW image thumbnails.** Use the multiselector to highlight the second RAW image to be used in the overlay. Press the OK button to select it.

9. **Adjust the exposure of Image 2 by pressing the multiselector up or down.** Press the OK button when the image is adjusted to your liking.

10. **Press the multiselector right to highlight the Preview window.**

11. **Press the multiselector up or down to highlight Overlay to preview the image, or use the multiselector to highlight Save to save the image without previewing.**

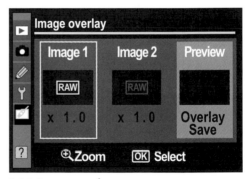

8.14 Image overlay screen

NEF (RAW) Processing

This option allows you to do some basic editing to images saved in the RAW format without downloading them to a computer and using image-editing software. This option is limited in its function, but it allows you to fine-tune your image more precisely when printing straight from the camera or memory card.

You can save a copy of your image in JPEG format. You can choose the image quality and size at which the copy is saved, you can adjust the white balance settings, fine-tune the Exposure compensation, and select an Optimize image setting to be applied.

To apply RAW processing, follow these steps:

1. **Enter the NEF (RAW) Processing menu through the Retouch menu.** Press the OK button to view thumbnails of the image stored on your card. Only images saved in RAW format are displayed.

2. **Use the multiselector left and right to scroll through the thumbnails and press the OK button to select the highlighted image.** This displays a dialog screen with the image adjustment submenu located to the right of the image you have selected.

3. **Use the multiselector up/down to highlight the adjustment you want to make.** You can set the following:

    • Image quality

    • Image size

    • White balance

    • Exposure compensation

    • Optimize image

    EXE (the last item on the list) actually sets the changes and saves a copy of the image in JPEG format at the size and quality that you have selected. The camera default saves the image as a Large, Fine JPEG. You can also use the Zoom in button to view a full-screen preview.

4. **When you have made your adjustments use the multiselector to highlight EXE and press the OK button to save changes, or press the Playback button to cancel without saving.**

 For more information on Image Size, Quality, White balance, and Exposure compensation see Chapter 2.

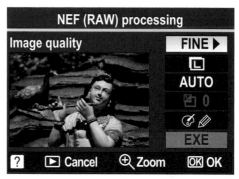

8.15 NEF (RAW) processing menu screen

Stop-motion movie

This option allows you to link together up to 100 images to be shown in a series and saved as a movie (AVI) file. Stop motion is used in animation to make still objects appear as if they are moving, similar to cartoon animation. Basically how it works is you take a shot of an object, move it slightly, take another shot, and so on. After these images are linked and played, the still object appears to move. The effect is sort of a crude, jerky animation. I don't find the need to use this option very often, but if you have some time and patience I'm sure you could put together some very interesting short movies.

Some other ways to use this feature would be to shoot an action sequence such as a skateboarder jumping a ramp and link it together to show the motion or even to put together a quick slide show of random images from your memory card. Follow these steps:

1. **After shooting a sequence of images, go to the Stop-motion movies option in the Retouch menu and press the OK button.** This brings you to a menu screen that gives you the options of Create movie, Frame size, and Frame rate.

2. **Select Frame size.** This allows you to choose how large the still frames in your movie are. The choices are:

   - **640 × 480.** This option stores your images at 640 pixels x 480 pixels. This is a suitable size for viewing on a small TV or com-puter monitor. This option results in a rather large file size.

   - **320 × 240.** This option is more suitable for posting to your Web site or to a site that hosts video such as YouTube or Flickr.

   - **160 × 120.** This gives you the smallest file size and is suitable for e-mailing.

3. **After you set your frame size, use the multiselector to scroll down to Frame rate and press the OK button.** This gives you the options for the *frame rate.* The frame rate, given in frames per sec-ond (fps), is how many still images are shown per second. There are four options:

- **15 fps.** This is the highest option and generally speaking 15 fps is about the minimum acceptable frame rate you can use before your movie appears jerky.

- **10 fps.** This shows you ten images per second and appears somewhat jerky.

- **6 fps.** This shows you six images per second. The video appears very jerky.

- **3 fps.** This shows three images per second.

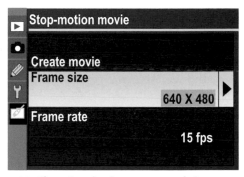

8.16 Choosing the frame rate and size

4. **After you choose your frame size and rate use the multiselec-tor to scroll up to Create movie and press the OK button.** This brings you to a menu screen where you choose a starting image and a stopping image for your movie.

5. **Using the multiselector, choose the image you want to start on and press the OK button to select it.**

6. **Using the multiselector, choose the image you want to stop on and press the OK button.**

7. **If you are happy with your choices, press the OK button again to save or use the multiselector button to highlight Edit, and then Press OK to make new choices.**

option then use the multi-selector left and right to scroll through the thumbnails. Use the multiselector up and down to set the images to be shown or not. A small check mark appears in the images to be shown; deselecting the image deletes it from playback (but not from the memory card).

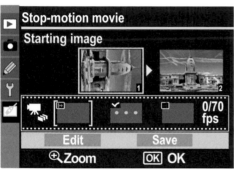

8.17 Choosing the start and stop frame

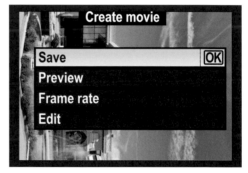

8.18 Create movie menu

8. **After you save your starting point you are shown yet another menu. There are four options:**

   • **Save.** This option allows you to instantly save the stop-motion move file to your memory card.

   • **Preview.** This allows you to view the stop-motion movie on your LCD monitor before saving to the memory card.

   • **Frame rate.** This allows you to adjust the frame rate as before: 15 fps, 10 fps, 6 fps, or 3 fps.

   • **Edit.** This allows you to change the starting and ending frame as well as to choose to not show certain frames in the middle. To choose not to show middle frames select the Middle frame

Before and after

This option allows you to view a side-by-side comparison of the retouched image and the original copy of the image. This option can only be accessed by selecting an image that has been retouched.

To use this option, follow these steps:

1. **Press the Play button and use the multiselector to choose the retouched image to view.**

2. **Press the OK button to display the Retouch menu.**

3. **Use the multiselector to high-light Before and after, and then press the OK button.**

4. **Use the multiselector to highlight either the original or
   retouched image.** You can then
   use the Zoom in button to view
   closer.

5. **Press the Play button to exit the
   Before and after comparison
   and return to Playback mode.**

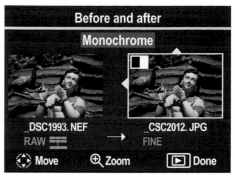

8.19 Before and after comparison screen

Appendixes

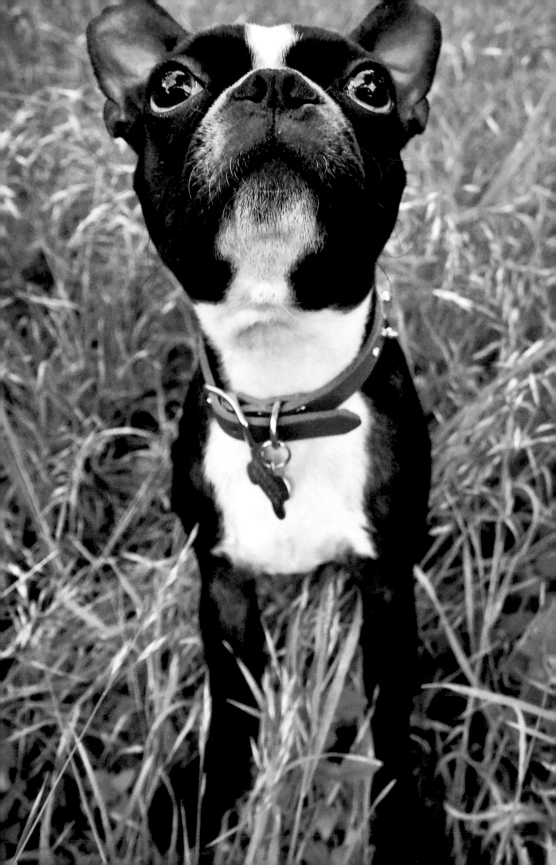

Accessories

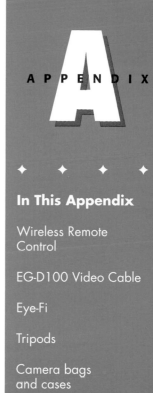

There are a number of accessories and additional equipment available for the Nikon D60. Ranging from batteries and flashes to tripods and camera bags, these accessories can enhance your shooting experience by providing you with options that aren't immediately available with the purchase of the camera alone.

Wireless Remote Control

Nikon offers the ML-L3 wireless remote control. This inexpensive little gadget is available for less than $20 and allows you to wirelessly focus and release the camera's shutter. This is a great feature for doing self-portraits or for hopping into group portraits. You can also use this device to make sure you don't shake your camera when you have it set up on a tripod for doing long exposure photography.

EG-D100 Video Cable

This cable available from Nikon allows you to connect your camera to a standard television for playback or editing your images in camera.

Eye-Fi

The Nikon D60 is the first camera to be "Eye-Fi connected." Eye-Fi is a company that makes an SD memory card that has a built-in wireless transmitter. Using an Eye-Fi card, you can wirelessly transfer your images from the camera to your computer. When you insert the Eye-Fi card into the D60, the camera recognizes that the card is present and automatically adjusts the power management settings so that image transfers aren't interrupted. At around $100 for a 2GB card, this is a pretty good deal to make your camera Wi-Fi enabled.

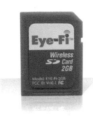

Photo courtesy of Eye-Fi

AA.1 2GB Eye-Fi wireless SD card

Tripods

One of the most important accessories you can have for your camera, whether you're a professional or a hobbyist, is a tripod. The tripod allows you to get sharper images by eliminating the shake caused by handholding the camera in low-light situations. A tripod can also allow you to use a lower ISO, thereby reducing the camera noise and resulting in an image with better resolution.

There are literally hundreds of types of tripods available, ranging in size from less than 6 inches to one that extends all the way up to 6 feet or more. In general, the heavier the tripod is, the better it is at keeping the camera steady. The D60 is not a very heavy camera, but if you happen to be using a heavy lens like the Nikkor 17-55mm f/2.8, I recommend purchasing a heavy-duty tripod; otherwise, the weight of the camera can cause the tripod to shake, leaving you right back where you started with a shaky camera. Of course if you're only using the lightweight kit lens a smaller tripod will probably suffice.

There are many different features available on tripods, but the features to consider include:

✦ **Height.** This is an important feature. The tripod should be the right height for the specific application for which you are using it. If you are shooting landscapes most of the time and you are 6 feet tall, using a 4-foot-tall tripod forces you to bend over to look into the viewfinder to compose your image. This may not be the optimal-size tripod for you.

✦ **Head.** Tripods have several different types of heads. The most common type of head is the *pan/tilt* head. This type of head allows you to rotate, or *pan*, with a moving subject and also allows you to tilt the camera for angled or vertical shots. The other common type of head on a tripod is the *ball* head. The ball head is the most versatile. It can tilt and rotate quickly into nearly any position.

✦ **Plate.** The plate attaches the camera to the tripod. The D60 has a threaded socket on the bottom. Tripods have a type of bolt that screws into these sockets, and this bolt is on the plate. Most decent tripods have what is called a *quick release* plate. You can remove a quick release plate from the tripod and attach it to the camera, and then reattach it to the tripod with a locking mechanism. If you're going to be taking the camera on and off of the tripod frequently, this is the most time-efficient type of plate to use.

The other type of plate, which is on some inexpensive tripods, is the standard type of plate. This plate is attached directly to the head of the tripod. It still has the screw bolt that attaches the camera to the plate, but it is much more time-consuming to use when you plan to take the camera on and off a lot. You must screw the camera to the plate every time you want to use the tripod, and you must unscrew it when you want to remove it from the tripod.

When to use a tripod

There are many situations when using a tripod is ideal, and the most obvious is when it's dark or lighting is poor. However, using a tripod even when there is ample light can help keep your image sharp. The following are just a few ideas of when you may want to use a tripod:

✦ **When the light is low.** Your camera needs a longer shutter speed to get the proper exposure if there isn't much available light. The problem is, when the shutter speed gets longer, you need steadier hands to get sharp exposures. Attaching your camera to a tripod eliminates camera shake.

✦ **When the camera is zoomed in.** When you are using a long focal-length lens, the shaking of your hands is more exaggerated due to the higher magnification of the scene and can cause your images to be blurry, even in moderate light.

✦ **When shooting landscapes.** Landscape shots, especially when you're using the Landscape scene mode, require a smaller aperture to get maximum depth of field to ensure that the whole scene is in focus. When the camera is using a smaller aperture, the shutter speed can be long enough to suffer from camera shake, even when the day is bright.

✦ **When shooting close up.** When the camera is very close to a subject, camera shake can also be magnified. When you're shooting close-ups or macro shots, it may also be preferable to use a smaller aperture to increase depth of field, thus lengthening the shutter speed.

Which tripod is right for you?

Considering there are so many different types of tripods, choosing one can be a daunting experience. There are many different features and functions available in a tripod; here are some things to think about when you're looking into purchasing one:

✦ **Price.** Tripods can range in price from as little as $5 to as much as $500 or more. Obviously, the more a tripod costs, the more features and stability it's going to have. Look closely at your needs when deciding what price level to focus on.

✦ **Features.** There are dozens of different features available in any given tripod. Some tripods have a quick-release plate, some have a ball head, some are small, and some are large. Again, you need to decide what your specific needs are.

✦ **Weight.** This can be very important factor when deciding which tripod to purchase. If you are going to use the tripod mostly in your home, a heavy tripod may not be a problem. On the other hand, if you plan on hiking, a 7-pound tripod can be an encumbrance after awhile. Some manufacturers make tripods that are made out of carbon fiber. While these tripods are very stable, they are also extremely lightweight. On the downside, carbon fiber tripods are also very expensive.

Camera Bags and Cases

Another important accessory to consider is the bag or carrying case you choose for your camera. These can provide protection not only from the elements but also from impact. Camera bags and cases exist for any kind of use you can imagine, from simple cases to prevent scratches to elaborate camera bags that can hold everything you may need for a week's vacation. Some of the bag and case types available include:

✦ **Hard cases.** These are the types of cases to get if you travel a lot, especially if you check your camera gear when flying. The Pelican brand of hard cases are watertight, crushproof, and dustproof. They are unconditionally guaranteed forever. If you are hard on your cameras or do a lot of outdoors activities, you can't go wrong with these. Recently, Pelican has started to offer soft camera bags; obviously they aren't waterproof and crushproof, but they are excellent bags, nonetheless.

✦ **Shoulder bags.** These are the standard camera bags you can find at any camera shop. They come in a multitude of sizes to fit almost any amount of equipment you can carry. Reputable makers include Tamrac, Domke, and Lowepro. Look them up on the Web to peruse the various styles and sizes.

✦ **Backpacks.** Some camera cases are made to be worn on your back just like a standard backpack. These also come in different sizes and styles, and some even offer laptop-carrying capabilities. The type of camera backpack I use when traveling is a Naneu Pro Alpha. It's designed to look like a military pack, so thieves don't know you're carrying camera equipment. When traveling, I usually pack it up with two Nikon dSLR camera bodies, two Nikon Coolpix cameras, a wide-angle zoom, a long telephoto, three or four prime lenses, two Speedlights, a reflector disk, a 12-inch Apple PowerBook, and all of the plugs, batteries, and other accessories that go along with my gear. And, with all that equipment packed away, there is space left over for a lunch. Lowepro and Tamrac also make some very excellent backpacks.

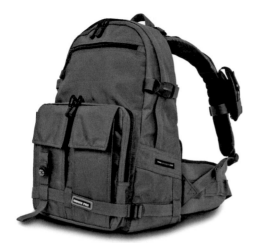

Image courtesy of NaneuPro
AA.2 NaneuPro Alpha camera backpack

✦ **Messenger bags.** Recently, more camera-bag manufacturers have started to offer messenger bags, which resemble the types of bags that a bike messenger uses. They have one strap that goes over your shoulder and across your chest. The bag sits on your back like a backpack. The good thing about these bags is that you can just grab them and pull them around to the front for easy access to your gear. With a backpack, you have to take it off to get to your camera. I also have one of these for when I'm traveling light. My messenger bag is the Echo made by NaneuPro.

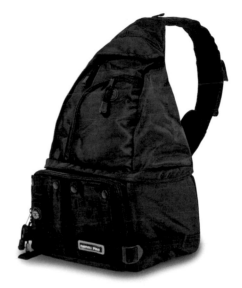

Image courtesy of NaneuPro
AA.3 NaneuPro Echo messenger bag

Monopods

An option you may want to consider is a *monopod* in addition to a tripod. A monopod connects to the camera the same way as a tripod, but it only has one leg. Monopods are excellent for shooting sports and action with long lenses because they allow you the freedom to move along with support to keep your camera steady. The figure here shows a photographer using a monopod to photograph racecars.

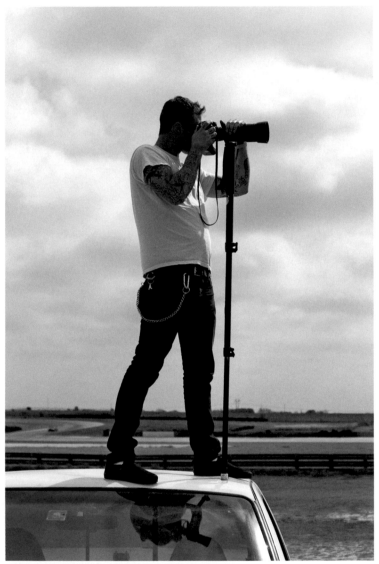

Photo © Destry Jaimes — nine2fivephotography.com

Online Resources

A lot of valuable information is available on the Internet for photographers. This appendix serves as a guide to some of the resources on the Internet that can help you learn more about the Nikon D60 and photography in general, as well as help you discover photo-sharing sites and online photography magazines.

Informational Web Sites

With the amount of information on the Web, sometimes it is difficult to know where to begin looking. The following are a few sites I suggest you start with when you want to find reliable information about your Nikon D60 or about photography in general.

Nikonusa.com

Nikonusa.com gives you access to the technical specifications for Nikon Speedlights, cameras, lenses, and accessories. You can also find firmware updates here should they become available. You can find the Web site at http://nikonusa.com.

Nikonions.org

Nikonions.org is a forum where you can post questions and discussion topics for other Nikon users on a range of photography-related topics. You can find the Web site at www.nikonions.org.

Photo.net

Photo.net is a large site containing resources like equipment reviews, forums on a variety of topics, and tutorials. If you are looking for specific photography-related information and aren't sure where to look, this is a great place to start. You can find the Web site at http://photo.net.

DP Review

One of my favorite sites, this Web site offers in depth reviews of almost every camera and lens released, from simple point-and-shoot cameras to high-end medium format digital cameras, and everything in between. You can find them at http://dpreview.com.

Photo-Sharing and Critiquing Sites

In the past few years there have been quite a few Web sites pop up that allow you to share your photos with friends and family as well as with other photographers. These sites allow you to interact with other photographers around the world to share ideas, find out where you went wrong, and get ideas on how to improve the quality of your images. These Web sites can provide you with an invaluable learning opportunity.

Flickr.com

Flickr.com is a site for posting your photos for others to see. The users range from amateurs to professionals, and there are groups dedicated to specific areas, including the Nikon D60. You can find the Web site at http://flickr.com.

Photoworkshop.com

Photoworkshop.com is an interactive community that allows you to participate in competitions with other photographers by providing assignments as well as giving you a forum to receive feedback on your images. You can find the Web site at http://photoworkshop.com.

ShotAddict.com

ShotAddict.com is a photography site that provides photo galleries, product reviews, contests, and discussion forums. You can find the Web site at http://shotaddict.com.

Online Photography Magazines

Some photography magazines also have Web sites that offer photography articles, and they often post information that isn't found in the pages of the magazine. The following is a list of a few photography magazines' Web sites.

Communication Arts
http://commarts.com

Digital Photo Pro
http://digitalphotopro.com

Digital Photographer
http://digiphotomag.com

Outdoor Photographer
http://outdoorphotographer.com

Photo District News
http://pdnonline.com

Popular Photography & Imaging
http://popphoto.com

Shutterbug
http://shutterbug.net

Glossary

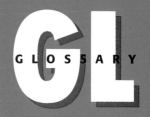

Active D-Lighting A setting in the camera that adjusts the exposure as the image is being taken and applies some tone compensation to achieve a better dynamic range and to avoid overexposed highlights and underexposed shadow areas. This is not to be confused with D-Lighting, which applies tone compensation to shadow areas as the image is being saved.

AE (Auto-Exposure) A general-purpose shooting mode where the camera selects the aperture and/or shutter speed according to the camera's built-in light meter. See also *Shutter Priority mode* and *Aperture Priority mode*.

AE-L/AF-L A camera setting that lets you lock the current metered exposure and/or autofocus setting prior to taking a photo. This allows you to meter an off-center subject and then recompose the shot while retaining the proper exposure for the subject.

AF-assist illuminator An LED that emits light in low-light or low-contrast situations. The AF-assist illuminator provides enough light for the camera's AF to work in low light.

ambient lighting Lighting that naturally exists in a scene.

angle of view The area of a scene that a lens can capture, determined by the focal length of the lens. Lenses with shorter focal lengths have wider angles of view than lenses with longer focal lengths.

aperture The designation for each step in the aperture is called the f-stop. The smaller the f-stop (or f/number), the larger the actual opening of the aperture; and the higher numbered f-stops designate smaller apertures, letting in less light. The f/number is the ratio of focal length to effective aperture diameter.

Aperture Priority mode A camera setting where you choose the aperture, and the camera automatically adjusts the shutter speed according to the camera's metered readings. Photographers often use Aperture Priority mode to control depth of field.

aspect ratio The proportions of an image as printed, displayed on a monitor, or captured by a digital camera.

autofocus The ability of a camera to automatically determine the proper focus of the subject.

Automatic Autofocus (AF-A) A focus mode in which the camera decides whether to use continuous or single AF. See also *Continuous Autofocus (AF-C)* and *Single Autofocus (AF-S)*.

backlighting A lighting effect produced when the main light source is located behind the subject. You can use backlighting to create a silhouette effect or to illuminate translucent objects. See also *frontlighting* and *sidelighting*.

bounce flash Pointing the flash head in an upward position or toward a wall so that it bounces off another surface before reaching the subject. This softens the light illuminated off the subject. Bouncing the light often eliminates shadows and provides a smoother light for portraits.

bracketing A photographic technique in which you vary the exposure of your subject over three or more frames. By doing this you can ensure a proper exposure in difficult lighting situations where your camera's meter can be fooled.

broad lighting A lighting effect created when your main light is illuminating the side of the subject that is facing toward you.

camera shake The movement of the camera, usually at slower shutter speeds, which produces a blurred image.

catchlight Highlights that appear in the subject's eyes as a result of the reflection of the light source. Catchlights are desirable as they give the subject's eyes a look of liveliness.

Center-weighted meter A light-measuring mode that emphasizes the area in the middle of the frame when you're calculating the correct exposure for an image.

colored gel filters Colored translucent filters that are placed over a flash head or light to change the color of the light emitted on the subject. You can use colored gels to create a colored hue of an image. Gels are often used to change the color of a background when shooting portraits or still life photos, by placing the gel over the flash head and firing the flash at the background. Gels are also used to balance the color of a flash to match the color of the ambient light in the scene.

compression Reducing the size of a file by digital encoding, using fewer bits of information to represent the original. Some compression schemes, such as JPEG, operate by discarding some image information, while others, such as RAW with lossless compression, preserve all the detail in the original.

Continuous Autofocus (AF-C) A focus mode that allows the camera to maintain focus on a moving subject.

contrast The range between the lightest and darkest tones in an image. A high-contrast image is one in which the shades fall at the extremes of the range between white and black. In a low-contrast image, the tones are closer together.

D-Lighting A function within the camera that can fix the underexposure that often occurs in images that are backlit or in deep shadow.

dedicated flash An electronic flash unit, such as the Nikon SB-600, SB-800, or SB-400, designed to work with the automatic exposure features of a specific camera.

depth of field (DOF) The area within an image from the foreground to the background that is acceptably sharp. DOF is controlled by manipulating the f-stop. The larger the f-stop (smaller number, larger opening) the shallower the DOF. The smaller the f-stop (larger number, smaller opening) the greater the depth of field.

diffuse lighting Soft, low-contrast lighting.

digital SLR (dSLR) A single-lens reflex camera with interchangeable lenses and a digital image sensor.

exposure The amount of light allowed to reach the film or sensor, determined by the intensity of the light, the amount admitted by the aperture of the lens, and the length of time determined by the shutter speed.

Exposure compensation The ability to take correctly exposed images by letting you adjust the exposure, typically in 1/3 stops from the metered reading of the camera. This enables the photographer to make manual adjustments to achieve desired results. Exposure compensation is usually used in conjunction with auto-exposure settings.

exposure mode Camera settings that let the photographer choose how the camera determines the exposure settings.

f-stop See *aperture.*

fill-flash A lighting technique where the Speedlight provides enough light to illuminate the subject in order to reduce shadows. Using a flash for outdoor portraits often brightens the subject in conditions where the camera meters light from a broader scene.

fill lighting In photography, the lighting used to illuminate shadows. Reflectors or additional incandescent lighting or electronic flash can be used to brighten shadows. One common technique outdoors is to use the camera's flash as a fill.

flash An external light source that produces an almost instant flash of light in order to illuminate a scene.

Flash exposure compensation Adjusting the flash output as compared to what the camera's meter sets the flash to. If images are too dark (underexposed), you can use Flash exposure compensation to increase the flash output. If images are too bright (overexposed), you can use Flash exposure compensation to reduce the flash output.

flash modes Modes that enable you to control the output of the flash; some of these modes are red-eye reduction, rear sync, and slow sync.

front-curtain sync Front-curtain sync causes the flash to fire at the beginning of the exposure when the shutter is completely open. This is the default setting. See also *rear-curtain sync*.

frontlighting The illumination coming from the direction of the camera. See also *backlighting* and *sidelighting*.

histogram A graphic representation of the range of tones in an image.

hot shoe A slot located on the top of the camera where the flash connects. The hot shoe is considered hot because of its electronic contacts, which allow communication between the flash and the camera.

ISO sensitivity The ISO (International Organization for Standardization) setting on the camera indicates the light sensitivity setting. Lower ISO settings provide better-quality images with less digital noise; however, the lower the ISO setting, the more exposure time is needed.

JPEG This is an image format that compresses the image data from the camera to achieve a smaller file size. The compression algorithm discards some of the detail when closing the image. Also referred to as a lossy file type. The D60 allows you to choose different levels of compression; fine, normal, and basic.

Kelvin A unit of measurement of color temperature based on a theoretical black body that glows a specific color when heated to a certain temperature. The sun is approximately 5500 K.

leading line An element in a composition that leads the viewer's eye toward the subject.

lens flare An effect caused by stray light reflecting off of the many glass elements of a lens. Lens flare is generally avoided by shades on the lens. Sometimes lens flare can be used creatively.

lighting ratio The proportion between the amount of light falling on the subject from the main light and the secondary light.

macro lens A lens that provides the ability to focus at a very close range, enabling extreme close-up photographs.

manual exposure Bypassing the camera's internal light meter settings in favor of setting the shutter and aperture manually. Manual exposure is beneficial in difficult lighting situations where the camera's meter may not provide correct results.

Manual mode Manually setting the exposure on the camera.

Matrix metering A light-metering system that calculates exposure by measuring the light from different areas of the scene and determines exposure by a series of complicated algorithms.

metering Measuring the amount of light utilizing the camera's internal light meter.

mirror lock-up A function of the camera that allows the mirror, which reflects the image to the viewfinder, to retract without the shutter being released. This is done in order to reduce vibration from the mirror moving or to allow sensor cleaning (when the shutter is open).

NEF (Nikon Electronic File) The name of Nikon's RAW file format.

noise Pixels with randomly distributed color values in a digital image that create a grainy look to a photograph. Noise in digital photographs tends to be more pronounced with low-light conditions and long exposures, particularly when you set your camera to a higher ISO rating.

noise reduction A technology used to decrease the amount of random information in a digital picture, usually caused by long exposures and high ISO settings. Noise reduction typically involves the camera automatically taking a second blank/dark exposure at the same settings that contains only noise, and then using the blank photo's information to cancel the noise in the original picture.

pincushion distortion An aberration in a lens in which the lines at the edges and sides of the image are bowed inward. This distortion is usually found in longer focal-length (telephoto) lenses.

Programmed Auto (P) On the camera, the shutter speed and aperture are set automatically when the subject is focused.

RAW An image file format that contains the unprocessed camera data as it was captured. Using this format allows you to change image parameters such as white balance saturation and sharpening after the image is downloaded. Processing RAW files such as Nikon's NEF require special software, such Nikon's Capture NX, Adobe Camera RAW (available in Photoshop), Adobe Lightroom, or a number of other third-party programs.

rear-curtain sync Rear-curtain sync causes the flash to fire at the end of the exposure, an instant before the second, or rear, curtain of the focal plane shutter begins to move. With slow shutter speeds, this feature can create a blur effect from the ambient light, showing as patterns that follow a moving subject with the subject shown sharply frozen at the end of the blur trail. This setting is usually used in conjunction with longer shutter speeds. See also *front-curtain sync.*

red-eye An effect from flash photography that appears to make a person's eyes glow red, or an animal's yellow or green. It's caused by light bouncing from the retina of the eye and is most noticeable in dimly lit situations (when the irises are wide open), and when the electronic flash is close to the lens and, therefore, prone to reflect the light directly back.

Red-Eye Reduction A flash mode controlled by a camera setting that is used to prevent the subject's eyes from appearing red in color. The Speedlight fires multiple flashes just before the shutter is opened to contract the pupils of the subject to lessen the amount of light reflected from the retina.

S-curve A leading line that is shaped like the letter S. See also *leading line.*

self-timer A mechanism that delays the opening of the shutter for some seconds after the Shutter Release button has been pressed.

short lighting When your main light is illuminating the side of the subject that is facing away from you.

shutter A mechanism that allows light to pass to the sensor for a specified amount of time.

Shutter Priority mode In this camera mode, you set the desired shutter speed, and the camera automatically sets the aperture for you. Often used when shooting action shots to freeze motion of the subject when the camera is using fast shutter speeds.

Shutter Release button When this button is pressed halfway the camera focuses, when the button is fully depressed the camera takes the picture.

shutter speed The length of time the shutter is open to allow light to fall onto the imaging sensor. The shutter speed is measured in seconds or more commonly, fractions of seconds.

sidelighting Illuminating the subject from the left or right. See also *frontlighting* and *backlighting.*

Single Autofocus (AF-S) A focus mode that locks the focus on the subject when the Shutter button is half-pressed. This allows you to focus on the subject and recompose the image without losing focus as long as the Shutter Release button is half-pressed.

slow sync A flash mode that allows the camera's shutter to stay open for a longer time to allow the ambient light to be recorded, resulting in the background receiving more exposure, which gives the image a more natural appearance.

Speedlight A Nikon-specific term for its flashes.

Spot meter A metering system in which the exposure is based on a small area of the image; usually the spot is linked to the AF point.

TIFF (Tagged Image File Format) A type of file storage format that has no compression; therefore, no loss of image detail — often referred to as lossless. Because the data is not compressed, TIFFs can be very large image files.

TTL (Through-the-Lens) A metering system where the light is measured directly though the lens.

tungsten light The light from a standard household lightbulb.

vanishing point The point at which parallel lines converge and seem to disappear.

Vibration Reduction (VR) A function of the lens in which the lens elements are shifted in order to reduce the effects of camera shake.

white balance Used to compensate for the differences in color temperature common in different light sources. For example, a typical tungsten lightbulb is very yellow-orange, so the camera adds blue to the image to ensure that the light looks like standard white light.

Index

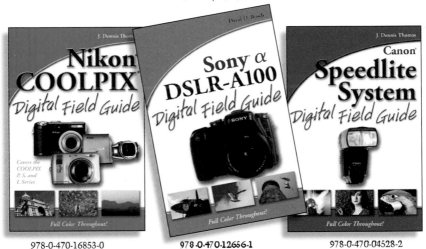
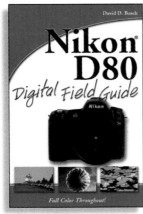
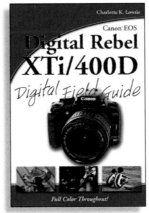
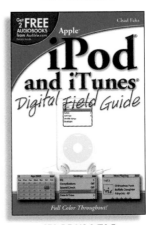